MOMENTUM

MOMENTUM

LANCE WEST

Momentum

An Introspective Narrative On Overcoming Bipolar Disorder With Meds, Music & Faith

Copyright ©2019 by Lance Wesley Hudson
All rights reserved.

Published by Rebel Press
Austin, Texas
www.RebelPress.com

No part of this publication may be reproduced, stored in a retrieval system, or transmitted in any form or by any means—electronic, mechanical, photocopy, recording, or any other—without the prior permission of the author.

ISBN: 978-1-68102-796-8

Printed in the United States of America

For Mom, Dad and Anne

who saw me through the literal ups and downs

Objects will remain in their state of motion
unless a force acts to change the motion

— *Newton's Law of Inertia*

I said a hip hop hippie to the hippie
The hip, hip a hop, and you don't stop

— *The Sugarhill Gang, "Rapper's Delight"*

MOMENTUM

Contents

1 So Many Firsts 1

2 Young Rejection, Growth and Rapper's Delight 10

3 A Transition from Sports to Music 26

4 Path to Plan A – Guitars, Girls and Grades 36

5 Pushing Through the Early '90s – A Diagnosis 51

6 Mental Challenges Ahead 75

7 A New Millennium 101

8 An Equal and Opposite Reaction 122

9 New Momentum – Leaving Dark Music and Alcohol Abuse Behind 141

10 Steps to Generating and Maintaining Momentum in Your Life 159

Editor's Note – Serendipities 161

Acknowledgments 163

About the Author 171

INTRODUCTION

Let me skip ahead in the story, for just a second, to introduce you to the man I am still becoming. Some super kind industry insiders have called me a "crafty singer-songwriter whose sound is fostered by his eclectic taste in music – born in part by his San Francisco roots and involvement in the '90s rock scene." My sense of self is intermingled with the musical influences of artists like Mat Kearney, Jason Mraz, Jimi Hendrix, Jethro Tull and Bootsy's Rubber Band (1970s funk at its most brilliant.) All feeding back to a spiritual center and my Christian faith. The music I create vibes across genres, often landing in indie rock with a message.

My original musical compositions include lyrics/vocals recorded over electric/acoustic guitar, bass, keyboards and electric piano tracks. I've been told my songs – based on the experiences I'm about to share – both uplift and inspire.

As I work on my new album *momentum* as a companion to this book, I can't help but reflect on my previous album *Gratitude* which was conceived and created to show respect and love to the very creator of creativity, God. I opened my heart wide channeling a unique blend of rock, soul, blues and Christian influence, with the mission of being a beacon of light in the all-to-often darkness.

Through it all, my momentum was building. Growing into areas of my life beyond the studio jam sessions and the lyrical writing. I decided to share more of my story here – my journey through music, mental illness and tested faith.

So, if you have experienced mental illness or want to understand someone who has, let's delve deeper into this topic together. Let's learn how to use momentum to overcome the fears that can keep us bound to an unfulfilling life.

1

So Many Firsts

Before I knew it, I had sunken into the morass of sorrow at an age not even in the double digits. It was a somewhat unfamiliar feeling I felt in times of duress. Blackie was a spunky 5-year-old collie with a single color to match his name, except for a little white patch under his muzzle that was often wet with doggy saliva. A week before, I'd been playing with him and picked him up. He squealed in pain, turned and bit me on the arm. I dropped him to the concrete there in our sculpted backyard of half grass half concrete, curving around the house like the sand and the shore. What was wrong? He loved me. He would always rush over and look up at me through the fence when I called his name.

One morning before school, I heard a heaving sound coming from the backyard. I pulled back the curtains and looked through the sliding glass door. There he was undulating on the pavement. Heaving uncontrollably. When I opened the door, the heaving sound increased dramatically and white foam was coming out of his mouth. I sat there on my knees next to him for what seemed like an eternity. Until his body was motionless and limp. I was just kneeling there next to him. My mom called my dad who took the day off from work to take Blackie to the pound for cremation.

My dad had one of those '70s Dodge van conversions with the bubble windows. So, I rode in the back with Blackie's body which was now stiff. As a lay next to him, gazing into his brown eyes that looked like marbles in his head, I wondered where was the Blackie I knew? Full of life and love. I knew he was no longer there. I don't think I realized at the time this happens to all living things. They cease to exist in the form we knew them. When we arrived at the pound, Dad had me carry Blackie in. I just remember he was light and stiff. I reached up on my tippy toes and handed him over to the proper authorities. That was the last time I saw him. Dad took me to Togo's for lunch to comfort me. I still remember that.

Later that week I went out to the backyard, welled up with tumultuous emotions. Frustration, anger, sadness. I wildly picked up a post along with the concrete base – way heavier than anything a child my age should be able to lift – and threw it to the ground, tears pouring down my face. I could taste the salt in my tears. A bitter reminder of my loss. After frantically picking the post up and throwing it down for several minutes, exhausted, I fell to my knees into the cool wet winter evening grass. Something in me died that day. And l feared that I would never get it back. The part of me that was attached to Blackie.

I can't describe the numbness and emptiness I felt. But it was to become a reoccurring theme in my life, both self-imposed and circumstantial. Perhaps I'd learned something that applies to life to this day. We are only here for a season. Do not get attached to the things of this world. Life is a moving thing that perpetuates itself and changes all the time in cycles. Blackie had completed his cycle and his spirit energy returned to the source of all light – the center where the spirits of that very light congregate. Pure energy untainted by the slightest careless doubts that we indulge in while here in physical form.

According to science, energy cannot be created or destroyed. It just changes form. Much like water, it cycles within itself. From the rivers, lakes, streams and oceans, up into the sky, then rains back down on us indiscriminately. Just as Blackie was made of water and his essence returned to its source along with the electric energy that flowed through his anatomy. I couldn't physically hold onto Blackie anymore. I was forced to let go. Little did I know that letting go is one of the most liberating and transcendent things we can do. I couldn't possess Blackie and keep him forever. He was his own being, sharing the same space and time with me. I don't think I fully realized the inevitability of death at that age. I just felt the hurt of loss. Too young to realize the same rules applied to me. And that someday, I would face the loss of loved ones.

The beginning and the end are where the most profound changes happen in existence. From conception. The actual creation of life. A seed being planted in a woman's womb. And the fruit of life growing for nine months, the perpetuation of life. The gift of creation given freely to all indiscriminately that your mother nurtures, feeds and unconditionally loves until that child too grows to bear the fruit. Perpetuating life until the setting of their own sun. The cycle is completed only to start again. In a sense, I was Blackie but just way earlier in my cycle than him. The same natural laws apply to all life. Some of the most profound lessons can be found in some of the most hurtful experiences.

Yet I struggled with the whys of loss. Why didn't Blackie live longer, if not forever? Why did he have to suffer so much? That was something else I had yet to learn. Sometimes we don't get an answer, we are forced to accept things. But it was my choice how I responded. I could have gratitude, that blessing of Blackie's doggy friendship in my life. I could remember how he would look up into my eyes and make a comforting whimper when he saw me cry. I could remember frolicking with him in the backyard, spraying him with the water hose in the summer as he ran about me in circles, barking and tail wagging. He was alive in my heart. He left a profound impression on my psyche. One that can only be lost when my cycle ends. When I too return to the Lord. I had not lost a friend, I had gained an experience that taught me profound lessons in life. Lessons I would continue to build on as my life unfolded. As a child, I could barely phrase these feelings in words and now I only try. Some of the joyful experiences I had at that age were almost transcendent. The thing that made these experiences so wonderful? Everything was new – so many firsts were unfolding.

Another profound first happened just after kindergarten. My mother Mable was a teacher and I was fortunate enough to attend the school where she taught. Often after school she would have meetings and teacher conferences. So I would stay with a babysitter for a couple of hours after school. My first babysitter was Mrs. Beckman. She was a white woman who'd adopted Julie, a black daughter my age. Julie and I were like peas in a pod. We would go out to the backyard on blistering summer afternoons and struggle through the thicket to reach the warm blackberries that could be found on their vines. Much like a rose bush. You could really get scratched up. But we roughed it and fought our way into the bushes. I remember the burst of flavor when I bit into the warm tangy berries and playing with the seeds between my tongue and cheek.

Mrs. Beckman was a strict disciplinarian and would hit Julie on the hand with a spoon if she misbehaved. Thankfully she would not do that to me, instead telling my mother I'd been acting up. Julie and I were your typical, curious little 6-year-olds. Discreet and shy. We had a cute little secret we were keeping. We would go upstairs and shimmy under the bed and play what we called love motion. Which was basically kissing and talking to each other. I think we had seen these things in movies and were trying to emulate it.

After about six months of this, Julie moved away to Pennsylvania. My mom told me I could write to her but that made me feel bitter. I didn't want to write or receive a letter. I wanted to continue to play with Julie. But this was a different kind of loss than Blackie and brand new to me. This was circumstances working against me. Circumstances taking someone out of your life makes you feel so helpless. I knew she was out in Pennsylvania, but it was light years away to me. I couldn't see her. She was out of reach. After a while, I didn't even think about her anymore. It was as if we had never shared those special fleeting moments of early childhood.

My mother was always showering me with attention as most mothers do with their little children. Letting me have candy before dinner, playing with my friends before my food had a chance to settle. My dad left for work early, so I would climb into bed with her. Snuggling up to her warm body as if I was still suspended in the comfort and safety of her womb. I had not been in the world too long. It was as if I were connected to her with a spiritual umbilical cord that could never be severed. We would lay there until the last possible minute and then hop out of bed, soles hitting the cold unforgiving floor. Often, I would go in the bathroom, close the door and lay on the floor to continue my slumber with a makeshift bed of the bathroom floor mat. Laying in the fetal position, to keep my exposed flesh from touching the cold bathroom floor.

I would hear my mom's voice: "Lance, time to go."

I would lay there until the final booming, "LANCE!! Let's GO!"

When my mom reached her limit – which happened often with a terror like me – she would yell. And I deserved it. Now with barely enough time to make it to school before the bell rang, we dashed out the door, jumped into the Maroon '78 Buick Electra 225. We floated down the street and hit the corner like evading criminals in a car chase scene straight from *Streets of San Francisco*. Only we were being chased by time.

Sometimes we would get to school early. In those days, teachers had to provide the lesson plans, worksheets, charts, even pencils and erasers. Plus, they had these manual ditto machines where you would put in a two-ply ditto master, like those old credit card machines, and attached it to a cylinder you'd rotate manually with a hand crank. The image would be pressed onto the blank sheets of paper. And she would hand the dittos out to the students, with all the addition and subtraction problems. I remember the machine had an ammonia smell to it. We usually had limited time to prepare for the class, so I'd wear out my arm, repeatedly rotating the cylinder to help my mom who was taking care of another task. I was her little sidekick.

The interesting thing is I was the only Black child on the campus. I didn't know it or understand any perceived difference between me and the other kids. It's interesting how some adults, who are supposed to be way more experienced and mature than children, couldn't understand the basic principal that we are all a part of the human race. Maybe their innocence was tainted by the hatred, intolerance and indifference of their parents. Maybe when they were children they never learned these fundamental principles and became set in their ways. Maybe it was a lack of exposure and positive experiences with those different than ourselves. Our perceptions are formed by our experiences or lack thereof.

Although my school was predominately white on the West Side of San Jose, I lived on the East Side where there was a wide array of cultural diversity. Asians, Latinos, Blacks, Indians, Whites. Being in an environment like that is a huge blessing to a person privileged enough to have it. Being raised in an environment like that, you're bound to form friendships outside of the cultural comfort zones. Beyond just eating their food and drinking their beverages. A real connection to their culture through the love for a person from that culture. The only thing that can derail that growth is peers and family members who teach and demonstrate intolerance and hate. Also, it can grow from a seed of feeling unloved. Neglect from a parent. Verbal, physical and maybe sexual abuse.

Most young children do not know true hate. They haven't had enough bad experiences. All they know is the feeling of being loved or unloved from what parents, friends and teachers say and do. And often things they don't say or do. One of the mistakes parents make is always pointing out and fixating on the negative with their children. Saying things like, you're lazy, you procrastinate too much, you're stupid, ugly, fat. These hurtful things are internalized and can eventually become their self-perception. Often someone, who had overcritical authority figures, feel they could never be accepted and become overly critical of themselves. Even unsupportive and cruel to themselves. A healthy perception comes from healthy seeds planted in the psyche and nurtured to maturity through kindness, support and an overall feeling of being loved unconditionally. I've heard some parents say: "I am not angry with you, I am disappointed because I expected more of you."

They always tie everything together with a general feeling of love.

Planting the right seeds in the first place is much easier than having to unravel an elaborate knot of self-doubt, insecurity and fear later in life.

It was not until I was verbally attacked by several white teens in my neighborhood that I learned some people hated me because of the color of my skin. Some perceived difference between us. Across the street from my house there was this huge walnut grove, about a 20-minute walk deep and about 10 minutes across. Must have been a 100 trees out there. I remember trudging through the big thick dirt clods, almost twisting my ankle with every step, to make it to the base of our tree fort which was really just a piece of wood stretching from one branch to the other. Just big enough for a couple of us to sit with our legs dangling over. There were several white guys in the neighborhood that didn't like my friends from the block, who were mostly Black guys.

There was this big pile of dirt in the field, like a little mountain in comparison to my youthful frame. I heard yelling from a distance. When I looked up, I saw several boys about my age emerging over the top of the dirt mound, like a rising sun. One of them was barking a word I'd never heard before in a combative tone, "N#$%r, Ni#$%r."

Before I knew what was happening, I saw one of them draw his arm back and swing it toward me, hurling a rock in my direction. Instinctively, I reached down into the clods without even looking, eyes trained in their direction. Haphazardly, selecting a rock to retaliate. As I released it, a barrage of rocks, bottles, anything they could pick up they hurled at me. Just then, my dad arrived home from work and witnessed the tail end of the skirmish. I ran home to meet him at the house and informed him of the melee that had just unfolded. He told me I'd done the right thing. He taught me to meet force with force and don't back down. I wonder if that was my nature or a learned response to conflict. It felt like instinct but who knows.

About a half an hour later, a woman appeared at the door of my house with an inflammatory demeanor. Telling my dad, I'd attacked her sons. My dad, not the back-down type, jumped to my defense. Having witnessed part of the skirmish with his own two eyes, he told her that was her problem.

Later that week, while riding my bike around the corner by their house, I noticed a flag I'd never seen before, hanging in front of their door. It was red with a blue and white X across it with stars in the X. It was ol' Dixie. I didn't know the correlation between that flag and the contempt those boys had for me. I wished it was just a flag and didn't represent what it did. Some say it's a sign of freedom and rebellion. I would follow the facts and look at history. The country was divided in part because the Southerners wanted to keep their slaves and the Northerners didn't agree with that. Had the Southerners had their way my family and I would be slaves right now.

Let me be clear, I believe in the oneness of mankind and anything that perpetuates division is the real enemy. We were just children who had been indoctrinated a certain way. If we had our way, we would have been sitting up in that old tree without a care in the world. But we had a lot to learn. And we didn't even know it. Hell, some of our parents may not have even known it. I was too young to understand. I was a lover by nature.

She had no idea I liked her. Lara, tall and thin, with straight blonde hair just past the shoulders. White-and-red '70s short shorts, white tank top with a rainbow in the center. Woolworth Brady Bunch blue loafers with white soles. White socks stretched all the way up, almost over her knobby knees.

Fourth grade had just begun earlier that week. A new chapter in the elementary school play they call campus. Today was the day. Sitting there in class before recess, I opened my Star Wars Trapper Keeper and tore a page from its center, making a ripping sound that caught the teacher's ear by not eyes thankfully. On it I scratched a single question with my No. 2 pencil: "Do you want to go around?"

This was our elementary school version of boyfriend and girlfriend in our childish circle. Along with two boxes with the words YES and NO next to them. Now I just had to drum up the courage to give it to her. So, later during recess, I saw her in the hall, threw the note at her and bolted out of sight around the corner. Within seconds, she was in hot pursuit around the corner past the tether ball poles, through the basketball courts by the library. I couldn't shake her. She was fast with those long legs. At the time, I was probably 5 inches shorter than her. Over by the principal's office next to the kindergarten, I finally ran out of steam. As I stood there winded, she opened the letter I'd folded into multiple squares, sloppy origami. I almost felt like I was getting in trouble or something, but I think she enjoyed the attention and the chase as much as I did. I don't recall what she said, but I do recall her not checking either box.

This was the beginning of me liking girls who did not feel the same way I did. Or so I thought. We were just kids obviously, but I felt a sense of rejection and wanted to be accepted and embraced by a girl I liked. A friend of hers wrote in my yearbook later something along the lines of "You need to stop pursuing girls that don't like you or your feelings are always going to be hurt." She actually said it way more eloquent than that, an elementary school Ann Landers before her time.

Often no one pulls us aside and gives us instruction as far as how to build healthy relationships. We just piece it together through experiences and long conversations with close friends and family members. In my case, I hardly ever told anyone about the experiences I was having and the problems I was encountering. I was raised with one sister and I didn't have an older brother figure growing up. I was always the one helping my friends and sometimes being an older brother figure to them. So, I didn't have a brother to discuss these things with. My brother may have told me it's stupid to give a girl a note and run away. He may have really given me a hard time about it. And that may have been a good thing.

I didn't go to my dad much with things that were embarrassing to talk about, like being rejected by girls. My dad was a very strong old school Charles Bronson type. He was not afraid to face adversity head on. He was and is one the strongest willed people I ever known. He really had faith in himself that he can handle any situation. No matter how difficult or insurmountable it seemed. See he had faced unspeakable conflict and adversity and never backed down. My dad was raised in Vernon, Texas, just south of the Oklahoma border at the bottom of the pan. He had experienced the racism of the South firsthand. The segregated school, water fountains, bathrooms.

One time he went into a soda shop much like a Denny's with stools at the counter. Kids would congregate there and have chocolate malts, ice cream, sodas. He went right up and hopped up onto one of the stools and ordered a Coke. The woman filled a glass with a fountain Coke. He sat there anxiously waiting for his ice-cold Coke as she went down to the end of the counter and walked out by the front door, Coke in hand. He reluctantly followed her, and she said, "You have to drink your soda here. You can't sit at the counter." He was about 10 years old.

When I think of the things I was worried about when I was 10, the contrast between our experiences was obvious. Dad didn't have the luxury of worrying about if a little girl liked him or not. He was in survival mode. There is such a dramatic difference between our experiences and different perspectives.

They say when it comes to conflict it is fight or flight. I have learned both have their advantages and disadvantages. If you put up a good fight and don't back down, you gain people's respect. Respect must be earned. That is how my dad deals with conflict. There is an old Jamaican saying, "He who fights and run away, lives to fight another day." That about says it all for the case of flight. I also think there are personality and character types with humans. We are much like the animals of the wild. There are predators and prey. Predators stay and fight for territory, food and respect, and prey eat grass and run when there is a conflict. Both creatures are trying to survive. They just have different methods of surviving. Both are integral to the cycle of life and the food chain. My dad is like a lion, I am like an eagle. It took me time to learn that I don't need to try to be like other people. My role is just as valid as anyone else's. I am not as aggressive and assertive as him, but I very introspective, analytical, like solitude and soaring in the clouds. I am also good at building bridges and resolving conflict.

There is a balance in nature. A harmony, a rhythm and reason to things. I truly believe God is in control and this is all written. There are lessons for every one of us. I believe no one leaves this world until they have served their purpose. Some people's lives are shorter or longer than others, but the big picture is like a moving collage of pictures, humans shining and fading as stars in the sky.

The '70s van was truly a conversion. It converted our lives, from the time we got it after sitting in the Dodge dealership for what seemed like an eternity. Playing with my two well-worn Bosch and Luke from Hoth Star Wars action figures. Sitting there on the floor, imagining the Imperial Walkers bearing down on the Rebel base. Pretending Luke had a fighter ship, which ended up being him just flying like Super Man. Bosch was the universal bad guy. Boba Fett, Darth Vader, Stormtroopers. Except he looked like a lizard with a space suit on. Five to six hours later I was slumped next to my mom's warm body on the lobby couch, limp from exhaustion and fatigue. Anne and I had also run around quite a bit as kids do. Much like Star Wars, this van was going to take us on journeys. This van represented freedom. An escape from school and work. A mobile sanctuary for our family.

I remember many times winding up through the mountain roads carved in the hills through the redwood trees. V8 engine wide open, air conditioner blasting. You could hear and feel the pressure of the wind being forced out through the little slots in the dash. My mom's cotton candy afro moving in the breeze, adorned in full '70s attire. Maroon bell bottom hip-hugging slacks, a multi-colored tube top and brown platforms. My mom always went with the flow when it came to fashion, changing with the times.

My dad was in the driver's seat, afro about two inches off his scalp, shrouded by a black stocking cap rolled up and tucked under, giving it a lip around his head. Beige corduroy pants and a cotton T-shirt that was dark blue on the top half and beige on the bottom, divided by a thin red line sewn just where the colors came together horizontally. My sister was in the back with her feet up on the railing that housed the bed when it was pulled down, hunched forward, face buried in a book most likely Judy Bloom at that age. She had two thick black, Pippy-Longstocking-style braids on either side of her head, sticking straight out. She was dressed much like my mom. The only real difference was the awesome '70s T-shirts she liked to wear. Like the hand with the thumb and pinky sticking out saying "Hang Loose" Hawaiian style on the front and "00" on the back like a team jersey. Often these T-shirts would have 3/4 sleeves and loud colors like bright yellow and green. I had an afro too, slightly longer than my dad's. I often wore terry cloth shirts that had a bumpy texture in neutral colors of beige, maroon, light gray.

I can still feel the cold root beer in my hand as I looked out the bubble window, watching the world go by like a fish looking out at the world from his bowl. From my vantage point, the world looked fascinating and intriguing. The redwoods stretched straight up and out of view as the sun and the shade flickered across the window like an old rotary slide show projector, flicking from picture to picture. Frames of youth going by before my eyes. I wondered what was beyond the redwoods? How deep did it stretch out back into the hills? What kind of animals call those woods home? Would I get to see any of them? Then I wondered if Big Foot was out there like I'd seen in the *Six Million Dollar Man* episode? And why was Big Foot hiding anyway?

My daydreaming was interrupted by the smooth tone of my father's voice. He was singing my favorite song:

"Daddy's home,
your Daddy's home to stay,
I'm not a thousand miles away ... "

As he went into the verse of the song, I not only heard love for my mom, Anne and me. I felt it. Dad never used the word love. He showed it. I really respect that. Often words can't do our feelings justice. There are things that can't be expressed in words. And I'm convinced these are the most meaningful things in life. His voice was like watching a sunset. That's how it felt. Magical. Love is often difficult to express in words. A mother can just look at her child and the child knows it's loved. Sound is truly a gift to me. I am really affected deeply by the things I hear, not just words but sounds. And not just words but the way they are said. The slight inflections and tiny nuances. I cherished those moments when Dad sang to us because it was a rare glimpse into his heart of hearts. Dad was also our main disciplinarian. If we got in trouble, he was usually responsible for our punishment. Dad was raised in a time where parents were really frustrated by the circumstances they found themselves in. My grandma and grandpa worked in the fields, pulling cotton where they made barely enough money to feed their family. That was during cotton season. The rest of the time Grandma ironed clothes for white people and was a homemaker. My Grandpa did numerous jobs over his life. Janitor, dishwasher, porter, garbage man, junk hauler. People then were barely surviving. Not to mention the racism. So, parents were not very patient when it came to nonsense with the kids. And in those days children were to be seen not heard. They did not talk when adults were talking, and they called them ma'am and sir. Often parents would go overboard due to the frustrations of life and discipline their children harshly and out of anger.

So, there was no playing when it came to my Dad. With Mom, there was a little more leeway. I remember the first time I went to a supermarket my dad told me, "Don't say anything and don't touch nothing on the shelves." Dad had this way about him where you didn't even try him. If you were foolish enough, you'd be disciplined accordingly. As a child, it was hard to understand corporal punishment, at least it was for me. A person who loves you is hitting you because they are unhappy with your behavior. It can be argued that a few little taps on the butt to let the kid know you mean business won't hurt. If not done in anger. But I feel the line is crossed when the child is afraid of the parent. It's possible to discipline a child and still have them know you love them. Let's face it, I was bad sometimes and needed behavior modification. Kids need to know there will be consequences when they behave counterproductively. Some people never learn about boundaries and basic right and wrong because no one taught them that they will be held accountable for their actions in this society, whether they understand and agree with it or not.

I believe in healthy, balanced discipline that shapes a person into a responsible adult, and then there is discipline that is counterproductive. That can cause a person to rebel and even spiral out of control later in life. We've all heard stories of abuse and the impact it can have on a person's psyche for the rest of their life. Overly harsh discipline can be handed down from generation to generation and perpetuate discord throughout the person's life. When a person feels abused, the underlying bottom line in their mind is this person doesn't love me and maybe even hates me. This may or may not be true depending on the relationship you have with the person. A deep seated feeling of being unloved or unworthy of being loved can be at the root of some of the most elaborate mazes of anger, frustration, depression and ultimately low self-worth.

It's imperative a child, teen, young adult know their parents love them unconditionally and they are worthy of being love. I truly feel that now but there was a time when I didn't. For some people, it's neglect by a parent or parents that abandoned them at an early age. And they are left feeling abandoned, thinking, "They didn't love me. I am unlovable."

I wrote a song years ago called "Love or the lack there of." Love is a pivoting point on which we all process our interactions with people in the world around us and our relationships with them. The need to be accepted translates to a need to be loved. That's why when a person feels like they are unaccepted, they start to generate hate and contempt for those around them. We all just want to be accepted and loved unconditionally. This can lead us on a path to the Lord. Often it is difficult to find true unconditional love. Everyone has their agendas and selfish, sometimes hidden motivations as to why they are in your life. That's why I advocate a loving relationship with the Lord as the foundation of a belief system.

If you truly believe God loves you unconditionally, you can have peace of mind, joy, hope, inspiration despite circumstances. If you truly believe God has your best interest in mind always, there is no reason to question him anymore. You can just rest assured he has it all under control. If we understand the nature of God's love and the broad role it plays in life, we can achieve true liberation.

2

Young Rejection, Growth and Rapper's Delight

Small rejections don't always come from peers like my grade school crush Lara. It often comes from adults like parents and teachers. The seeds planted in a child's psyche, regarding their worth to people they so desperately want to be accepted by, grow into self-perceptions, whether accurate or not. When a child is called stupid, lazy and ugly, they are forced to process that and react to it somehow.

When I was a child, I was energetic and rambunctious with seemingly endless energy. I could just run around like a banshee all day. I was playful, creative and a leader. I was always the one breaking branches off trees, peeling the bark off and wrapping electrical tape around the handle for makeshift swords. I was the swashbuckler creating tree forts out of scrap plywood and cardboard boxes. Nailing boards up the side of the tree to climb up. I lived to play and let my mind run wild outside where I belonged. My mom would call me in for dinner and I would sigh at the idea that I had to interrupt playing to eat. I remember she used to tell me I couldn't go back outside until my food digested, which was eternity as far as I was concerned.

When it came to school, I was a terror. I craved attention, so I would be the one shooting spit wads, pulling the girl's hair, making strange noises that seemed to only make the other true dorks in class laugh. The school had a system of discipline where they would write your name on the board and mark checks next to it. It seemed I only got attention when I was doing something wrong or being scolded. Although I enjoyed the attention that getting my name written on the board attracted, it only reinforced the idea of only getting attention from authority figures by being bad. When I was particularly bad, I would get sent to the principal's office, where I was formally reprimanded and sometimes faced in-school suspension.

In these meetings with the principal I was made to feel rejected. Children are like a sponge and a mirror combined. They soak up everything we expose them to and reflect it back. The message I was getting from the top authority at the school was I was a bad kid that did not fit in, whose behavior wouldn't be tolerated. I didn't feel loved. I have come to realize that is really the bottom line. Maybe that is why I was acting out in the first place. Never once did the authority figures in my life attempt to address the root causes of my behavior and try some sort of real meaningful behavior modification. Looking back, I feel as if the principal and teachers were too busy to deal with children who had emotional problems and truly needed extra care.

Children need a holistic approach. Some children are introverted and internalize their true feelings and become secretive about it. They blame themselves and can become downright cruel to themselves, leading to depression later in life. Others are extroverted. Their attitude is no one is going to hold me back. I'm going to go forward and overcome this and excel. Others fall somewhere in between, like me.

The holistic approach to building self-worth in a child should include mind, body and spirit. If a child is unhappy at home and feels unloved, how can they wrap their mind around the idea that God loves them? Even child logic would say, if one or both of my parents doesn't love me why would God?

I was not raised in church. My mom is Christian and one of the kindest loving and righteous people I have ever met. She gave me the most precious gift that I believe was my saving grace – unconditional love. I never went to church, but she showed me how God loved me. My father did not believe in God and always questioned Christianity. How did Moses fit the animals from all over the world on Noah's Ark? Why didn't the Bible address the dinosaurs and that the planet is billions of years old, not thousands? See, my dad is very practical. He wants evidence of things. Facts. Something tangible to go on. Religion requires faith in God. My dad is one of the strongest people I know, and I really commend him for his strength to face things head on.

I have come to realize that faith is precious and required to have a healthy balanced life. I think some look to God, others go it alone or with the help of others. Christian faith is not taught in schools like it once was, nor are any other religions. But a child must believe in something and love themselves. This is imperative. I cannot stress this enough.

I suffered a great deal for many years because of feeling unloved and lacking faith. Honestly, I still struggle at times with these things. But as I build momentum writing this book, the music for the *momentum* project and the band music, I grow each day. With each visit to the gym and writing session, I feel better and better about myself because I'm building integrity with myself and God, keeping my word.

Once negative seeds have been planted, they grow like weeds. The more positive seeds also grow. But if these negative seeds aren't dealt with, they can kill the good plant in the person's heart – just like an abandoned, dilapidated house with an overgrown front yard. Most children don't know how to sort through positive and negative input and disregard the negative and nurture the positive. Many adults don't even know how to. There needs to be a permanent solution to the problem rather than just constantly weeding.

I remember when I was a kid, I saw one of the neighbors put a black plastic ground cover around their plants and cover it with tan bark. That way there was nowhere for the weeds to grow. Then they could just focus on watering and nurturing the good plant. But with humans it's a little more difficult because we are getting negative input from external sources and then internalizing it.

One of the first steps is knowing the truth. If you tell a child you love them, they are special, you believe in them and God loves them, that is their reference point. As the authority figure in their lives, you are giving them a foundation for their self-image. They may get conflicting information from some people at school. But with constant positive reinforcement, they will forge a rock-solid self-perception. Too often some parents, teachers and peers rarely express love and acceptance to the child, especially if that child is acting out due to issues. They may see the child as an annoying pain in the neck. I think this mainly falls on the parents. If the child doesn't feel supported and loved by one or both parents, they have no foundation. No good plant to nurture, just weeds.

Maybe some parents are imbalanced themselves and have no clue how to nurture and support a child. I don't want to short change parents here. I know the overwhelming majority of them would do anything for their children. But often we fail to see our own flaws and how they will affect the development of our children. Love is so powerful and so pivotal to development. Feeling unloved or having no concept of true unconditional love can be devastating to the developing mind.

When a child perceives they are being rejected or abandoned by their parents, they take this on as their identity and self-perception. Sometimes the child will gravitate toward other children who also have a less than favorable perception of themselves. Once a child has settled into the idea that they are not good enough, unwanted, unloved, that they don't fit in – the next natural step is to start developing low self-worth or even self-contempt, blaming themselves. Unfortunately, what often follows is destructive behavior. Aggression directed toward themselves or others.

When a child feels unloved, they feel deeply hurt and over time, that hurt turns to sadness and anger.

"They don't love me, so F#$% them."

"They won't accept me, so F#$% them."

"They don't appreciate me, so I will find other people like me who accept me the way I am."

Even in elementary school I was beginning to act out. With this sense of needing extra attention all the time, I remember killing bugs. I am sure all kids do this but looking back that was a destructive expression toward living things. And it even made me feel a little guilty.

I used to go out to the field and lift a board that had been there so long, the earth under it had taken on the flat surface of the board. And the exposed big black crickets would scatter. I would take a rock and smash them, beige bug guts jutting out from under the rock, as the others scrambled to get away. Looking back, I think it was a feeling of power. I felt helpless in the situation I was in, not fitting in, so this was a place where I had power. This is a byproduct of what feeling unloved can do to a child. It can perpetuate destruction and self-destruction. I am sure kids in some neighborhoods were doing far worse with beating up, stabbing and shooting other kids. So, it can be serious when children act out from feeling unloved.

What made me feel guilty and remorseful toward the crickets happened a few days later. I was laying on my bed on my back, looking up at the ceiling, and I heard a scraping sound over and over. Not knowing what it was, I turned on the light to investigate. After looking around the room, I located the culprit. It was one of those black crickets from the field across the street. He was eating some of the paper off a paper grocery bag sitting in the corner. I didn't kill him, I just went back and laid down. A few days later, I felt a funny feeling on my arm. When I looked down, it was one of those crickets on my arm. I quickly jumped and knocked it off my arm and it scurried away. That showed me maybe I didn't have as much power as I thought. Like the old saying, "What goes around, comes around." It's all about perspective. That is why respecting life is so important. But those poor crickets that were minding their own business had to be killed for me to learn that. That is one thing I really believe is true. Often there are lessons in bad experiences.

For me, self-destructive and escapist behavior began in my mid-teens or earlier. When I was in elementary school, I was doing self-destructive things, but I didn't know it. I was obsessed with sugar and it is amazing I didn't get childhood diabetes. When I was about 10, my friend's brother let me have a sip from his Colt 45 tall can. I remember it tasted terrible, but it was cold. I didn't even get a buzz, but I never had the perception that drinking was bad or potentially even self-destructive behavior.

By early high school, I'd really set into my low self-perception and was looking for an escape. I was shy but extroverted at the same time. I loved to make people laugh and get attention but had very few friends, and girls thought I was immature and stupid, at least that's what I thought. But when I was alone in my bed at night, I was deeply sad and dejected. What I learned quickly about trying to escape from reality via altering of consciousness is you wake up the next day in the same life situation.

You have two choices. To drink and get high again or address how you really feel and the root cause of it. Obviously, I didn't know this at the time, so I often took the first choice. I realized there was a major problem with my heart at that time, so I began to seek answers and solutions by studying psychology. I didn't even think to read the Bible at the time. From what I'd been hearing from my father, that was not the path to the peace of mind I was seeking. So, I studied about coping mechanisms and all that, but I was in no position to apply those principles to my life. I was in emotional turmoil much of the time through constant disappointments.

In times when I found myself isolated by fear and insecurity, I eventually learned to turn to God. But in the early days of youth, I had not even developed a real belief in God or any higher power. I was leaning on my relationships with people to give me a sense of belonging, which often fell short of really fortifying me as I needed.

As early as I can remember, music became my place of solace. I would listen to the radio in the Buick 225 maroon boat of a car I spoke of, on the little transistor AM radio my mom kept in the classroom to listen to after school. Other times, I turned on the big furniture-looking '70s console player, with the turntable and 8-track set down in it. I remember you'd slide the cover over it and it would just look like a dresser or something. I even had a little miniature boombox I could listen to on headphones. In those days, you'd make cassette mixes of music you liked. DJs made more elaborate versions but most of us just recorded songs off the radio. My sister was really into R & B and radio pop when we were little. Groups like the Gap Band, DeBarge, Mtume, Cameo. I was really into how funky those arrangements sounded.

One time I went into my parent's room at night, when their lights were out, because I was shy and sang in my undeveloped higher voice the Manhattans:

"Honey you are my shining star,

don't you go away,

gonna be right here where you are

'til my dying day."

I loved those old Doo Wop ballads. I could feel that music in my heart. It was an outlet for believing love existed and was awesome. There was something so comforting and soothing in those melodies. I believe that is what those artists tapped into that made the experience so special. I felt God's love before I even knew there was a God. That was the evidence of his existence that I was not even seeking at the time. These melodies were hard wired into my brain, to the point where I can hear them in my head until this day and still know most of the words. Those lyrics were my life's blood as far as emotional and spiritual support. There was such an innocence and hopefulness in some of those melodies and phrases.

My grandmother on my father's side lived in this small town in Texas just south of the Oklahoma border in the bottom of the Panhandle. My dad was raised there, from right up until about 10 years old, when his mother and father divorced. We would drive out there summers to visit her. Over the years we went in several different vehicles but this time we went in the Dodge Van conversion. I loved that van so much. It had a seat in the back that folded down to a bed. That was my favorite thing. So many adventures in that van.

One of the things I loved the most about those trips is we had air conditioning, and we would frequently stop to get Lay's sour cream and onion chips, sodas, Ding Dongs, Ho Hos and my favorite you could only get in the Bay area. I can't remember what they were called but it was two little banana bread cups with this banana cream filling. I remember when I opened the package the frosting would stick to the plastic wrapping, and I would quickly lick that first, to not miss an ounce of the cream.

I could also bring along my action figures and little cars and make elaborate scenarios with the characters I created. Video games were just coming out around that time too in the early '80s, like the first major system Atari 2600. Which were pretty much just blips moving across the screen when it first started, just like Pong which was basically like tennis. But my favorite thing in the world at that time, which provided hours of enjoyment, were the little hand-held games. By the time we went on this trip to Texas, Pac-Man Fever was in full swing. That was the first huge breakout game that everyone loved in the arcade and at home. But my favorite hand-held game was Scramble. The casing was beige, and it looked kind of like an over-sized calculator, with a black screen about 3 inches by 6 inches with green graphics. The early games were like that, with no multi-colored graphics, just either green, orange or white lines. I would navigate a little ship horizontally across the screen from left to right, dropping bombs and shooting enemies coming toward me simultaneously with one push of the button at a time.

I considered the drive to Texas a huge adventure. There was such freedom on the road and new things to experience. The vast deserts of Arizona stretching out as far as the eyes could see. The unbearable blistering heat when we had to turn the air conditioner off, so the car wouldn't overheat, a problem with those old cars. Especially in extreme heat. I recall almost being delirious from the heat. As it blazed and rippled off the road in clear waves you could see, we approached the oasis in the form of a mom-and-pop convenience store. The kind you see every 100 miles that you must stop at because you didn't know when you would see another.

When we hopped out of the van, I could feel the heat baking the soles of my sneakers. I think if I stood there for more than a minute, my shoes would have melted and fused with the ground. We rushed and threw open the doors of the store, hoping it would be dramatically cooler but it wasn't. When I reached into the cooler and grasped the ice-cold Coke, it almost hurt my hand – there was such a contrast between the temperature of my hand and the Coke. As we were heading out of the store, I popped the lid and tilted back my head gulping the cold beverage straight down.

I felt loved when I was in that van with my family. I felt love and awe when I looked up into that sky.

Texas was just like a road cutting right down through the middle of a barren flat landscape as far as the eyes could see. Except for an occasional small town like Henrietta, Texas, where we would stop at Dairy Queen and get a hamburger and shake. Sometimes when we passed a town, we'd see these huge silos that looked like partially build rocket ships neglecting to lift off – almost looked like those rockets from the old Road Runner cartoons. A cylinder with a funnel-shaped top. In Texas, the roads in opposite directions were far apart like about 100 feet running parallel to each other.

When we arrived in Vernon, which was just a few exits long, we pulled into the Black part of town which was not paved and slowly drove through the community to Grandmas'. When we got to her street, I noticed some of the houses were visibly vacant and half-burned down but still standing. Grandma's house had a porch on it, raised up about 3 feet, just deep enough to fit a couple chairs on. She jumped up from her seat when she realized it was us and headed out to the van to greet us. She was thin and about 5 feet 4 inches with a pleasant, calm face and a sweet voice.

She hugged me and said, "Goodness gracious, grand mommy." I loved when she would say that. I felt so warm and invited. The outside of the house looked a little rickety but inside, she kept perfect house. It was obvious she took immense pride in her house and her cooking. It was so rich, sweet and flavorful. And it would put us to sleep. I swear she could have packaged that stuff and cured insomnia for millions. At Grandma's, I also felt love. That was the best part of the trip. It made it all worthwhile. I enjoyed the adventure of the road, but it was exhausting. These were the experiences that planted the seeds of love, I needed to nourish and take care of. I just didn't know how to hang onto those feelings. There were contrasts between those experiences and some of the ones that fueled my struggle as a child going into adolescence. There was always that sense of malaise playing in the background, like a haunted Halloween record.

The trouble was I didn't know how to maintain that sense of self love. I am not aware if I had a concept of self-love. I needed to get it externally like a patient needs an oxygen tank to survive. I didn't feel that sense of love and support consistently from some of the people I needed it from most. Looking at it now, I think that is what a lot of us are doing. Living from day-to-day, seeking and getting love from wherever we can find it. The truly blessed may find a relatively consistent source of love from a spouse and children. But circumstances change. When we become too attached to another person, we can be devastated if they leave our lives. But God is consistent. He will always be there. He has been with me my whole life. Even times when I didn't know it.

I look back on some of the experiences I have had and situations I have gotten through and know he has been with me. There were times when I was wrong, and I had trespassed. What I deserved was to face the consequences for what I had done. But I turned to the Lord in desperation and asked for his help, and he got me through those situations without condemnation. What I have learned is Jesus died for my sins and took the punishment for them, so that I can be forgiven when I sin. It's not that I deserve it and I didn't always earn it but that is the incredible gift of his grace. He is indiscriminate, just like rain and sunshine. He rains on both the sinner and the saint, the righteous and the wicked. He will forgive anyone who turns to him with a true, sincere heart willing to change.

He has done it for me. He loves us and is just waiting for us to return to the fold. He is not expecting perfection from us. Christians are not here to judge and condemn, we are here to love and show God's mercy like he has shown us. The idea of being perfect must be abandoned. We are perfect in our imperfection.

In music, we often stumble on a better part by making a mistake. This happens a lot in jazz music and jam sessions. In the band's last practice, it happened. If we are afraid to make mistakes, we may never discover that next blessing.

As with most people, my family built the foundation for my sense of belonging. With them I could be myself and not be judged. However, outside of the home, it was a little more difficult. I think many of my peers were put off by my constant reaching for attention. Even in elementary school, I had a yearning and longing for love that was beyond my years. I was overwhelmed when it came to the expression of feelings toward girls and later women, although it became subtler when I grew up. When I was in my teens, one of my friends told me that I, "come on too strong." I had that all-or-nothing mentality that lends itself to depression. When I was liking the girl, I would build up my expectations and courage to approach her. When I did approach, I was shy but somehow bold at the same time. When the feelings were not reciprocated, I would be devastated. Sometimes it would work.

When I was about 12, right around the time I was liking Lara, a family moved in next door. They were from Santa Rosa. There were about five or six kids ranging from 2 to 16. The father was a war vet that looked like John Cougar Mellencamp from the early '80s, only with dirty blonde hair. (Give John Mellencamp a Google.) The dad always wore those white, short-sleeve T-shirts with the pocket on the front that you can pick up at Sears in a three pack and straight-cut 501 jeans. His face looked weathered and leathery, like he'd been out in the sun for years. His vacant eyes sat suspended in their sockets. The son closest to my age name was Joseph. He and I were about the same height and build, 5 feet and thin. He spoke with a Southern drawl, much like his father, only his was with a not-so-subtle lisp.

Joseph and I would often play war in the streets with our plastic guns, not knowing the potential destruction that could lead to if taken all the way down the line. War is taught. Us and them is taught. Just as talking things out and seeing the other party's view is taught. But Josephs' dad couldn't talk to his enemies. At that point, it was too late. He was being shot at.

One day we went into Joseph's house to get Otter Pops, to ward off the baking heat of the summer. Instead of running straight out the door to resume playing, he quietly led me up the hall without speaking. He opened the closet door and pulled back some of the old clothing hanging there, including his father's old avocado green army jacket from the war. His last name sewn on a black patch with white writing. I could see what first looked like the handle of a vacuum cleaner. But upon further inspection, it was a huge military rifle. Most likely an M60 from the war. It consisted of a black barrel about one inch in diameter and about three and a half feet long. You could see the slot on the side where you would feed in the ammunition. Next to it was a wintergreen metal box about the same size and shape of the box on the rifle. It had a handle on top like those old metal Space 1999 or Scooby Doo lunch pails from the '70s. There was a latch on the side.

When we popped it open and lifted the lid, there were bullets about the size of an adult index finger, chained together like a belt. The bullets diameter was larger at its base at about two- thirds of the way down, it tapered to a point. I later learned this is the projectile that leaves the barrel and pierces through skin, bone and organs limiting the chances of survival for the victim. I wondered if those bullets would ever be fired? Or would they just stay there in that closet dormant, waiting for their chance to explode and destroy? I know now that only man could do that. It is anger, frustration and fear that makes a man pick up a gun. Fear of being killed, fear of never seeing your family again. I wonder if Joseph ever went off to war. I was going to say we should stick to the plastic guns.

But I'm going to get radical ... let's dispel the fear and hatred that divides man and pits us against each other. It is hard for us to believe but there are countries with few guns. Gun violence is the furthest point away from love and respect for one another that you can get. On the opposite side of the spectrum is patience, kindness, love and respect for one another's differences. If we want a world where we can have peace, not lock our doors at night and trust our neighbors, it starts with that vision and faith that it can be a reality.

I once saw a documentary about gun violence where they went to Canada to ask people about their perceptions regarding fear for their safety. One lady said she's not afraid, so she doesn't lock her doors. She trusts her neighbors and she can't imagine anyone wanting to harm her. It turns out many people in her neighborhood felt the same way and said the same thing. And people in Canada have plenty of guns. They use them for hunting and for sport. Not to kill people. However, if you go south into America and told somebody they shouldn't lock their doors, they would call you crazy. But the truth is, there are many people here in the United States that believe in non-violence and effective, positive conflict resolution. A friend of mine and his wife have never had a gun. When I asked them why, they didn't feel as if a gun would help them and they didn't want blood on their hands. They are using faith as their defense, even in this tumultuous, dangerous sometimes chaotic society we live in here in America. In fact, many people are using faith and just good old-fashion minding their own business to stay out of drama and potentially dangerous situations. I have a gun my dad gave me. It is a nickel-plated Beretta Cheetah .380 automatic with a wooden brown handle. Even though I have it, I am not convinced I could bring myself to have blood on my hands like that. I know there are circumstances in which I may have to defend my family. So, far God has done the best job of that.

"Live by the sword, die by the sword" and "Thou shalt not kill." These are the principles I want to live by. If I am blessed enough to be a father, I want to teach my children to love and respect the lives of fellow humans. And to exhaust every possible resource before turning to violence in defense or offense.

In the end, I would like to be able to stand before God and say I did the best I could. We can have a world where violence is rare and contained when it flares up. But violence is like a wheel, once it's in motion, it perpetuates itself. The only way for the wheel of violence to stop turning is for the individual to take responsibility and refuse to perpetuate the violence by participating in it. I realize that may be very difficult when the wheel is already in motion. It may take great faith. But it can be done. In this life one person may see the world as this wonderful amazing creation they are blessed to enjoy and explore. And another may see it as this dark terrible place, with no hope or mercy, that wants to destroy them. Same environment, two different perceptions.

The reality of the world exists whether are perceptions are accurate or not. But maybe our perceptions affect the way the world sees us and responds to us. The way we interact with the world. Maybe our perception is the pivotal point upon which reality is affected. If we understand that the Lord loves us, will protect us and bless us, then we are not entertaining fear or letting it in. We are creating a foundation for a healthy perception of reality. I've heard that optimists live longer than pessimists.

I once worked with someone who was extremely negative. I think she was severely depressed and I am unaware if she was being treated for it properly if at all. She was so down I would give her constant positive reinforcement all day. She had been through a lot in life with many bad experiences. One thing I learned from that experience is I do not want to do that to God. Constantly turning to him, insecure with fear. Asking him for the same things in prayer over and over. Desperately wanting him to bless me or spell out a clear answer to something I was inquiring about. I realized I'd been doing that. Coming to God in fear not faith.

The wonderful thing about the Lord is his patience. I will never forget what a trainer at work Annie Heffley said to me on my first day:

"Ask me anything, no question is stupid, even if you ask me 100 times, eventually you will know it and you will never ask me again."

That is how God is with us. He wants us to come to him in faith. But he knows people are in various stages of development. Some people need constant support when their faith is weak or undeveloped. I think we all do at some point in our lives. Think of a child learning to walk for the first time. They crawl around on all fours for a while, until they realize they may be able to stand up. With their parents holding them up under their little arms, demonstrating for them what they will at some point do on their own. The child may fall 100 times, but the parent never gives up. They know the child will eventually learn. They have faith in that. That is what Jesus did. He was patient and helped countless people. People from all walks of life. All that he required is that they have faith.

God has a great abundance of patience but even he will eventually expect us to grow. Just like a child is expected to walk eventually. There is a difference between being insecure and just needing a little re-direction and ignoring and insulting God. I learned that insulting God is called "grieving the Holy Spirit." Sometimes we sin simply because we are doing what we want to do. Not to intentionally hurt God. But that is like saying I drove drunk because I like drinking, I didn't intend to kill a pedestrian. I believe that as we develop in our relationship and walk with God, we start to progress to higher levels. And different things are expected of us as we mature in faith. At some point, knowledge begins to hold you accountable. You can no longer claim ignorance. This is the point I am at in my walk with God. I am at the "walk the walk" point. It took me 46 years to get to that point and it feels so good to make him proud.

Sometimes I still struggle even when I cannot claim ignorance. That is where prayer comes in. When your prayer is asking God to help you be righteous, he is always there to motivate and inspire. I have wanted to write a book for years. I conceived the idea of *momentum* a couple years ago and I am finally doing it. When God puts something on your heart, it becomes your calling. You must do it. It is part of your destiny. I hope to provide you with the keys to unlock the potential momentum that lies inside. Momentum based on divine inspiration. Inspiration that doesn't wear thin. An unyielding driving energy.

My friend Joseph had three sisters ranging from 3 to about 16 and a brother about 15 named Gary. The middle girls name was Rona. She was around my age too. It was like I had two sets of peers – the ones from Terrell Elementary the West side of San Jose and the neighborhood kids on the East side. So, when things didn't work out with the girls at school, I had the local ones. Thankfully, some of my social disappointment at school was sometimes balanced out by other more positive neighborhood experiences.

Shortly after they first moved in, I'd see Rona playing in front of the house and thought she was cute. So, much like with Lara, I had to find a way to let her know I liked her. In keeping with my m.o., I composed one of my letters. Only this time I had a better strategy. I was going for the sympathy angle. While she was playing in the garage, I pedaled up the sidewalk toward her house. When I was right out in front of the driveway, I dropped my bike to the side. She immediately ran down the driveway, knelt beside me and said, "Are you ok?" I can't remember what I said back, but I am sure I must have been awkward and shy. We played together for the rest of the afternoon. Trudged through the huge dirt clots in the field, narrowly missing twisting our ankles and headed out to my favorite walnut tree in the middle of the field. It was the tallest one, yet still easy to climb. This was before we started building the tree forts, so we found the biggest branch that could comfortable support our tiny wiry frames and climbed out away from the tree. Sitting there next to one another. Feet dangling down. She was a tomboy who liked to do all the boy stuff. But she usually wore almost Sunday church type dresses with cute little shiny patent leather black shoes. I am sure we must have looked funny up there. Me with 10-year-old boy soiled clothing from playing all day and her looking all prim and proper.

We would just sit up in the tree sometimes for hours. Being up in that tree was like being on the top of the world to us. We didn't want to come down. Our expectations were not high about anything. It was totally organic and natural. It didn't cost a thing. We were happy to just be. Up in that tree there was no homework, no class, no chores, just pure freedom.

There were several neighborhood kids that were staples in my childhood on our street Whinney Place Way. Three really stand out. James, Dani and Marlene. I met all of them in early childhood. James mom was from El Salvador and her name was Blanca. She used to call James "Jaime" with a heavy accent. James and I were inseparable. He was like my little brother. I clearly remember those summer afternoons. Playing for what seemed like endless days. We lived to play.

One time we road our bikes around the corner and over by the frontage road on Highway 101 up by this old farm house. There were rumors the farmer up there would shoot kids with rock salt shot gun pellets if they trespassed. But that was not our intention that day. The farmers house was at the top of a steep hill. When we got to the top after vigorously pumping our pedals, leaning all the weight that our little frames had to make it up the hill, we could see all the houses below. There was something about being at the top of the world and looking down that was so soothing. A chance to reflect on things. Even at that age. Everything looked so peaceful. And it was quiet. Just like being up in a tree. We really loved seeing things from that perspective.

After a few minutes of resting from our arduous steep uphill climb, we tried to prepare ourselves for the exhilaration that was to come. Turning our bikes around perched at the top of the hill just like the slopes at the winter Olympics. We looked at each other, looked down at the steep incline in front of us and shoved off. Immediately picking up speed, like being shot out of a rocket. Hair flying back in the wind. Going so fast the bike felt a little wobbly. As if it were on the brink of falling apart. Like a makeshift rocket we designed from the ground up. A side of me wondered what if I hit a rock or a pothole right now. But the exhilaration of the moment quickly brought me back to reality. As with most exciting things in childhood and life, it ended quickly but was worth the effort of the climb.

It was these experiences that made childhood so special. It didn't cost a thing and it was there for our joy and amusement. There was an innocence at that time too. I don't remember our parents worrying about us. We would ride our bikes miles away from the house and they wouldn't even worry. There wasn't such a sense of impending problems that we have now surrounding children's safety.

When Dani and I were little – I was about 9 and she was about 7 – we walked all the way to the nearby creek. Up through the residential area and up Silver Creek Road, up to a steep hill much like the other spot James and I took our bikes to. In San Jose in the summer, the fields had this beige-colored straw that would grow wildly. Once we got off the main road by the creek, we stomped by through that foliage down through a trail that led to the little creek. There were lots of creeks like those in the area. There wasn't much water in the creek but if I remember right, there was a rope swing. We found a little watering hole where someone had been eating crayfish they'd caught. We wondered who this person was? We never saw them, but we knew they were back there in those woods somewhere. Which gave me a kind of uneasy feeling. I was a curious kid that was always looking for adventure and new experiences.

After hanging out there for a while, we headed back down Silver Creek Road toward Whinney Place Way. In those days, you had to be back for dinner or your parents would get mad. It was a little chilly, so I took my sweater and put it over her shoulders. I don't know where I got being a gentleman. Probably from Dad and the movies I had seen on TV. But it really made me feel good. Like it was a respectful way of showing how I felt and appreciated a girl. Dani was also a tomboy who even played street football with us. She was like a little sister to me. Partly because she was an only child.

It was summer of '82 or '83 when the song that changed my life first came on the radio. This was a time when radio changed many lives. Radio was all we had. No iPhones or tablets. We were glad to have cassettes.

The song started with a Congo drum beat and a bass intro à la "Streets of San Francisco" (and for those of you who do not know that means "funky as hell.") After a few bars of that, it broke into the fattest groove I'd ever heard in my life. The beat was so solid and driving and the bass just flowed. Smoothly hugging the cadence of the rhythm. You couldn't help but bob your head the instant you heard it.

That was the beginning of my long love affair with hip-hop. The song was called "Rapper's Delight" by the Sugarhill Gang. But the music had been lifted from Chic's 1979 "Good Times." Hip-hop had been going strong on the East Coast since the late '70s, but this was the first time it had been played on mainstream radio. It was riding the tail end of disco. If you YouTube "Rapper's Delight," in the video you'll see the old color-coordinated baby-blue bell bottom suits with the dark blue strips of felt, sewn down the length of each leg. The huge afros. The disco dancing-machine ladies with the maroon elephant bottoms with platform shoes and rainbow-colored tube tops with the Farrah Fawcett hair. Everybody moving their body every which way to the beat. But, no video yet at the time. I was just listening to it. And even though it was in heavy rotation on the radio, I recorded it on cassette so I could listen to it whenever I wanted.

First thing early on Saturday mornings I would slip out into the morning dew and climb up onto the fence, just under Rona's second-story window. Blasting the Sugarhill Gang groove until she came to the window and looked down on me, smiling from ear to ear. Although I thought I was quite the player when I was little, kissing several of the little girls in the neighborhood, I don't recall any "love motion" with Rona. After about a month of our courtship, it soured. She began to be mean to me and argue. Looking back, I think she was affected by her parent's constant arguing, which seemed very passionate and heated. She may have been acting out a bit.

"Rapper's Delight" had such an influence on me, it affected my choice in relationships. One of the lines was, "If your girl starts acting up, then you take her friend." Well, I graciously took that advice. See Rona had a friend named Teresa. She had light brown hair and hazel eyes. Her parents had money, so she was always wearing designer jeans. Most kids looked sloppy compared to her, even most of the girls. What I liked most about her is she liked a lot of the pop R & B my sister was exposing to me at the time and, of course, my new passion rap. She was what we called a "fly girl."

While I got along with most children, there was one kid that was particularly obnoxious and unpleasant toward me. His name was Buddy. One day I was walking with my squirrely little friend across the blacktop, past the tetherball pole chain tapping against the metal, echoing across the playground. Buddy emerged seemingly out of nowhere and buried his fist deep into my abdomen. I dropped to my knees, hunched over, head down with a string of drool hanging from my bottom lip. I could see his black Converse low-top sneakers with the circular white emblem on the side, laces dingy from kicking up dust. Before I could stand up, he dashed away blurting out a cruel, twisted cackling laugh in the tone of a 12-year-old whose voice had not changed yet. This is the same kid that later bashed my teeth into the metal water fountain, busting my lip and causing my gums to bleed. How could a child be so cruel to another child? I didn't know the answer to that at the time. I just knew he enjoyed making me suffer.

My mom, being a teacher at the school, had Buddy's brother Sam in her class. He was really a behavior problem. To the point where the principal had to intervene many times. Including having parent-teacher-principal private conferences. When mom spoke to his mother, it seemed he had a father who was emotionally unavailable, physically and mentally abusive. I am sure my mom only got half of the story. God only knows what Buddy and Sam were facing when they returned from school every day. I saw them as unbearable to be around. But they were children that didn't choose their set of circumstances. They were simply reacting to the adverse situation they found themselves in.

No matter how bad the abuse the child only has two choices. Leave or stay and take it. Thank goodness for divorce, grandmas and loving aunties who will take children in. The unfortunate other option is for kids to take to the streets. And that is not unusual either. It depends on how unbearable the abuse is. But then, ironically, they go out into the world only to find the abusers have many faces. Somehow, they feel they have more control over their life when they are running. It's difficult to wrap my mind around the idea of children having to face things that some adults have never even faced. I realize now it wasn't Buddy that punched me in the stomach, it was his father's frustration and anger channeled through Buddy. And where did Buddy's father's frustration come from?

Love can stop the cycle. One person having empathy and compassion despite their frustration can stop the cycle. Two unconditional arms stretched out wide open to receive the broken with sensitivity and kindness. Buddy and I could have been the best of friends if we had the luxury to put our weapons down. When we see ourselves in others, it's easier to have compassion for them. But first we must have compassion for ourselves. Kindness and love toward ourselves. If you can empathize with yourself, you can understand the true nature of God's love. His unwavering support. The Lord knew I would learn something from that punch in the stomach. I am thankful for that. I experienced something unpleasant that taught me to have empathy for one of my peers. It was not just an unpleasant experience it was a lesson under God's tutelage.

Many people like Buddy go on to find compassion and love in their hearts through the birth of their first child or maybe sooner with that long first walk down the aisle. I am sure many men who were bullies as children go on to feel empathy for their victims knowing they wouldn't want their children to be harassed at school. That is just the learning curve and the evolution of an individual's spirit. But some men may not learn in this lifetime.

Having two groups of kids to play with had its advantages. If I had a rough day at school, I could come back to the neighborhood and enjoy my friends there or vice versa. For the longest time I was walking everywhere but there was one form of transportation that was about to revolutionize my life. It all started with my first bike – red with silver flakes that caught the light and shimmered as it moved. It had a long black banana-shaped seat with a crisscross pattern sewn into it in a diamond pattern. The wheels were black too but with the thick white wall design, like the ones on old '50s cars. The handlebars stuck right out to the side.

When I threw my leg up over the seat and attempted to turn the pedals, it was as if I was trying to ride the bike through sand. I was working up a sweat to pedal just the stretch on the front sidewalk of our house. My friend and I walked down to the bike store and told the man behind the counter the wheels wouldn't turn right, and it was hard to pedal. So, he said he would fix it and took my name.

Later I told Dad I'd taken the bike to the store to get fixed. Dad was upset the man had received the bike from me without him present, so we went down there. Dad let the man know he was not pleased with the way he was doing business, got back the bike and asked for his money back. My dad is very direct when it comes to confrontations. He doesn't back down. It's just not in him. So, when the man went to give him his change, he had broken 5 to 10 dollars' worth of change into a large amount of coins nickels, dimes, even pennies just to be a jerk. When he did that, it set my dad off.

He took the change and threw it across the counter. You could hear the change chattering on the floor.

I just remember telling him, "Dad we better leave."

I was afraid we were going to get in trouble. My dad stormed out of the store with me trailing behind him. I didn't understand why my dad had gotten so angry. I had not had the experiences he did. So, there was no way I could have understood as a child, just above his knee, looking up at him towering over me. This was not the first time my dad had encountered that type of adversity.

What I realize now is different people have their own ways of dealing with confrontations. But it's still basically like nature – fight or flight. I never had to face the level of opposition and adversity my father had, so I couldn't relate to the level of anger he had inside.

When my dad was 5 or 6 years old, he was in the cotton fields of Texas with his family. At that age, he was not expected to really pick. He was just being groomed for future long days of grueling work in the relentless heat. See, during cotton season the whole family and much of the Black community were out there. It was a time where plenty of money could be made. The adults had sacks that looked like pillowcases but made of burlap and about 8 to 10 feet long. As they slowly worked their way down the rows hunched over back and legs aching, they would fill up the sack. My dad and his other little siblings had sacks the size of a regular pillowcase. When they got tired of playing and picking a little wad of cotton here and there, they'd hitch a ride on their mother or father's sack. Sliding along behind them through the field as if they were on a magic carpet. I am sure the children's minds wandered. Pretending to be Errol Flynn or Daniel Boone. He said there were even snakes slithering through those fields looking for a rat or gopher meal. Dad didn't have a bike. In fact, very few people in his neighborhood did. He may not have had a bike yet, but he had some awesome adventures with Grandpa Curtis Senior.

When my dad was about 10 years old, he went to live with his father. In those days, Black men's job opportunities were limited to say the least. But Grandpa was a hard-steady worker. His jobs included gas station attendant, janitor, porter at a bus station, garbage man to name a few. He also kept an old truck for hauling garbage privately for people. One of the places Grandpa worked was a janitor at the police station. Dad learned his excellent work ethic from Grandpa. So, instead of running around like a kid which he was, he brought his shoe shine box to the police station and told all the officers he would shine their shoes for free. So, he did. This went on for months and months until Christmas came. He arrived at the station as usual to shine. But all the officers were gathered around a shiny brand-new bike. Much like the one he would later buy me. The difference is – he earned it. It didn't come without sacrifice and work. And he was not expecting it. He was doing it because he wanted the officers to look sharp when they went out on the beat. He was proud of that bike. He had profound respect for the officers and it meant a lot to see the fruits of his effort. Dad knew the true value of that bike. Not what it cost in dollars and cents but what it was truly worth. He was the only kid in his neighborhood who had a new bike.

Dad had respect for authority. But he expected it in return. Not as a handout. Because he earned it. However, in the South in the '50s and '60s, no amount of arduous work would be rewarded fairly by some. I say by some because there were always good white people who knew racism was wrong. My dad said that. Many of them marched beside Marth Luther King, Jr. on Selma, Alabama, risking their very lives for what was right.

It's difficult to understand the effect that being oppressed has on the human psyche. Simply because many have never been in that situation themselves. Perspectives are developed through experiences and observations. Some may be able to relate to it ideologically, but they haven't felt it to the core of who they are. But I feel it's possible for someone who has not experienced racism firsthand to empathize. Just human compassion. But it starts with some having love for themselves.

It's impossible to hate an entire group of people without hating a part of yourself. If you hate a portion of the humanity of which you are a part, you hate a part of yourself. Often, if not most of the time, hatred is born from within. As I've said, it's all about love and how we see ourselves in relation to the world around us. I believe it is impossible to love yourself and hate others at the same time. Like a person who has a cancerous tumor in their body that you can't see from the surface. If it goes unaddressed for too long, it can kill its host. Hate is like that tumor. It just keeps growing and growing slowly, eating all the healthy tissue around it.

This makes me think of the mass shootings plaguing our country for the last 20 years, from Columbine to San Bernadino. One thing I'm sure we all noticed is most of the shooters kill themselves after their rampage. We can say it is because they didn't want to go to jail, but I think there is another factor. I think after they have killed, they implode and direct their hatred inward, which is where it was all along. I believe some of these people have been detached for so long they are just on autopilot for the enemy. They don't question or challenge the negative thoughts and ideas they are having. The cancer grows to a point where the host person is given over totally to destruction which is the ultimate manifestation of hatred. Much like cancer if detected early enough the hatred can be located and addressed at its source. Then be removed and the person can return to a normal life.

But often hate goes undetected. We don't pay attention to the little comments that sound like a joke but become more and more frequent. We fail to notice the changes in behavior. We are unaware of the extent someone is struggling. So, we assume they are ok. Sometimes that is not the case. They are far from ok. It is then time for them to look themselves in the eye and be honest.

Why am I so angry?

Why do I hate people?

How do I feel about myself and why?

We have a society that enables hateful people and validates them. They simply seek out other people that believe the same thing they do to create a perception that what they are thinking and believing is normal. A good gauge is asking yourself, "Am I agitated, angry, frustrated, bitter and just generally miserable?" I would suggest you question if that is normal or how you really want to feel. It is a very uncomfortable place to be. What I haven't addressed much here is the condition of one's spirit. Sometimes a person has a heart problem in the core of who they are. Many have severely broken hearts that desperately need to be healed. One may have spiritual cancer where their spirit is sick, keeping them prisoner to negative feelings.

I've had my own mental and spiritual challenges that we'll explore. These conditions of the spirit are just like any other medical illness. There are certain symptoms and certain treatments. I hope we can use our collective experiences as a guide through the eye of the storm. Where everything is peaceful, despite the swirling torrent all around trying to block our momentum toward God.

3

A Transition from Sports to Music

Going from elementary school on the West Side to junior high on the East Side was like making it to the next floor in the Bruce Lee martial arts movie "Game of Death." Some of the kids on East Side were living hard with the gangs in low-income neighborhoods. I made a few friends who were enduring terrible things in their home lives.

In my household, Bruce Lee was held in the highest regard especially by my father. With the constant themes of seeking vengeance for the killing of family members and friends, Lee was always outnumbered but never once showed fear. He carried himself with an air of determination and confidence. It was his destiny to avenge the lives of those he had lost. Much like the old video games of the '80s, there were different henchmen who had to be defeated to move to the next phase of the game.

Thankfully my foes were not literal in junior high. It was my fears and insecurities that were my greatest adversaries and would prove to be ongoing opponents throughout my adult life. At the end of each Bruce Lee movie, he would face his ultimate nemesis and of course defeat him.

These films captured my imagination.

In the summer of the year between elementary and junior high, my friends and I would walk down to the Gould Dollar Cinema, about an hour walk, and watch the latest Karate movies. They seemed to be popular then. I remember that summer it was *Ninja Assassin* that showed ninjas using grappling hooks to climb over high concrete walls to come and kill their enemy in the night. We were so intrigued by these movies we would buy the karate magazines. In the back, they had catalogues where you could buy real metal throwing stars, sais and nun-chucks also made popular by Bruce Lee. The stars were actually dull and had to be sharpened to stick into a tree or the fence. That summer, I decided to enroll in karate. It seemed like a natural next step. My father felt it would build my confidence by giving me self-defense skills.

Tae Kwon Do is a Korean martial art that emphasized striking and offense. Most classes consisted of practicing the different kicks and punches in groups. Toward the end of each class, we would do free sparring or fighting. When I first started, I was insecure about the fighting portion but as time went on, I got used to it. One thing I learned is the fantasy is always different than the reality. No matter what it is. For one thing, getting kicked didn't really hurt that bad. One time I was fighting a guy bigger than me, and when I lunged forward to go in for the attack, he perfectly timed a side kick right as I was coming in and took me off my feet to the ground. There was no time for fear. The next thing I knew, I was just getting up off the floor.

Our teacher Sah Bum Nim Mike taught us to only use martial arts to defend ourselves, not in anger or to hurt someone. But anger is an opponent within itself. Feeling we have something to prove is another. Even at that early age, some of my frustrations were bubbling to the surface in those karate sessions. When we would spar, the teacher would split us up into four groups by our level of talent. This day I was in group two out of four – four being the most aggressive and talented kids.

The kid I was sparring with was tall and skinny with glasses I was considerably shorter than him and equally thin. That day I was frustrated that I was in the lower group. I saw an opening between his arms, where he was attempting to block his abdomen, and proceeded to swing kick him as hard as I could in the stomach. When he hunched over, that triggered me to go in for the kill, so to speak. In just a few seconds, I kicked him five or six more times. It was like everything was silent in my head when it was happening. I was so focused. The teacher stepped in and moved me up to group three. I remember feeling a little bit sorry for the other guy after I'd done it. After all, I had let my anger get the better of me and I was basically rewarded for it.

When I advanced to the next level, I proceeded to immediately get my ass kicked by everyone on that level. Which provided me with another lesson. No matter how good you are, eventually you are going to run into someone better. At some point being on top just is not as important as you once thought it was. You start to put other people in front of yourself and mentor others. That is an awesome part of the process and journey that many are blessed enough to experience.

When I was in karate, I wanted to make my dad proud, as would any child. But Dad had the bar set high for me. He wanted me to be the best kid in karate class – the Black Bruce Lee, if you will – and so did I. Sometimes I didn't apply myself enough and Dad would reprimand me. One time, the whole class was going to jog down to the junior high and back, and Dad took it like a race where I should be leader of the pack. But I was not inspired enough that day and was all the way at the back of the pack. He was disappointed and for the first time that I can remember, used some adjectives that were hurtful to me. Looking back there may have been some truth to it, but it was very hurtful and affected my self-esteem going into junior high and high school. He said I was a lazy procrastinator and I was content doing the bare minimum. The truth was, I just wanted to be accepted and loved by my dad unconditionally. I didn't want to have to prove something to him.

I went on to proudly become a red belt in Tae Kwon Do by the age of 13, just one belt under black. The competition started to get stiff and I knew the tournaments were coming which I was intimidated by, because people get knocked out and you had to fight two people simultaneously to get a black belt. Also, I had been playing a lot of street football in the summers and wanted to try my hand at football in high school.

Even though I lived on East Side, Tae Kwon Do was not something I needed for survival. I hardly ever got in fights because I got along so well with people. I ended up living by the code that Sah Bum Nim taught me to only use it in self-defense.

Time had gone by so fast. Suddenly it was my first day of freshman year in high school. A dreaded transition for me. Becoming a little fish in a big pond. That first day was so important. I really wanted to be on point. This was fall of '84, so I had all the current fashion choices. Black parachute pants with zippers all over. Some horizontal, some diagonal, some vertical and some seemingly random with almost no purpose. I think some of them were not even pockets. They were just there for looks. Then I had a black cotton T-shirt with green showing under the sleeves with a diagonal zipper that when pulled down exposed the same color green of the sleeves. The jacket was most likely the black 501 Run DMC button down. I was super into their music at that time. I also remember Velcro being popular on shoes. But I was rocking the Adidas white shell toes with black stripes ("The ones I like to wear, when I rock the mic ... " – Run DMC.)

First day, first class of the day, I met Gary in Mr. Pointer's history class. I knew him from LeyVa Junior High PE class. He really stood out to me because he was not competitive at all in track. I was the total opposite I always felt I had something to prove and took competition as an opportunity to shine and gain acceptance. I remember laughing out loud about the fact that he came in toward the back of the pack when we ran the mile. Much like I had done in Tae Kwon Do. He just didn't care, and I thought that was hella funny. Little did I know how much he had to offer as a human being and how long our friendship would last from then until now. More than 30 years so far.

Up until that point, I'd listened to mostly R & B and the fresh music that had just blown up. Rap. *Purple Rain* had just come out and I remember that being one of the first things I asked Gary had he seen it or not. My friendship with Gary was a turning point for me. I was about to be turned on to the world of rock 'n roll. Plus, Gary and I had a similar take on school. We were not very social, but we enjoyed making people laugh.

I had been playing a lot of street football in the neighborhood. Our block against other blocks. And I had become good at throwing the pig skin. For some reason, none of us ever thought of going down to the high school and playing tackle. Personally, I was not all that suited for it anyway. I was 5 feet 6 inches and about 120 pounds. So, by the time I tried out for football with the Silver Creek Raiders Junior Varsity, I had no experience with tackle football and I was this little guy. I didn't make the team along with another kid that looked just like me named William who would later go on to play the next year. I remember feeling really dejected when I didn't make the team. I felt as if I was not good enough despite how much football I'd played in the streets. But the coach told me he was afraid of me getting hurt. Looking back, it was probably one of the best rejections that ever happened to me. Often God closes doors to guide us to the right door. By process of elimination, we eventually find the right one.

"Ask, and it shall be given; seek, and ye shall find."

When I told my parents and they saw how disappointed I was, they decided to seek other alternatives to high school football. We had a program in the area called the Police Athletic League (PAL) that would just let you play for fun. You just had to pay for the uniforms and to participate. Our uniforms were yellow and blue. We were kind of like the Rams.

Within the first week of being on the team, the coach noticed what was holding me back. Fear. I was afraid of tackling. Which was essential to the game obviously. He knew I needed to overcome my fear. So, he did something dramatic. At least it was from the perspective of a 14-year-old who was 5 feet 6 and 120 pounds. He put me on one end of the field and the whole team on the other end. Like a punt return, only I had no blockers. It was just me and a whole team coming at me like a wall. I was terrified to say the least. But like a scared animal, I did what I had to do. It was like karate – the next thing I knew, I was just on the ground wondering what hit me. Jumping back up and doing it all over again.

Much like with karate, Dad didn't feel like I was being aggressive and competitive enough. Like the coach, he noticed I was scared and just wanted to give me a little tough love to get me up to speed. My dad didn't realize how intimidating he could be. I was really scared of him at times. And I am sure he didn't realize it.

One day after practice he told me, "If you don't tackle, you better be afraid of me, not your teammates."

Dad was not aware of the effect these things were having on me because we never discussed it. I didn't understand at the time Dad did love me. He just wanted me to succeed. After a couple months, the pressure got to be too much for both Dad and I in PAL, so I quit. That was like the closing of a chapter to a dream for me. Something I loved. I never thought about playing pro or anything. I just loved the game and enjoyed it on so many levels. That broke my heart deeply and was internalized as a monumental failure for me at the time. I didn't know what God's plan was. It was really the close of the sports chapter of my life. I haven't participated in any sport seriously since. It is something I would like to take up again sometime. Without the pressure. Knowing I have nothing to prove.

The truth was, in the wake of that perceived failure, I kind of hit the f@$%-it-I-don't-care switch which would dramatically change my direction.

When I was about 10 years old, my friends brother used to joke around with me and say certain things put hairs on my chest. Beer, women and hot sauce. So, one day he gave me a sip of his tall can of malt liquor. It was even named after a gun – Colt 45. I remember almost spitting it out as it touched my young palate but keeping it in my mouth and forcing it down, so I could look like a grownup. He laughed. At the time, I had no interest in it. It tasted disgusting and I didn't even know it would give me that treasured buzz I'd become so accustomed to later.

But after the PAL disappointment, I felt I had a reason to escape into the realm of self-defeating behavior. It was the beginning of doubting myself and feeling like I didn't measure up. That was what would go on to comprise a big part of the foundation of my low self-esteem.

When I started high school, I also entered the Esteem Program for kids a teacher felt had low self-esteem. Looking back, I think our junior high teachers most likely pointed out the students they felt would benefit from the program. It started the first day of freshman year. As a student that was in the program, I felt it was a bit hurtful to be pointed out publicly as a kid with low self-esteem. They could have been a bit more tactful with the name of the program. But just like most things in the '80s, they were not very PC.

The teacher I remember in the Esteem Program was Mrs. Jusa. She was in her late 30s and what stood out the most is she would wear Kangaroo sneakers, the ones that with the Velcro flaps that keep them closed instead of laces. Looking back, they may have even been the no name brand knockoffs you could get at Kmart, and I recall us making fun of that too. We also thought it was funny she wore sneakers with a long jean skirt and a long-sleeve turtle neck sweater. She used to say one of the only things I still remember from the program:

"When a peer is insulting or humiliating you, tell them – you know, that's a put down and it really hurts."

We thought that was hilarious. We couldn't imagine saying that. They would really go in for the kill. I vaguely remember us sitting in groups and each of us saying things about topics prompted by the teacher. They were all just surface things. It is good they noticed which students were struggling with low self-esteem, but I feel they should have went for the foundation upon which self-esteem is built. Which is feeling loved and worthy of love. Most of the acting-out by teenagers is low self-esteem directly related to a feeling of being misunderstood or unloved by parents and peers.

On my campus, much like some of the teen movies in the '80s our campus had about 10 to 12 groups most kids fell into one way or another. The jocks, the preppies, the mods, the punk rockers, death rockers or metal heads, stoners, nerds, surfers, cholos, R & B hip-hop kids and the misfits that didn't even fit into any of those categories. Gary and I had friends in several of those groups who we'd entertain with our dorky brand of humor. I know I personally was borderline annoying and overbearing. We would never get invited to parties. We really felt like outsiders. I don't think I ever went on an actual date, but I flirted like crazy. I remember my friend Will saying I came on too strong. I was 15. I really didn't like academics and studying. It bored me and made me sleepy because it didn't interest me. My dad really pressured me to focus on my studies. He knew I needed to be educated, to have a professional career to take care of a family. But I was just a kid who couldn't grasp an adult perspective. I just wanted to have fun and make everybody laugh.

By sophomore year, the I-don't-give-a-f@$% switch was ripped out of the wall and thrown out the window. I had rejected myself. Repeatedly shooting myself in the foot. One night after a spaghetti dinner at my parents' house, Will came to pick me up. I was a huge Star Wars fan and I remember laying on my back with my feet up on the dresser. Playing Star Master on the Atari 2600 game and pretending like I was Luke in the cockpit of an X-wing destroying the Death Star. (I am sure I was not the only kid doing that. Now we have a whole new generation doing it.). I jumped up and bounded out the door with my friend. Hanging out with Will and Gary was super cool because I was having new experiences. I had never gone out in a car with friends and stayed out until midnight It was pure freedom. An evening to just do what I wanted, without the constraints that school and parents put on me.

Will knew older guys that had bought him a 12 pack for us to drink that night.

It was hidden in a bush near his house. We drove over to a nearby school after dark and walked out onto the campus, 12 pack in hand. We busted it open and started to drink them. It was harsh in taste but cold and refreshing. I half heaved the first few sips because my body was not used to drinking a whole beer. Four beers later, the guys and I were ready to go down to the stores and hang out. The stores being a strip mall along Aborn road in San Jose. There was a liquor store, 7-11, pizza places and the videogames. Different stores had different games.

That night we went across the street to Lucky's cause our favorite game was there. As I was watching my friend play, I started to feel a little queasy and wobbly on my legs. After a few minutes, I rushed out the automatic sliding door and proceeded to empty the contents of my stomach on the sidewalk right outside the door. The spaghetti, the beer. I hobbled away, one foot going one way and one going the other and wound up flat on my back in the ivy next to a bank. World spinning around. I remember saying out loud, "I will never drink again." I had yet to keep that promise. But I think I had the right idea for sure. I grew to like the feeling of being buzzed and the break from reality I got from it. My mom always said she likes having her faculties, so she doesn't like being drunk. That is exactly what I liked. It was unhealthy then and it is unhealthy now. That was the first time I had altered my state of consciousness to cope with my problems and have fun. That was one of the several ways that I'd come to escape.

When I got up the next morning, I learned a valuable life lesson. Your problems aren't resolved because you got drunk or high. Reality is waiting for you the moment you sober up. What I needed to do was channel my negative feelings into something constructive that would build me up. Much like what my sister had done. She was three years older than me, so she was a senior. Despite pressures from life, she was a yearbook editor. Plus, a track runner and vice president of the Senior Class. She took circumstances that were not perfect and channeled her energy into something that would build her life up, rather than tear it down. Anne didn't struggle with alcohol. She was too busy building the life she had envisioned for herself. Anne looked at adversity as a motivating force. Not something to bring her down. She would go over, around or under it.

My mom had a teacher tell her when she was in school, "You will run into obstacles but don't let that stop you. Create a way out."

I say, "Be like MacGyver. Make a grappling hook out of an old umbrella and some twine you found beside the building and scale that wall." The differences between Anne and I prove that two people can grow up in the same environment, with very similar sets of circumstances. One can wallow and get stuck in a rut and one can flourish and grow to their fullest potential. Anne was also very extroverted. She knew all the popular people, the latest dances, styles.

I, on the other hand, am a thinker. Analytical and capable of focusing on a task. Meticulous to detail. I have always loved religion and philosophy. High school is when I first began to study psychology. I wanted to see why I was so unhappy and how I could overcome it. But no matter how much I read the circumstances of my life were not changing. I didn't understand the world around me was reacting to me.

If I acted insecure, it came off as a lack of confidence.

If I acted overbearing, it was a turn off.

But confidence had to be earned. If not, it can wear thin when you're put on the spot. You can only fake it for so long.

We didn't speak much of God in my household through my childhood years. And when we did, my father spoke against the Christian church from experiences that he had in his youth. The people in his church were living lives that directly contradicted the Word of God that they were supposed to be living by. And that had a profound effect on his perception of the church and God. He felt as if people used their positions of authority in the Church for personal gain, whether financially or to commit adultery and other sins. He was convinced that preachers wanted to take advantage of people because that had been his experience. If those people only knew how much damage they had done to his perception of religious authority figures, they'd be beyond ashamed. But they were human beings.

Human beings have a nature to sin and struggle. The goal of a Christian is to love and be Christ like, but God knew that we would make mistakes. He loved us so much he allowed room for us to make mistakes. What my father didn't understand is those people did not represent God. They were humans with flaws that were struggling with their own demons.

The truth is, God loved those people that were a bad example to my father. Everyone has a story. We are all at various levels of development and here to learn something. It was in the early 1950s when my Father had these experiences in the Church. There was a lot of racial tension in the South at that time and people had a lot of frustration, anger, sadness, disillusionment surrounding the situation they found themselves in. Many people used sexual pleasure and alcohol to cope with their negative feelings. To escape if only for a few minutes or hours from the constant oppression and being made to feel inferior to the white people of the time. There was a lot of fear there too. In my grandfather's generation, Blacks were being pulled out of their houses in the night and killed. So, there was a lot of constant tension that needed to be relieved. In many southern Black Communities, there were very few outlets for entertainment. It was either Church, the bar or a little of both. Many Black people, my dad included, may have been wondering if God loved them. And if so, why they had to exist within this set of circumstances?

I believe one of my dad's saving graces was his father Curtis Senior. Grandpa worked hard, and he taught Dad to work hard. That if he had a job, he would be able to take care of himself. When Dad was 10, his father and mother divorced, and he went to live with his father. There was no babysitter, so my dad went with Grandpa everywhere and I mean everywhere.

One time he brought Dad into the bar and the bartender said, "Curtis, you know you can't bring that kid in here. He has to be 21."

Grandpa said, "He's with me." Grandpa was over 6 feet and about 250 pounds of solid muscle from all the labor jobs he had done over the years, so the bartender said "Ok" to avoid a confrontation.

Dad was exposed to things no one his age should even hear about let alone witness. But these experiences made him mature fast. He was not babied. When he got a spanking, he had to lick his own wounds. No mother saying, "I'm sorry, baby." I think being a sidekick to Grandpa empowered him and showed him he could do things and take on responsibilities usually reserved for people well beyond his age.

When I look at where my father was at 10 and where I was at 10, I see the dramatic difference between our experiences. But our hardships are relative and real to us nonetheless. I learned from Dad that a man works to provide for himself and his family, period. That was never a question. Not everyone is taught that. And I am truly blessed to have learned that. For many young men that did not have a father in their life, things may have been different. Some of them were taught to pursue fast illegal money and ended up part of the prison system that houses so many of our bright young men that made serious misguided mistakes when they were young.

But my dad was there for me and worked hard to give us the life he envisioned for us. I love him for that.

My friends and I were looking to escape from the confines of suburban, middle-class teen life. We were somewhat socially inept and didn't engage in many of the activities other teens considered everyday life. Like getting a girl's number at school, going out on dates, good night kisses. Our weekends consisted of going over each other's houses. Listening to classic rock 'n roll records and watching videos. We loved horror and sci fi movies too. Videogames and many a Friday night at Chuck E. Cheese pizza time theatre, which would become my first job.

Another thing we liked to do is go up to the mountain roads, curving up into the darkness. Not knowing what was around the next corner. It was symbolic of our lives at the time. We didn't know what tomorrow would bring, but we were zipping around the corners in the darkness, often right along cliff edges that descended into the darkness like an abyss. There was something exciting about the edge being so close and the danger so eminent. It made us feel alive. It was adventure, we were in control. Not our parents or the school. That was a feeling of power I had not yet experienced and it was intoxicating.

One of my friends had been smoking pot and turned me on to it. This was another step further into the unknown. My mom said she didn't have to experience being high. She was told it wasn't healthy for her, so she just didn't do it. Me? I was the type that wanted and felt I needed it to cope with and, more specifically, escape from reality. Pot introduced me to seeing things from different perspectives. I had never really thought much about those things with my sober consciousness.

Like I am tiny when I look up at the sky and realize the sun holds Earth in orbit.

Am I a mere dot in someone else's sky?

All those little dots like an old Lite Brite toy set are suns. I am almost microscopic compared to that. But when you look at my skin under a microscope, the cells that comprise my skin look like canyons. And there are space aged looking creatures crawling all over my skin that can't been seen with the naked eye. That the inner space is almost as vast as the outer. Just as the Planets revolve around the sun every atom that comprises the matter that all things are comprised of has protons and electrons revolving around the neutron. That is passion to me. It opened a world of curiosity and questions. So many unknowns in the equation of life. The things that are known being like stars in the sky that we can connect, to try and create a universal shape that ties everything together.

One time I'd been out with friends and we'd bought some pot and smoked some. I had a little left in the bag, so I shoved it down the front of my pants into my underwear. When I got home, I walked down the hall to my room and it dropped out.

My dad came up the hall and said, "Is this your grass?" (Grass being what they called marijuana in the '60s, which always makes people laugh when I tell them this story)

I said, "No, it was my friends." Then I said I'd only done it two or three times. By that time, I had been doing it for a few months relatively frequently. Often before school in the field. I even had a little bong made from a little jar we got in chemistry class. I even put brandy in it instead of water. I used to keep it in my locker and sometime my inside pocket of my jacket. Well my dad wanted to know who this friend was that I was smoking pot with. I was always with one friend at the time, so he assumed that it was him. So, he forbade me to hang around with him.

I'll never forget what he said to me next. This was top notch parenting here because it really worked.

He said, "You disrespected the family by bringing this in here. Be prepared, because your mother might cry when she gets home, and I tell her."

When she got home, she took the bag out of his hand laughed and said, "So, this is what marijuana looks like?"

My dad said, "It's not funny." So, it blew over for the time being. But what stuck with me is that I had been disrespectful. I quit smoking at that point in sophomore year, but that was not the end of my exploration of altering consciousness. Since then, I smoked maybe three times in my early 20s.

Now that I could no longer hang with my main friend outside of school, I started to hang with Will. One time he asked me if I had ever done acid. I'd heard about it because I was really getting into everything '70s retro, and I knew the hippies did it, including one of my favorite rock icons Jimi Hendrix. So, there was a lot of curiosity surrounding it. I'd heard people would see things melting and morph right before their eyes. Really dramatic stuff.

Sitting in his early '70s Vega, he took out a little piece of foil with two little square pieces of paper on it. I put it on my tongue and just let it dissolve, he did the same. We then headed over to the movie theater by the Winchester Mystery House in San Jose. In the trailer for one of the movies, a man was crucified on a cross I believe it was supposed to be Jesus, but I didn't know it at the time. He went over a waterfall while on the cross and went down a violently rushing river. For some reason, this was funny to me and Will. I mean really, really, funny. I mean absolutely, hilarious. The next thing we knew, we were hunched over, damn near falling out of our seats. When we looked to our right, a couple that had been sitting just a few seats over from us were on the other side of the whole theater.

The interesting thing is, at the time, I hardly had a conscious relationship with God and no concept of Jesus. I was just struggling and trying to ease the pain. The sad part, I felt just as helpless as a person would feel in that predicament. Hands bound, tied to a cross and rushing down a river. Unable to control things due to bondage and circumstances that were out of my control.

When I got home that night, I was too high to be paranoid about my dad thinking I was high. He was watching a very strange movie to cap off my very strange and interesting night. A Jamaican Rastafarian karate movie. Very campy bad acting but totally rad. It was as if God had shined down on me that night. I just laughed a little with Dad and went to bed. I had come down considerably.

One day, Will told me something that would make an indelible mark on me and shape my behavior for years to come, all the way to this day. He said never do any powder drugs. Like heroin, cocaine or speed. That was a powerful message coming from a peer that I had drank, smoked pot and done acid with. I never have, and I have Will to thank for that. And I did thank him recently – he saved me back then from making a bad situation worse with a condition I didn't even know about yet.

4

Path to Plan A – Guitars, Girls and Grades

I think a teen has a lot better chance of avoiding drugs and alcohol if they have a support network of friends and family they can talk to and address the challenges they're facing directly and honestly. So, their struggles can be resolved in a healthy productive manner. What I did was surround myself with other teens that were struggling just as much as I was, who were using unhealthy habits to cope with the stresses of teen life. I was getting support on some level because we were going through similar experiences and feelings. But we were also enabling each other to engage in self-destructive and counterproductive behavior.

I had a friend in high school who was having such a hard time emotionally and spiritually he had to be admitted to a psyche ward by his parents. His father was controlling. They came from a culture where the father played the dominant role in the family and women and children were subservient to the father. Much like me, he had only one main friend he hung out with all the time at school. They were super into the Beatles which gave us something in common. Since Gary and I were really getting into '70s rock 'n roll. Although the Beatles were not really our favorite band. More like Led Zeppelin, The Who, James Gang, Black Sabbath. My friend told me the people in the psyche ward had no clue what he was going through and talking to me for an hour was more valuable to him that a week at the facility.

He told me his father didn't like him listening to American music and his sister was gravitating toward American boys when they preferred arranged marriages in their culture. His father ripped all his posters off the wall and threw out his records. He was just a kid trying to find his own way, express himself and adjust to a new culture. He had not chosen the situation he was in. He was just trying to be himself and get by.

I think it's common for children and parents to not totally get each other. The parents were raised in a different time and were socialized in a totally different environment. So, their perceptions of things can often be dramatically different. Also, parents have an enormous amount of experience. Some of the lessons they learned are applicable to their time frame and some are universal lessons that transcend trends and time periods. This generation gap can be bridged with patience and a healthy dose of love from both the parent and child. For two people to respect each other, they need to care about one another's feelings. If a child feels unloved and doesn't think the parent cares about them, they are more likely to rebel and fall in with peers who are also rebelling.

I had a female friend who was dating one of my friends tell me something awesome about how her mother got her to be obedient.

Her mother said, "I love you and when you go out and do not call me or come home late, it worries me, and I stay up on the edge of my seat by the phone."

The key word there was love. Her mom communicated that she loves her first and wants her to be safe. She knows her mom's concern is motivated by love and although it may seem smothering, she just wants her to come home safe.

Contrast that with a teenager coming home an hour after curfew and the parents yell, "Why did you disobey me? I told you to be home at ten! Go to your room! I do not want to see your face!"

A child dealt with like that feels the parent doesn't love them and just wants to keep them from escaping and enjoying their friends. So, it is all about communication and perceptions. Just think of the long-term effect that ineffective communication could have on a person's self-worth over an extended period.

Psychologists say a child's basic character is formed by the time they are 12 years old. Really think about that. Being a parent is the greatest responsibility a person can ever have. But as Jesus said – if we learn nothing else from his teachings – is love one another. If that could be our guiding principle, everything else might just fall into place. After all, that is all anyone wants is a little love and respect. Love breaks down barriers, walls and fear. Hate builds walls that imprison.

Once the wall is up, it is hard to communicate with a wall. We must work to bring the wall back down, to communicate with the person again. Hate is isolating and can create an almost unbearable environment that can lead to lashing out in violence. We need love. Without it we can develop "cancer of the spirit."

My band had a song titled "Cancer of the Spirit." It is about the spiritual malaise that can develop if a person goes too long without love and the perception of not being loved. All the manifestations of fear, sadness, confusion, frustration, disillusionment, contempt for one's self and others. Living with these downward spiral emotions all the time can be beyond unbearable and feel insurmountable, to say the least. Prison is often self-imposed, out of becoming comfortable with a level of suffering and fear of greater suffering if one steps outside of that comfort zone.

There have been times in my life where I have been self-aware that I was a prisoner but often I had no idea what to do about it. There was an artist in the late '80s named Richard Marx who had a line from his song "Hold on to the Nights," which really resonated with me. I know he has dealt with depression because only someone that has would think to phrase it like this, "I don't know how, to stop this feeling this way, hold onto the night, hold onto the memories." In my early years, I spent countless hours indulging in self-pity and morose. Now I realize what a waste that was. I could have been experiencing life and enjoying myself, but I chose to perpetuate the problem by sitting in that prison, comfortable with my discomfort. Now that I know and understand love more, that truth is liberating.

Maybe this is all an opportunity to learn about building up a child's natural strengths in character and gifts. Inspire them to develop those gifts. And teach them how to stay motivated by setting short-term goals and plugging away. Going easy on themselves when there is a setback and honing their craft. I truly believe everyone has a specific purpose and has the potential to become the highest form of themselves, with diligence and effort. Many people go on to spend many years doing things they aren't passionate about. That do not use their core strengths, giving them the feeling that they are not serving their higher purpose.

A sense of worthlessness. Just punching a clock to pay bills.

When we have so much more to offer as a human being.

As people, we have been sold this lie. That we must live passionless mundane lives with no spark. The truth is, we are choosing to do that. There are a lot of other choices. Like many kids, when I first picked up my guitar at 17, I had an idol – Jimi Hendrix. Someone I looked up to as an icon. A reference point of greatness. But I was told …

It was a far-fetched hobby.

I needed something to fall back on.

I needed to be sensible.

I had to pay my bills

To build my life around Plan B. Not to focus all my extra time and passion on Plan A and just do plan B to fund plan A until it popped.

When I was in junior year, I met a special person named Tom Choi. Even though Tom was only in high school, he had his own style and sound. He was in a band called Ear Wax with a few of his friends from the other side of town. What I loved about those guys was there was no security net and playing it safe. There was no Plan B. Plan A was their passion.

We all have separate roles in life and some people find their peace in Plan B. But the Plan A people continue to intrigue and inspire me. One is a path of fear and one is a path of faith. Think of the kid who joins a tongue-in-cheek punk band like Ear Wax, but his Dad wants him to be an engineer. He has no interest in that and is not passionate about it. Plan A being the punk band and Plan B being the engineer job. There are potential rewards with both paths. But one path is a passion and one is a safe, tried-and-true route.

In situations like this, what should a parent tell the child? As adults, we know regret can be a tough pill to swallow. And it is something we start to face later in life. Not having a Plan B can be terrifying to a person who is pragmatic and logical. It is the unknown. But not having a Plan B is an adventure to the person of faith. The truth is, there is a place in this world for every type of person and we go through distinct phases in our lives.

Ear Wax transformed into a more serious heavy outfit called Asbestos Death and later Tom formed his band ItIsEye. His bandmates. Al, Matt and Chris went on to form Sleep. All these guys except for Chris had no Plan B through their 20s, 30s and 40s and are recording artists until this day. I remember one-time Matt, Tom and I went to the mountains. We were drinking, and Matt walked right up to the edge of a cliff with a vertical drop of about 80 feet. I wouldn't even go all the way to the edge. About three or four feet out from the edge was a rock. Without hesitation, Matt jumped from the edge of the cliff on to the adjacent rock. There was no fear, apprehension, doubt or safety net at the bottom of that cliff. He trusted in his own ability to make that jump safely. I on the other hand stood in awe, "Wow, dude."

Matt just followed through, trusting himself every step of the way and is now and has been for many years a Rock Star. Matt's father didn't believe he would make it to his goal and tried to discourage him. The truth is, it was Matt's destiny to be where he is. A lion will always be a lion. It is so inspiring seeing he didn't let fear impede his progress. Matt and I are alike in so many ways. We had similar experiences coming up. And both of us are passionate guitar players. And we both believe in living the dream.

Young people need inspiration and fuel for their dreams. I am not implying every child out here should aspire to be an athlete or entertainer – unless it's something they are passionate about. They can explore the vast amount of interests and find something that really resonates with them.

Senior year had finally come, and I was desperately trying to graduate. Thank God you could get a few Ds and still graduate, or I probably wouldn't have. It was getting toward the end of the year and prom was coming. There was one girl I was really into. Her name was Stephanie, at 5 feet 10 inches, light brown hair, hourglass figure, the cutest smile. What I liked about her most was how playful she was.

One time I bought her these miniature squirt guns of about four in a package. I remember how easy it was to just rip the packages open at the top. We had so much fun squirting each other with those little guns. Just like many of the other girls I liked in high school, I think she was overwhelmed by me. I was playful boarder lining on childish for that time, although I was still just a teen. I wanted to ask her to the prom, but she always hung around with this other kid. I found out later he was not even her boyfriend, I was jealous because I wanted to spend time with her too.

I was too insecure to ask her to prom. I was certain that she would say no, so I didn't even bother. At that age, I thought I had a lot to prove due to insecurity, so I would often make a fool out of myself. I was so busy trying to talk the girls who didn't like me into liking me, that I didn't even notice the ones who did. I was not even aware of any girls that were crushing on me. And I am sure there had to have been a few. Another thing I had the tendency to do was anticipate rejection before it even came. Often not even bothering to try.

The night of the prom had come, and my friend and I went over to the Zippy Mart where they sold beer to minors. Sometimes we had to ask adults to buy for us or an older brother, sister or cousin. When I went up to the counter, the palms of my hands were moist with anticipation. Was he really going to sell it to me? Was this the right cashier or do all of them sell it? At that time, a 12 pack was about 10 bucks if I remember right. He quickly pulled out a brown paper bag from under the counter and bagged the beer quickly before anyone could see. And barked, "20 dollars."

I jammed my hand down into my pocket and pulled out my wallet, retrieving a 20 and handing it to him. We darted for the door as if we had just stolen something. I was not aware of them ever getting busted for selling to minors, but it seemed like a shaky operation to me.

As we pulled out of the parking lot into the intersection, I noticed a car behind us that looked like my parents' car. I was not supposed to be hanging out with my friend due to the weed thing, and he had a 12 pack of beer on the floor board between his legs. I felt as if the cops were behind me with their lights flashing. I gunned it from the light and made a left. With a couple quick maneuvers, I'd lost them. A few minutes later we were in the Chuck E. Cheese parking lot in East San Jose, pounding beers in the car. It was Friday night and I had a buzz, but this was prom night.

I wondered what I had been missing all that time. Never having even been on any date, let alone a prom date. That night I killed it at Rush 'n Attack, a videogame based on the beef we were having with Russia at the time. I was an American fighter, running from left to right on the screen shooting, bombing and incinerating my enemies on the screen indiscriminately pounding on the machine, cursing every time I lost a man. That was my outlet. My way of venting my frustration, anger, bitterness. I learned how to cope with my problems with alcohol, pot, violent movies and videogames. By the end of High School, I had not even developed the basic social skills to get a girlfriend, and I felt as if I was in a state of perpetual rejection and coping with those feelings.

Music was to become a driving force to me. A reason to carry on. A platform on which I could stand with confidence and honor. But I didn't know it at the time. I had just picked up my dad's 1960s Yamaha acoustic guitar. My grandpa had played a little, so my dad picked it up at a pawn shop and hardly even played it. When I first went to strum it, the strings were loose and impossible to tune. But I tried to play it anyway and broke a string. (I told my mom I broke the string and was afraid my dad would get mad because it was his guitar.) When I finally got it strung and tuned, I learned a few power chords. These were simple because it only required you hit two strings at a time.

My friend Tom was in Ear Wax at the time, so my first songs were simple with power chords. My first song was called "Societies Humanoid" at the time I felt like everybody I knew on the campus was trying to fall into some preset category. That they were not really searching for their core identity and just falling into some default idea of what they were supposed to be. The truth is, we were all trying to establish an identity and just gravitating towards the scene that most fit our personalities. That had people that we identified with.

I am a Black guy from an upper middle-class family, I went to an all-white elementary and lived in mixed neighborhood. I identified with the average white kid with friends from all the different minority groups. I was in a unique situation. I was really blessed to be exposed to that kind of diversity. We used to always imitate people's accents like many of the comedians at the time were doing. Personally, I was not making fun of other people's way of speaking and culture. I loved diverse cultures and was fascinated by the different ways people spoke. I loved the way it sounded so I wanted to imitate it. Then I could hear it whenever I wanted.

Gary was really gifted and always got A's through high school. He got accepted to

San Diego State, a real party school close to the Tijuana border. I barely graduated and was not accepted to any college. I don't even think I applied. I did do well on the SATs.

Then my parents and I moved to Stockton in the last six months before graduation. They didn't expect the house to sell so fast, but it did. So, I finished out the year commuting. We would drop off my dad in Santa Clara. Then my mom and I usually stopped and got donuts at Winchell's. Then across town to West San Jose as she still taught at the Terrell the elementary school. Then she would reverse it on the way home. Commuting absolutely sucked. I would get home and just pass out on the bed for a couple hours. Then take a shower when I woke up. I am still shocked I graduated. It was tight.

After graduation, I found myself in this new Central Valley town of Stockton. I didn't know anyone and was still socially awkward, so I decided to attend San Joaquin Delta College, the local community school. I absolutely hated school and was only going because that was what I felt was expected of me. And I was young and needed the comradery of my peers. I took a regular load of classes.

My father had bought me an entry-level electric guitar called a Dean Z Jammer II at the local Mr. C's music store, a little combo that they sold as a pair for like $99. I was really stoked about this. It sounded terrible and fed back when you turned toward the amp, but it was my first guitar. At the time, I wore a little Fender Strat keychain on my belt loop wherever I went. Which caught the eye of a stoner looking kid named John. He saw the chain and asked me if I played guitar. I said yeah.

He invited me over his house in Lodi to jam with him and his friend Phil who also played guitar. John had a cool style of playing drums, kind of like Mitch Mitchell of the Jimi Hendrix Experience meets Ginger Baker of Cream. He had a real sense of groove. Really organic drummer. And it matched his personality. He was a huge KISS, AC/DC and Pink Floyd fan. Phil played a Gibson SG, the kind of guitar Angus Young from AC/DC played. And he used Marshall amplification.

Around the time I started jamming with these guys, I'd been working for Target in security for almost a year. On layaway, I had a cream color Fender Stratocaster with a white pick guard and a maple neck. I religiously went and made payments on that guitar as my checks came in. I will never forget the day he lifted that black guitar case up onto the counter and turned it around toward me. Almost like when they make you a pizza and present it you before you walk off with it – but 100 times better.

The inside of the case smelled like the interior of a new car. Just sitting there, waiting to be played, and it was mine. Little did I know the journey of a lifetime was about to begin as I walked out of the music store with a definite pep in my step. I decided to use solid state Fender amplification, which would later lead to my powerful punchy sound.

There was a lot of anticipation the first time I drove up to John's house, popped the trunk, retrieving my gear. The first thing we did was popped the caps off a few beers. Then we headed to a small middle room in his parents' house where he had his drums set up. He had a pillow in his bass drum to muffle the sound. We couldn't rock like we really wanted to in this environment, but the experience was liberating. We had the freedom to just express ourselves without anyone's input, opinion, critiques or judgments.

It was like a conversation with the clock running. It was the first time I had played music in unison. Johns incessant groove, Phil's droning guitar sounding like a freight train coming down the tracks. And me wailing over the top of it with shrieking guitar runs. I had never known a feeling like that. It was as if a part of me that had been dormant had finally come back to life. It felt like I was continuing a conversation that had been interrupted.

There was something about playing over a beat that I absolutely loved. It was in that little spare bedroom I fell in love with playing guitar. I think to have a lifelong love affair with music there must be passion there. A love for the craft. Something that you will do anyways. No matter what the rewards or the lack there of. I truly believe God put that calling on my heart to play guitar until the end.

Inspired by our jam sessions, I decided to take guitar lessons. I think I found the teacher through a flyer in the music store. I came from the era of shredding guitar licks. Guitarists like Eddie Van Halen and Slash The majority of guitarist shared the goal of playing clean and fast, usually with distortion. My guitar teachers name was Ritchie Rojas. Which I thought was a cool name because one of my favorite popular guitarists was Ritchie Blackmore from Deep Purple and Rainbow. Ritchie taught me scales and song structure, which would comprise the foundation for song writing and guitar playing. I had developed a lot of bad habits before I took lessons that I needed to unlearn. With Ritchie's tutelage, I was finally able to play and write in key.

Armed with this knowledge, I began to pen my first song in A minor. It didn't have a title at the time but would go on to become "Leave it Alone" on the record *Art of Solitude*. It happened at work. Standing next to the EAS system at Target. You know the alarm that goes off when a person leaves the store without paying? I heard a part in my head. At the time, I didn't have a handheld recorder yet to remember parts. So, I just thought about the part all day. Couldn't get the infectious rhythm and melody out of my head. All the way home up I-5, down Turner Rd, along to School Street – it was still in my head. I rushed in. Went into my room, where I had my little boombox with an onboard mic you could record on. I pulled out my guitar and recorded it. When I played it back, I discovered my second love – producing. Having ideas in your head and putting them together to make a final recording.

I was really stoked to play it with Phil and John. One of us played the clean, picked guitar part and the other the lead. Around that time, I bought a Casio keyboard with preset beats you could play over. I discovered that if I took two little boomboxes with external mics, I could record two tracks at the same time. I would record the beat and rhythm guitar on one box and play it back, while playing the keyboard line over it and recording it on the second box. By then, they already had multitrack recorders. I was just unaware of it.

Eventually I got a 4-track cassette recorder. With that, I could record four tracks with over dub layering.

There was a girl at Target named Robin. She was a typical '80s rocker/stoner chick and I loved that. She loved bands like Bon Jovi and Skid Row. She drove a maroon late '60s Camaro. She was fricken bad ass. I really dug her, but she acted kind of aloof toward me. She became the inspiration for my second song. The ironic thing is I only liked her for about two weeks, but this song would eventually find its way onto *Art of Solitude* too, a collection of songs that I compiled from the early '90s through 2008. Under the name "Robin," this was the first song I did an almost full arrangement for, minus bass. Keyboard, guitar and vocal. At that time, I was immersing myself in music theory and loving every second of it. Scribbling on little pieces of paper and recording parts into my handheld recorder. I had found one of my true callings. Being creative for me was like breathing. I didn't feel alive unless I was doing it on a regular basis.

For the first time in my life, I was out on my own and living with friends in Lodi. After a few months, my Dad bought me my absolute dream car although I may not have totally known or totally appreciated it at the time. A light green 1970 Pontiac Firebird 350 with a two-barrel carburetor. My friends loved muscle cars like a lot of the small town young adults did in those days. There was not much to do. So, they would buy cars and soup them up. My friend had a Maroon 1955 Chevy 396 with a 4-barrel carburetor. His was an absolute monster. It idled like a drag racer. Car moving left and right with every pop and hiss. It was so awesome driving up to the house in my car. My friends were stoked. It was such an awesome car it didn't really need any souping up. Something about those old muscle cars, the music we loved and whiskey/beer went hand in hand.

Through John, I met his brother Dave, Dina and Bob who I ended up living with. John and Dave both had girlfriends, Bernadette and Michelle. Almost everybody in the scene was coupled up and we hardly ever had additional single girls in the scene. I was like the fifth wheel. I had to seek girls outside our little scene. Usually girls at work. One day, I saw a short cute Mexican brunette walking by my post at Target. It was like things were in slow motion, like those campy movies with "Dreamweaver" playing in the background. Just kidding. But she was rad, total Phoebe Cates *Fast Times at Ridgemont High* moment for me. She was short and petite. She lived in a small-town East of 99 called Linden. We would literally talk for hours on the phone. About every topic you can image. She shared her dreams, her desires, her darkest fears. She told me some things I think were most likely just stories she was trying to be dramatic. After about a month of chatting on the phone, she agreed to let me pick her up in Linden on the side of the road. I suspect she didn't want her parents to know her business that she was dating me. I think her whole family spoke Spanish. As I was driving, "Ice Ice Baby" by Vanilla Ice (or should I say Queen and David Bowie) was on the radio. It was a hot song at the time. I knew all the words.

When we got back to the house, there was nothing else to talk about. For the first time in my young adult life, I made out, but I was too unconfident to follow through. I was 20 years old. One of my friends later said "she wanted you to take charge." By this time, I had seen a lot porn. I had older friends, so alcohol and porn were readily assessable. From what I'd seen, the woman would just start doing everything with the guy. What I quickly learned is the reality is always different than the fantasy. It is one thing to watch other people have sex and another to experience the sensations. Those movies never gave me a clue as to how to develop the kind of relationship that would lead to a sexual encounter. 9 times out of 10 my insecurity would ruin things before they could ever develop.

I am from a generation that was literally raised on porn. I have met girls who say they learned about sex from watching porn. And some that are grossed out if you even bring it up. But for a young man it is like a rite of passage in American society. When I was in elementary school, two of my friends and I found a porno mag over by the kindergarten benches. The guy was giving a lady oral sex. I didn't really know how to process what I was seeing. So, I read the text under it. I will never forget what it said, "I want to see your tongue in my nice hot juicy cunt." To the young me, the words shocked.

Later in junior high, a friend of mine had me and a few other friends over after school. And we watched a porno. At that age, I was starting to become aware of my sexual desires, but it felt awkward being around other people. Later in life, I went on to watch it in private as most do. In my case it became more of a crutch than something that liberated me. Without possessing the social skills to build a relationship, the fantasy of porn would become an escape just like alcohol, drugs and junk food. Children need to be taught to build healthy functional relationships where they are respectful and loving to women. With porn as most men's reference point, how will men learn that a big part of the connection comes from having love for the woman? Not just getting off. Porn is basically like watching a prostitute and a john have sex. Except both are being paid. But it serves its purpose to the person that is just looking to get off with no strings attached. But it can lead to other trespasses like sexually promiscuous behavior that could lead to disease. Sex itself can become another crutch that one uses to cope with their problems. There is a relief of tension that comes with it that is healthy. But when used in an unhealthy manner, it can be destructive to ourselves and others.

After the encounter with my first girlfriend was not fully consummated, things quickly fell apart for us. I didn't understand at the time but one lady I met said that if the guy doesn't follow through it makes her feel insecure. Like she is not sexy. It validates her insecurities. I don't even think I realized that young ladies were struggling with insecurity too and probably were just as shaky and embarrassed as I was in those first few encounters. At the time, I internalized this encounter in a negative way and considered myself a failure for not following through.

One thing I have learned is we must develop the ability to be kind, supportive and patient with ourselves. People with low self-esteem can be incredibly cruel to themselves.

Constantly repeating negative scenarios over and over …
How could I have done that? I am so stupid.
Giving themselves all or nothing self-chatter …
I am never going to get a girlfriend.
I am never going to make the team.
I will never get into college.

That was one of my worst habits. Things can seem dismal when we put them in hopeless terms using words like never and can't. It's rare that those words truly apply to a situation. Those are limitations we often set for ourselves. It is like tethering yourself to a tree with a 10-foot rope like people do to make dogs aggressive and mean. If you set limitations for yourself long enough that can become your comfort zone. You know what bondage feels like, but you somehow feel like you have more control. You have some comfort in your level of suffering. And fear if you venture outside that 10-foot self-imposed parameter, you may face even greater discomfort and suffering. This plays into a helpless cycle of hopelessness. It is impossible to have joy when you are in a state of hopelessness. I know that sounds obvious. But I didn't realize that for years.

Hopelessness was my reality, my comfort zone, my reference point. If someone came and removed the rope that tethered me to that tree, I probably would have stayed right there in the yard. Growing and changing can be very intimidating and uncomfortable for a person with low self-worth and limited expectations.

What would happen if I chose to fill myself with positive, uplifting and hopeful things? With wild dreams that get your heart pumping, make the palms of your hands sweat?

That make you feel like you are so light you could float up through the clouds?

At that point in my life I had not even felt those things. I had not allowed myself to. But often in my dreams, I would soar. I would feel the cool wind whisking across my face. Feeling the hair on my limbs standing on end. Hovering high above landscape I had never seen before. Pure freedom. No bondage. Pure exhilaration. This was the real Lance. This is where I belonged. No expectations of me, no judgments. Just being the bird, I was meant to be. Not to be accepted by people or get accolades. Just to do what I was designed by God to do. My role in the big picture.

Then I would awake and instantly feel disappointed I was tethered to this life. Bound by circumstances beyond my control. I found it difficult to feel that sense of exhilaration I had in the dream in waking life. Waking life felt confining. It did not feel liberating. I hated having to roll out of bed to do some stupid job I didn't care about. But I did enjoy some of the little simple things that kept so many of us going. Well, maybe not everybody made the kind of morning joe I did.

I would make this incredibly unhealthy concoction to wake me up when I started working at Chief Auto Parts warehouse. I had to be at work at 4 a.m., so this is how I'd start the morning (don't try this at home … you've been warned):

- Set aside a 64-ounce Big Gulp.
- Boil a cup of water in the microwave.
- Dump about four heaping spoons of instant coffee into Big Gulp cup,
- Along with an equal amount of creamer.
- The kicker … pour in can of Mountain Dew (because friend said it had the most caffeine.)
- Fill with ice until almost to the rim.

I wouldn't have made it through without "that frozen concoction that helped me hang on" (in the words of Jimmy Buffet.)

Another thing I loved in waking life was hanging out with my roommates on the porch of that old country house on School Street in Lodi. We had an old couch and one of those La-Z-Boy recliners. We would sometimes sit out there for hours, sipping Schafer's and Wild Turkey, talking until the wee hours of the morning. It was so nice to talk to peers covering every topic. At a certain time, every night, we heard the train come through in the distance. Just a friendly reminder that our little town's heart was still beating. There was something so peaceful about those nights.

Maybe those moments that I loved were my soaring, my exhilaration, my reason to carry on. Maybe we needed each other to get through our awkward, more dependent years. Maybe that was only a glimpse of the joy I could experience if I were to believe in and expect lofty things. Maybe flying was a choice. Maybe I never had to wake up. Maybe I could focus on the things that gave me the fuel, motivation and inspiration to fly.

I've heard people ask, "If you could go back and tell your 20-year-old self one thing, what would it be?"

I think I'd say, "Live your passion. Make your life a dream that you never want to awaken from, through trust, faith in God's purpose for your life and diligent work."

I've learned that what we focus on becomes our experience.

If we anticipate rejection, we approach a situation dejected before we start. But if we anticipate the life the Lord wants us to have, refrain from developing unrealistic expectations and avoid trying to control every detail, good things will come with time, hard work and faith in the destiny God has written for our lives.

I sometimes think where would I be had I taken my mother's advice to pursue education in music? Or where would I be if I had taken my junior college teacher's advice to pursue an education in creative writing? The truth is I had voices speaking to me, but I didn't follow through. I was concerned about the things my father said. "How are you going to pay the bills with music? You need something to fall back on." But he has expressed his support for me writing a book. I remember at the time he was leaning towards me being an Engineer or a CPA, both seemed logical but not using my natural talents or skills. Having played with John and Phil, I was starting to develop the dream of making it big in music. Although it seemed like the goal was on the opposite side of the planet to where I was then, it was starting to become a dream.

Sometimes it takes decades for people to take good advice and follow through. I have produced four records in the last decade but never written a book. This is my first crack at it. What I found is, just like with producing a record …

Start with a single melody.

A single chord progression.

A verse of lyric or a chorus.

Then a theme.

One day, while returning to Stockton from Pacifica after helping my sister move, I saw a license plate frame on a car that said "Momentum." I started to think about how important it is to develop momentum when you are pursuing any goal. And realized that it took momentum to achieve all the things I had done thus far. I had received an anointing from God when I produced my last album *Gratitude*, that gave me the momentum I needed to follow through.

I wrote for seven months straight and I never drank alcohol that whole time. At that moment, I had a clear picture of what it was that I wanted to achieve. I just needed the motivation and inspiration to follow through.

Later in this book I'll share a step-by-step process as to how I developed and maintained a sense of momentum throughout this project and how you can do it too.

Realize that no obstacle you have created in your mind is insurmountable. And very few things are impossible to do. Just look at the advancements that human kind has made in the last 100 years. It is absolutely astounding.

One thing that you can use right now is this.

Have you ever had a friend who loved you dearly and supported you through thick and thin? Was honest with you but gentle? Shared the good and troubled times with you?

You can learn to be that person to yourself too. You spend more time with yourself than anyone. Self-love makes the experience of daily life so much more pleasant and emotionally healthy. That self-love is going to be the foundation for the joy you are going to experience.

In my late teens, I had very little love for myself but desperately wanted to ease the pain of rejection I was feeling from myself and others. Sometimes to see things clearly you need a bird's eye view. When you are amid a situation and immersed in the emotions surrounding it, being objective can be difficult. I believe this is where vacations come in handy. From long prolific, life-changing vacations to laying on your back with your eyes closed, music either blaring riffs into the head phones or subtly soothing and relaxing every muscle in your body. In those days, vacation out of the country was not even a thought. It was so unattainable it was not even considered an option. My vacations had to be within driving distance and no more than a tank each way. A change of environment and context often creates a change in perspective.

The weekend had finally come, and it was time to head up north to Arcata to visit my Lodi friends John, Murphy and Phil. The warehouse job at Chief Auto Parts had become routine. Almost to the point of a rut. I was basically living to drink, play music and hang out with my friends. That was keeping me going. But there was still this incredible undertone of spiritual malaise I was struggling with. A malaise I associated with the life I had back in Lodi. There is something so liberating about jumping in an old Chevy truck and heading way north. To a destination I had never even heard of, let alone seen and experienced.

From what my roommates said I knew it was near the beach. That was about it. There was also a lot of anticipation since I had never been on a road trip with friends. I always went with my family. On the way up there, we had a blast making fun of the town names. Like Garberville, Weott, Fortuna. We wondered what people did in those little towns of just a gas station/general store and bar. Some towns seemed even smaller than Lodi, which I considered a small town because I was from San Jose. You could literally fit 10 Lodis in San Jose. My old East side of town was bigger than Lodi. We imaged what an average Friday night would be like in a tiny town like Fortuna. Something told us it would involve a lot of drinking and maybe sex. If you were lucky.

When we arrived in Arcata, John came out to the car. It really felt like seeing a brother who went off to college. And it was that to Dave. Knowing we were coming, John had planned a little party to welcome us. I can't remember if it was at his small apartment or a house. I think it was a house. I can just hear David Bowie's "Fame" blaring loudly as he opened the door and we stepped in. There were about a dozen people, six or seven of which were people I knew well. I love those kinds of parties when there is some sense of familiarity. There is an instant sense of belonging. And depending on the environment, you know there were a few people that had your back. (In Stockton, that was way more necessary than in Arcata.)

As I stood in the kitchen chugging my first beer to make me feel less awkward around the people I didn't yet know, I noticed a girl standing alone looking as insecure as I felt. She was about 5 feet 7 with light brown hair hanging in curls, haphazardly, as if she had just rushed out the door in excitement without looking back. She had cute chubby chipmunk cheeks, naturally rosy from the cool evening air as she had just arrived. Her bottom lip was full enough that it could easily be suckled between mine. She was wearing a pastel sweater that came down over her waist with a big thick belt diagonal across her hips. Stone wash jean skirt just above the knees and a well-worn pointy pair of light brown cow-girl boots. I mean this girl was Rad. Totally late '80s hot.

Unaware of what possessed me or gave me the courage, I just walked right up to her and said hey. Easily and smoothly, starting a conversation. It was like I knew exactly what to say and when, and it didn't seem forced or awkward. I was not overbearing. I think what I had found was a woman that genuinely clicked with me. I didn't have to be something I was not to impress her. She already liked me. That was not a common occurrence for me. After hours that seemed like minutes of flirty banter, my ride was leaving back to Johns. Everyone was planning to go to the beach the next day, so we planned to see each other the next day.

That next morning, I woke up so horny. The tension between Denise and I had border lined on overwhelming the night before. I felt we both were anticipating a greater connection to come and hopefully soon, as I was only there for the weekend and lived six hours away. When I saw Denise the next day, she was with a friend. With this friend around, the energy between Denise and I changed dramatically. It appeared as if she was trying to hide how she felt now. When I tried to talk to her, the friend would eye her like she was doing something wrong. Looking back, I think Denise had a local boyfriend that was not around that weekend or something and her friend was giving her a hard time for giving me time.

As we walked down the beach in a group, I kind of lagged a bit. Hope and excitement was quickly turning to disappointment. I was much more accustomed to the feeling of disappointment than I was the exhilaration of a new romance. But it really sucked. And we both knew it was now or never. It was not feasible for me to have a romantic relationship with that kind of distance between us. I would never see her. And I didn't know her relationship status. We never discussed it. Circumstance had claimed another budding relationship.

It is funny how we can so easily find love outside of our area and comfort zone and then return to it because things did not work out. So for me, at the time, it was nothing ventured nothing gained. The hardest things about these summer or weekend romances is never getting another chance to tell her how I felt.

That summer Gary came from San Diego State to visit me. Chief Auto Parts was having a picnic at a park in Stockton and we decided to put a set of cover songs together to play there live for my coworkers. We were really into '70s rock. A couple songs from Jethro Tull including "Nothing to Say" off the album *Benefit*, and I know we did "Rat Bat Blue" by Deep Purple. It was really cool playing a live set with my brother Gary.

The last time I attempted a live performance alone it had been a disaster. I had recorded a backing track consisting of keyboard beats to play the songs over. My stage was the little plot of concrete steps behind the back door of the small three-bedroom house. The backyard was where the crowd would form, which consisted of my roommates Bob, Dina and Dave along with a few friends. I still had my Dean Z Jammer II and a little Dean Markley combo amp my dad bought me.

I believe the first song was "Johnny B Good," a Chuck Berry song famously remade by my guitar idol Jimi Hendrix. I had rehearsed over these backing tracks for hours. I was actually considering this a show. It was a show for me. I had never played in front of my peers before. But it was the perfect audience. They liked all the same music I did, and they were supportive, even though it was just me playing guitar over a backing track alone at a party. I had drank about half a bottle of Carlo Rossi wine from this big ol' jug about 8 inches in diameter and about as tall as a regular bottle of wine. So, I was well lit. I think beyond the point of being able to play guitar well.

For me drinking heavily and playing guitar live do not go together. It makes my playing sloppy and I am more likely to forget what I rehearsed. So, I made my grand entrance swinging out the back door with my guitar strapped over my shoulder, stepping out onto the top of the three-step back porch. Which was just big enough to fit my little 10-watt amp with a little room left for me to stand. I reached down and hit play on the same boom box I'd rehearsed with. Immediately, the beat started, and I rifled into the intro of the song. Looking at my left hand the whole time, nervously avoiding eye contact with the few people not talking amongst themselves and probably wondering why I had such a desire to entertain them at all cost. About half way through the song I missed the bridge and totally got out of synch with the backing track. My head dropped, chin touching my chest, eyes buried in the grass in front of the porch.

I stormed off my would-be stage back into the comfort of the house. Realizing I'd made a total fool of myself or at least thinking I had. A few steps behind, Dave followed me in and said, "Come back out and keep playing. We want to hear you jam." I reluctantly went back out and played a couple more songs. But with all the wind out of my sails. I just couldn't perform as I expected of myself.

The truth is my friends and I were just enjoying a Saturday night together. It may have been a little dorky, if not extremely dorky, that I thought this would gain me some sort of accolades or a fan base. But it was the beginning of my dream. Dave understood how much this meant to me and was supportive as a friend despite everything.

In that moment, I was extremely cruel to myself. I felt that I had something to prove. I was not just jamming and having a good time. I wanted the acceptance I felt I never got from my peers and adults. I wanted to get good at something, if not great. I didn't realize success and building up your confidence is a process. Comprised of a lot of little steps. And what I had just taken was a little step toward a dream that felt enormous and extremely unattainable from my vantage point at the time.

I'm sure the first man that landed on the moon was once a kid running through the halls of his parents' house, cape trailing behind him in the wind. Toy airplane in hand. Imagining soaring through the air above the clouds and into the heavens. That was the beginning of his trajectory toward the goal of being an astronaut. The truth is, the first step down the hall with that plane in hand was just as important as that first step on the moon. It started him down a road that lead there. I had no idea how important and special it was that I took the first step and performed live. In fact, each step was as important as the next. It was a trajectory that had to be set.

Often a person doesn't know where their journey will lead them. They just know they are not happy with where they are and want a change.

When my dad was in his late teens, he left for Mexico with his dad and his girlfriend. About 10 miles out of town, they began to argue.

My father told them, "Stop the car and let me out! I am not going to listen to your arguing all the way to Mexico."

So, Grandpa drove him back to town and left for Mexico with his girlfriend. It was supposed to be for the weekend. But a week went by, a month.

After about a month and a half, Dad assumed something must have happened to Grandpa down there. So, he decided to join the service to get out of the South and the small-town racism. He took the test at the Army and flunked, Marines and flunked. By the time he got to the Navy, he knew a lot of what was going to be on the test and passed. Little did he know this was the beginning of an adventure that was not just going to get him out of Abilene, Texas, but would take him all over the world and eventually to California.

After Dad did his three months in boot camp, he returned home to Abilene. He asked around for his dad Curtis and was told by a friend where he was. It turned out that Grandpa's girlfriend had slipped him a drug and ran off with another guy down in Mexico. When Grandpa came to, he tried to drive back to Abilene half high and lost control of his car and ended up in a white woman's living room with his '59 Chevy. Obviously, this was a serious crime. He was unable to make any phone calls to his family. When he finally got out of jail he came back to Abilene and settled back in.

By now Dad was already on the military trajectory. Knowing his Dad was fine, he could now go out into the world and experience things he never imaged. After boot camp, Dad had a choice between somewhere on the East Coast and California. When he heard California, he thought "Movie stars!" It was California for sure.

The military paid for Dad to ride out there on a train. He had his own little room in one of the cars. He ate and drank to his heart's content. A luxury he rarely had growing up. Where Dad was raised everything is flat as far as the eyes can see.

He said, "I couldn't believe it when I saw all that water." He had never seen the ocean before. Something I can't relate to. I was born in California and was taken to the beach as an infant.

I am so grateful for the lifestyle my parents provided me. I didn't even eat ramen until I moved out on my own with Dave, Bob and Dina. I didn't realize Mom and Dad had to pay a lot of dues to give Anne and me the lifestyle we had. Sometimes it is easier to focus on what we lack and neglect to see all the things we should be grateful for.

5

Pushing Through the Early '90s – A Diagnosis

It was 4th of July in the summer of '92. My San Jose friends and I were heading to Marriot's Great America to watch the fireworks. When we arrived the energy was electric, vibrant, exciting, even dangerous. There were thousands of young people out there drinking, smoking pot. That night a friend of mine had magic mushrooms and I was going to be partaking. So, I gave my friend Tom the keys to my beloved Green '70 Pontiac Firebird. I didn't want to be driving around high.

Once the shrooms started kicking in, it felt even more electric. Like anything could happen. I looked up at the sky and heard the booming of cannons reverberating through my head. You could almost feel the concussions from the blasts. I always wondered if this would be traumatic for a person with PTSD. Somehow it didn't affect me.

Shortly after each boom, the sky lit up with huge plumes of bursting light that shined like moonlight on our faces. My mind's train of thought cycled through. It was as if my brain had locomotive gears turning without thought into oblivion. It was like being on a mission but not knowing what the mission was.

After about a half an hour, my friend Tom came rushing up to me, looking distraught.

"I'm sorry, Lance. I'm sorry."

"What happened? Just tell me what's wrong?"

He said, "You can hit me if you want to!"

"I don't want to hit you, just tell me what happened."

He said, "It's your car."

My heart sunk in my chest. At that point in my life, my car was all I had. It meant everything to me. Freedom, passion, access to anywhere the road could take me. I think it may have meant a little too much to me. I was attached to it.

He said, "Your car is stuck on a curb! Angie and I tried to get it off, but it's stuck."

Angie was a girl I was enamored with. A magical person. As we rushed back to the place where my car was, Tom kept repeating, "You can hit me if you want" despite my constant assurance I didn't want to hurt him. I loved Tom like a brother. I just wanted my car to be in one piece and work.

When we arrived, it was indeed still stuck. I got in to see if I could do something to remedy the situation. No luck. When suddenly a lively group of random strangers got together and pushed my car off the curb, causing damage to the linkage that changed gears on the transmission. Now that it was off the curb, I couldn't get it to move. So, we called a tow truck and had it towed to a friends' house.

That night I stayed at Tara's, a powerhouse of a rocker chick's place. I rode in the back of her old orange pickup. I couldn't get my car out of my head. I didn't know how much damage had been done. So, my mind just kept coming back around to it. It almost sounded like an old transistor radio playing in my mind.

After that weekend, I decided to stay in Sunnyvale with some friends Tom had. Mike, Christina and their son Sebastian had a nice 4-bedroom house in the suburbs, but Christina had been dealt such a hard hand to play. Her mother had died of cancer in the hospital, her father in the home of a heart attack and her brother was hit by a car and killed. Her entire immediate family was gone, and she was taking it as any 20-year-old young lady would. She took the money they left her and bought tons of clothes and partied.

I was told I could live there rent free if I helped them clean up the house, which had become a mess. That first few weeks I was there were spent with Tom and I working around the house to clean up. Tom and I would go to Shakey's pizza and get the all you can eat lunch. It felt so liberating to be on my own and away from my family. Just me and my friends against the world. And that's exactly how I wanted it. I quickly learned to live without my car. Walking mostly and riding the bus when it was too far to walk.

Within a month I'd found a job at Kinko's in Mountain View, which was about a 40-minute ride on my newly purchased bike. When I started, I was working swing from 3 p.m. until midnight. Then I'd ride my bike down El Camino home. I decided I didn't like living in the house because things were just too unpredictable. A lot of people were coming and going. So, after we cleaned out the garage, I moved up into the loft. You know, the little space above where people keep their skis and things. I put a mattress up there, with a boombox at the head of the bed along with a cassette holder and some writing pads. I felt like I was hidden up there. Like I had more control over my situation. Often when I would get home, Mike would be up milling around in the living room. Drinking a beer. Tinkering with things. One of the things he liked to do was play with his ham radio and talk to the truckers as they went by on the freeway. It reminded him of the '70s *Smokey and the Bandit* trip with "Breaker, breaker 109. How's it goin' Lead Foot" and the trucker would reply.

By this time our band Wood – me on guitar, Phil Romero on drums and Gary Niederhoff on bass – had been jamming for a couple months. At practice, I'd come up with this haunting repetitious part consisting of nine notes and seven notes that sounded kind of like Rush. I couldn't get that riff out of my head. It really stood out in the practice to me.

Momentum

When I arrived home from practice, the garage was open and Mike was playing with his ham radio loudly. It was about 1 a.m. I took my electric guitar out of the case and continued to play that riff I couldn't get out of my head. I was quiet and to myself because I was not plugged into an amp. Mike was about 10 feet away from me, facing me in a seated position. I looked down and to the left at my hand to watch as I played the odd series of notes together.

Before I could look up, Mike was at my feet with his back to me facing the opposite direction. Something that totally defied physics. There is no way he could have jumped 10 feet from a sitting position and land in the opposite direction. Mike quickly shuffled back into the garage toward the door that leads into the house, eyes popping and bugging out of his head. Speechless at what had just happened. Once he settled down a bit, he went on to say he and his friend had seen a white form in the backyard earlier that evening and went back there and nothing was there. This could easily be dismissed by saying, "Are you high dude? What have you been smoking?" but it didn't explain what I had just witnessed in the garage with my own two eyes.

I believe there is a spirit realm and we are unable to comprehend the ins and outs of that world while we are in a body. Christina's dad died in that house. I think he was annoyed with Mike and pushed him. Plus, Mike and his cousin said this has happened to Mike before. Things that defied physics. I had to sleep in the loft that night. Just to be safe, I said to the room and whatever was inhabiting it that I couldn't see, "I mean you no harm and I am here to help your daughter."

Christina often called me Montel Williams, a popular inspirational talk show host at the time. I was always delving deeper into the causes of people's hurt and how they could overcome them. The truth with Christina is she felt guilty for the way she treated her parents before they died. Partying, coming in late. She loved them and never had the chance to experience any closure with them directly. I told her sometimes we must forgive ourselves, so that we can move on and build healthier relationships in the future. One night, Christina really had a breakthrough as we were talking about her feelings. She really tapped into her empathy and regret, sobbing quietly with me there to listen and comfort her. That night I went up to the loft to go to bed. It was late. After a few minutes, my muscles were really starting to relax, and I was on my way to la la land. Just on the cusp of falling into deep sleep when I felt a soft warm hand gently stroke my left cheek. As a mother would with her child, laying in her lap. It felt heavenly, nurturing and comforting. I continued to feel and enjoy these soft strokes against my cheeks until the reality of the moment kicked in. I was up in the loft by myself. Not laying in my mom's lap like a child. I immediately jumped up to a half-sitting position, which is about as much as I could sit up due to the limited space in the loft.

Was that a rat or something? But there was no rat to be seen. After a few minutes, I settled back under the covers on my back, wide awake. Suddenly I felt comforted again in my heart. Realizing that was Christina's mom thanking me for comforting her daughter. Although many logical people would not come to that conclusion, I truly believe that in my heart until this day. The spirit realm is something that we may not understand but sometimes it reveals itself to us as a ripple effect to our reality. It shows us a glimpse.

Another time I was up in the loft with my feet dangling over the edge, playing my guitar, when the garage opened. I climbed down the ladder that lead up to the loft onto the counter and next to the entry into the garage where the button was located. I pushed the button. The garage door closed. Then I climbed back up into the loft to resume my guitar playing. Within seconds the garage door opened. I climbed down and closed it again. After the third time, I just left it open. Maybe this was Christina's brother playing with me. The whole thing had a playful energy. I was not annoyed by it. Mike said it was probably just airplanes flying over. Sometimes they trigger the garage door. Who knows but it would be neat if it was her brother.

I had a friend that refused to go in the house because he could feel that spirits were there that I guess conflicted with his energy. I haven't had a lot of experiences with ghosts like that, but it hasn't been often that I have been around that much death surrounding one environment.

Mike and I often talked at length about our lives, as many people do when they're young. Mike had a father he never met and a mother who abandoned them because she was an alcoholic and couldn't take care of her kids. Mike had a brother and a sister. He really struggled with alcohol and was unemployed the whole time I knew him. Mike had a lot of wisdom about life considering how young he was. I guess he had experienced way more hardship than the average person his age.

He said when in foster care he lived with every type of family. Many different religious beliefs and backgrounds. When he met my father, he told me he could tell my dad loved me. I told him my mad and I didn't always get along. He said that being a father himself had taught him something. When you have a child, it is like an extension of you out into the future. He said, "You are a part of him that he can't be, you are more like a sensitive side." And he said, "There is a part of him that you can never be, but the place that is in between is where you meet in the middle, that is where you are similar." After that conversation, I felt compelled to tell Dad how I felt about our past relationship.

One weekend I went home and told my dad I felt unloved by him because of the way he treated me coming up. He said there was no manual on how to raise a child and he did the best he could. He was raised with corporal punishment. And his parents didn't have time for a lot of nonsense. He was raised in the South with lots of hardship from working in the fields and racism. So, his parents had a short fuse. He also said I had it way better that he did.

After our conversation, we both understood there was mutual love there that had just not been expressed much until then. This changed the dynamic of our relationship dramatically for the better. I used to always feel I was rebelling against Dad and authority. But now I knew he really did have my best interest in mind. Even when he was suggesting being an engineer instead of a rock star. He just wanted me to have a stable life where I could have peace of mind and not worry about where the money was going to come from, to put food on the table.

One day I was hanging out at the house having a beer and I got a call from Gary.

"Dude, guess where I am?"

"Where?"

"Lollapalooza selling T-shirts."

He was in college radio at the time and sometimes would have access to events like this. Just the idea that he was there was so exciting. This was the first year and they had an incredible lineup: Jane's Addiction, a crazy psyche rock band with one of the raddest guitarist of the time Dave Navarro and Perry Farrell on vocals, both who liked to use a lot of delay effects which sounded spacy and cool. David also used a lot of jazz chords with distortion. I loved the way that sounded.

Living Colour was also playing, an all-Black pop-rock-funk outfit with a blazing out-of-this-world guitarist Vernon Reid. He was like the Jimi Hendrix of that time to me. I was inspired by wild blaring distorted licks and he used some jazzy sounding parts too.

Ice-T and Body Count were on the bill too. This was Ice-T branching out in music and forming a dark sinister punk rock/metal band. I remember he had a wall of brothas in front of the stage wearing all black with Syndicate T-shirts on.

Butthole Surfers were absolutely crazy coming out, firing fake shot gun rounds out into the crowd. At least I think they were fake. I can't remember what their music even sounded like. Siouxsie and the Banshees were on the bill too. Not a huge fan, kind of endured as you sometimes do at festivals and shows. Plus, besides these bands on the main stage, about four or five little satellite stages where smaller indie bands were playing throughout the day too.

The thing that stood out most to me at the show was Vernon Reid from Living Colour sounded like three guitarists playing at once. And Perry Farrell climbing the rafters to dangerous heights, to our amazement and awe. I wouldn't have had the courage to do that.

It was during that performance I heard a quiet voice in my mind I'd never heard. A steady, reassuring voice. "That is you down there ... you just have to go through a spiritual change."

I'd never experienced anything like this before. So, I didn't know what to make of it. I figured it must have been God or a spiritual guide informing me it was my destiny to entertain on that level. I was already starting to head on that trajectory. I didn't know what the spiritual change was or what it would entail. I didn't know if it was something I had to do, or something God would do. I just knew it had to happen before I could go on to fulfill my destiny as a performer.

After the band had rehearsed for five or six months, we arranged to perform for the first time with little notice in just a few days. At the time, there were tons of bands in the San Jose area and very few practice places. I think we were at 3B sharing a room with Jigsaw a progressive rock band. We had a band next door that always was practicing at the same time. Almost every time, they covered this one Steely Dan song that I still love to this day because of them. One of the other practice places in downtown was Rock Gardens which you could rent by the hour on the fly. There was no stage – just a room with our gear in one corner and everyone else crammed in there. Gary started with this groovy stoner bass line much like early Black Sabbath. I immediately went into warm, smooth, slightly bassy distorted blues runs. It sounded so good with Phil pounding away on the drums. And to get the immediate response of our peers. Banging their heads and standing there, eyes and ears fixed on us. Nothing could have ever prepared me for the exhilaration I was feeling. It was total freedom to release all my pent-up emotion which consisted mostly of anger and aggression, under which I'm sure was deep-seated sadness from all the disappointments I had experienced thus far.

Soon after our first party, we arranged our first gig at the long-standing punk rock venue 924 Gilman Street. Many bands had been through there including our close friends' bands. I think we only had a few songs and the rest consisted of jams, our signature when playing live. I remember stressing over every detail including bringing candles on stage, wearing a worn-out dashiki from a thrift store and a stocking cap pulled down over my eyes, so I didn't have to make eye contact with the crowd. I was so self-conscious I was in my own world throughout the performance. I was also having trouble hearing the guys because the sound guy was running our entire band mix through some wild effect that really made us sound muddy. All in all, I would say it was a wash out. But we were just glad it was over, and we made it out in one piece. Which could be a problem at Gilman. In the skinhead days, some people got stomped pretty bad. I was always with a lot of friends from East Side San Jose, so we hardly ever had a problem.

One thing I learned right away is playing shows can be a grind. It's loading gear around 7 p.m., driving to a venue that's often an hour or two away. Playing early on the bill and hanging out for hours after you play to get paid. But the best part of the whole thing was the performing and the hanging out with friends.

On the way to the show we would stop at a store like Thrifty and buy those gallon bottles of rot gut vodka and whisky. If we had money, we might get Kessler or Black Velvet. Then we would sit in the van and get drunk, it was like a roving bar. People would bring bongs and smoke pot. Some would even take acid and do speed. I had some of the most fulfilling, meaningful conversations in the back of those vans. Exploring every social, political topic imaginable. And music. We would talk for hours about our favorite bands, music blaring from the '70s house speakers we were able to hook up to the van's stereo.

As the band began to practice more and more, three times a week in our heyday, our sound began to get more and more dark and progressive. With a lot of clean, metery odd-timed parts and riffy-distorted parts.

The guys and I often ate at this burrito shop called Emma's in downtown San Jose, owned by relatives of Phil's. I mean it was an actual grandma in the back making homemade Mexican food. At the time, I ate a lot of Chicken Super Burritos with everything.

One day in '93 while enjoying a super burrito, I said to Gary and Phil, "We have some solid songs now. Let's set a recording date."

At the time, there was no internet. So, you would find recording studios by looking in music newspapers like Metro and BAM Bay Area Music. After researching I found a studio called Pyramind Sound. All digital, which was new at the time. Most recording engineers were still using 1-inch 16-track or 2-inch 24-track tape. But with digital everything was in the computer. You didn't have to cut the tape anymore to edit it.

Recording is an adventure. To put music into a fixed form and immortalize it like a snapshot of where you were as an artist and a person at a given time. By the time that day came, I'd listened to so much music and been inspired by so many artists. I had to find my voice as a guitarist.

A few months earlier I'd stumbled across a picking technique that allowed me to play fast and clean. It came natural to me. I could double and triple pick and isolate my picking on each string as needed. A big part of the technique is grounding the right picking hand by pressing with the pinky finger on the pick guard. Like an anchor. Which makes it easier to isolate the picking. I went in the studio armed with this technique. I also liked how Buzz from the Melvins used distortion to create feedback. I liked the idea of layering multiple tracks of feedback.

One of the first songs Wood wrote was "Sao Paulo" about the capital of Brazil in South America. The band was focused on pointing out the injustice in the world and offering solutions to age-old problems. We, like many young people, felt we had some answers to the world's problems. Who knows maybe we did on some level. We just needed to follow through. Anything positive adds to the good of everything in the big picture. That year in '93, I believe Sao Paulo had the highest murder rate on the planet. This was a cause close to us as the murder rate was also skyrocketing here in the USA at that time. With crack flooding the streets and gang warfare. Much like the USA, Sao Paulo was suffering.

I guess the question the song asked was what causes a person to want to do drugs and who is profiting from it. Who stands to lose the most from its eradication? And how do you stop a cycle of violence? These things were addressed in the lyrics of the song. At the time, I was atheist and believed we could solve things with logical solutions only. Now I believe in a combination of the spiritual and the logical coming together. Spirit and science. I truly believed then and still believe now to the core of my being that there will come a day when people will be shocked at the fact that people killed each other in the past. They will think we lived in a barbaric time. People will become so intelligent and logical that us killing each other just won't make sense and it will rarely happen if at all. I think there needs to be an emphasis on us being one people with the common goal of loving, nurturing each other and sharing resources so that all people on Earth can be brought up to a minimum standard of living. The greed of a handful of people is what is hindering the progress of the whole.

It was my birthday in '93 when my friends from Sleep were playing a show in downtown San Jose. They were popular at the time and still are. Our band had played quite a few shows and were generating a small fan base. We however had not played out of the South Bay besides Gilman.

Sleep was really taking a leap of faith and set on the vision of living their passion. I think it was their infectious bluesy, riffy, stoner sound. You could really groove to their songs. I think that resonated with people. It was dark metal with a sense of pocket. Although Al Cisneros and their drummer Chris Hakius had started with tongue-in-cheek punk rock, they evolved dramatically when Matt Pike joined them to form Asbestos Death. Tom Choi was also in the band for a time. I was absolutely captivated by the Asbestos Death tracks I first heard on a cassette. Yeah, cassette. These songs delved deeper into the psyches of these young men in their late teens. The angst they were feeling was evident in the bludgeoning distorted parts and the clean guitar parts that would balance out the sound and give it contrast at times. There was one song that resonated with the feelings I had experienced throughout my life up until that point. Tom Choi had this spacey clean part on guitar and he was using a chorus effect on it. He was running it through a Crate half stack. Although that amp brand didn't last, I loved the tone and how Tom handpicked that sound for the recording. These four guys inspired me beyond belief. From their infectious sound to our close friendships.

By September '93, Sleep had played many times outside of the South Bay, including Los Angeles and San Francisco as the big ones, to build a viable grassroots fan base in the U.S. Many of the bands in the South Bay scene simply did not know how to book shows in LA and SF. My only knowledge was you had to be able to draw for the real clubs to book you.

Once I tried calling the booking agent for Great American Music Hall in SF and spoke to the booking agent. He said he listened to and really enjoyed our music and wanted to book us. But it was not about his opinion. It was about selling 100 tickets at 15 bucks a pop. He said, "If you can do that, you can get on a bill here."

In San Jose, it was a little more relaxed. You could work your way up the bill. The first time we played Cactus Club, a staple for most of the bands locally, we opened on a Monday. That is the most entry-level spot you can possibly have at a club. And we were going to see the drawbacks of that slot. The problem is people pay to get in to see the top two bands of the bill, which play toward the end of the show. The opening band is lucky if the bartender and a few passersby catch the set. So, it was basically like a practice playing on stage. But eventually we would work our way up the bill and to better nights of the week like Friday and Saturday.

In the early '90s there was a big emphasis toward getting a deal with a record label. To turn a garage band into a nationally touring house hold name overnight. Around this time, music that used to be underground was becoming quite mainstream. And there was a much darker theme to popular music borderline dismal at times. A garage band from Seattle that played catchy, heavy music was about to become one of the most iconic bands of the '90s symbolizing the growing angst of a generation. Ironically the fame was unwelcomed from Nirvana's perspective. The fame coveted by so many bands that attempted to sound like them.

What I learned from watching my friends band grow is that artists make most of their money from touring. And that advances must be paid back once the record sales come in. This is how so many mainstream bands sold millions of records and ended up broke. They were getting such a small fraction of the record sales it was ludicrous. And they had to pay for the tour busses, food, beverages, and their entourage. But the label provided some valuable services. Marketing being a huge one, plus management and booking. Like Sleep's second label Ear Ache was small but they toured multiple times on that label and got exposure that would build an enduring fan base.

Another thing I learned from Sleep is they really pursued the opportunities they got. They spent an enormous amount of time on the phone, pursuing the next step in their careers. Many of the bands in the scene assumed they were just getting more opportunities by default. I think they just had an undying vision that they were not going to let any set of circumstances derail them.

Along the way, I was starting to become aware of a spiritual malaise that would just sit in my stomach up in the loft. My dreams and aspirations were in the clouds.

But it seemed like it was a million miles from where I was. My band was barely playing a few bars in San Jose, we never played huge shows. What I didn't realize at the time is that Shoreline was not a million miles away. There was a path to Shoreline and it would start with me changing how I think about playing there. I think the first thing I had should have done is brought things out of fantasy world and into reality.

Shoreline is a venue people play every night. It is a goal not a dream. There are hundreds if not thousands of musicians who have played there and many more will in the future. Why couldn't one of those people be me?

I'm sure there are just as many people who have stood at the base of Mount Everest or El Capitan.

Too many say, "It's impossible to climb to the top."

Others only wonder, "I am someone, why can't I do it?"

And fewer yet say, "I can do it."

These few keep asking the golden questions, "How were my predecessors able to do it? What obstacles did they encounter? How do I prepare myself to face these obstacles?"

And most importantly, "Is it my destiny to climb this mountain?"

There is a good chance it may be if you have gotten that far in the thought process. The next step is to breakdown the things that need to be done to prepare yourself into a timeline. And set a goal date for when you are going to attempt it. Now it is no longer a fantasy. You have entered the passionate world of action.

In my case with Shoreline I have an advantage because God has already given me the green light. But much like the Israelites and the Promised Land in the Bible, I questioned and doubted God's revelation of my destiny. I think people often look at destiny as a destination and not a journey. Every step is leading to you serving your ultimate purpose. I truly believe we cannot leave this world until we have served our purpose, or we wouldn't be here.

We are making decisions every day that affect our ultimate destinations in life. What we chose to believe effects these decisions. I think we can attract opportunities simply by having a positive, hopeful and gracious attitude. I have met a few people in my life that were just hell-bent on being miserable. They are choosing to be miserable. I know because I am one of the people who has struggled with this.

'We don't always have control over our circumstances, but we do have control over the way we react to them."

A choice we make every day. Many times, I would get my hopes about things going the way I wanted them to. I would create an expectation about a situation and then be emotionally destroyed when it didn't happen the way I envisioned. What I learned is God is in control of the circumstances that affect our lives. If we try to control circumstances, we are going to end up frustrated and bitter. Therefore, it is so important to have a healthy, respectful and loving relationship with God.

I found that if I was in a constant cycle of sin and guilt, I would never feel comfortable in my relationship with God. That is one of the biggest reasons I never attended church to that point in my life. I felt I had to be living a clean perfect life to be acceptable to God. What I learned through studying the Bible is that is not true in Christianity. It is a misconception and a cliché that some Christians have wrongfully spread. Telling people that they are going to go to hell because they can't meet the impossible standard of never sinning, ever. God knew sinning was in our nature and that sometimes we would make mistakes. So, he sent his son Jesus as a sacrifice. To make atonement for our sins. Jesus knew no sin. He was truly the lamb of God. He was something a human could never be. The only thing the Lord asks is we confess that we sinned and repent as we try our best to refrain from that behavior. I also believe at some point he expects us to reach a level of spiritual maturity where we are almost sin free.

During this time, I really began to understand the importance of having a loving relationship with God. Feeling loved and worthy of love from him is so instrumental in building a healthy self-worth. And for those who are in a state of disbelief, reach out to God in prayer and ask him to reveal his glory to you. He will do it in subtle ways most of the time. I know in my case I didn't believe there was a God or if there was, he must not love me. I felt what I needed was the love of those I felt were withholding love from me. Primarily the women that I liked. If they didn't love me, why would God? I was selfish. What I didn't realize is God was trying to get me to turn to him for love and support. He wanted me to lean on divine guidance and love. A love that would sustain me through my life in this body and beyond. God is the only thing to become attached to. He was there before you were born and will be there after and beyond into infinity. People will die. God is a constant. Like the sun in the sky. The center of the universe that all life revolves around.

He is the energy that permeates all that exists.

Every atom that comprises all living things.

The Nitrogen, the carbon.

The light, the darkness.

He touches everything in the universe simultaneously. He is at in the deepest darkest recesses of the oceans, to the furthest corner of the universe. Knowing all life intimately. Beyond languages, words and inflections. A unilateral feeling across all of existence. Yearning to know, love and comfort us. Not to punish, inflict harm and judge.

He is patient. He knows that learning is a process and we all are developing. There is no gap to bridge. We are all one right now. I believe the discord we are experiencing is the growing pains of mankind. We are slowly growing. Little by little. Kind, patient loving deed by deed. The growth of mankind is measured step by step. Billions of people interacting with one another daily.

My sister has a female friend was raised in the notorious Compton, California. She knows people who lived there all through the '90s up to now. Some of them do not believe in guns. Instead, they believe in God's love and protection.

I'll never forget some of the imagery visually from the South-Central LA riots in the early '90s. One photo I can still see vividly in my mind. A white man on the ground, beaten and bloody, at the feet of a black priest with his hands in the air, face fraught with turmoil. It was as if he was there to remind those so frustrated and angry from years of oppression to have empathy on this man who just happened to be white. But this had been their experience for years in that environment. Living under the constant threat of being robbed or shot or beat by cops. It was the Rodney King incident that ignited this inferno of rage in the community. After the world witnessed a brutal beating of an unarmed Black man, we discovered it was a widespread practice. I often wonder how the average Black male in the inner city perceived guns in early '90s of South Central LA. A tool for survival, an equalizer, something that provided power to someone that felt powerless in the situation they found themselves in.

One day when I was working at Kinko's in the early '90s, I noticed a new employee working at the 5090-copy machine. The one with all the bells and whistles. He was Black and in his early 20s. We didn't even speak or make eye contact the first few times I saw him working at the machine. He had a somewhat angry look on his face. It may have just been the slight scar on the corner of his mouth that had healed bad. It almost looked like a burn. When we finally spoke, it took no time for us to become friends. His name was Jay. He would invite me over his apartment for pizza and we would talk about everything that was going on in the world around us.

He was originally from the East Coast. He began to share stories about his experiences living in the inner city in his late teens. His father had passed away when he was young. So, like many young men without a positive male role model, he was raised by the environment he lived in. Many young men around him were unemployed and struggling to survive. Some took to crime as a means of making fast and lucrative money. He told me where he lived everything was divided into neighborhoods. You were affiliated with whatever neighborhood you lived in. So, you immediately had enemies just due to where you lived. And if you wanted nothing to do with the guys on your block, they would beat you up every time they saw you until you finally conformed to the way of the street.

One day he stepped onto the porch of his house and was rushed and attacked by three guys who punched, kicked and bludgeoned him until he was almost incoherent. A beat down, he said. In his environment, beatings and shootings were common occurrences. And the death toll was always rising, reaching out to engulf some of his teenaged friends without remorse. He said many of his friends had been shot, some killed. He said it was always happening. He would hear they got so and so on such and such street. However, on one fateful day, he was there when the shots rang out. When the gun smoke dissipated, and the shooter had fled, all that was left was his friend laying there on his back. Vacant eyes rolling back into his head, barely able to breath as his lungs had been punctured by the bullets. He just knelt at his friend's side and scooped him up under his neck. Pulling his lifeless body closer, not wanting to let go of all the things they'd experienced and said together. As his friend exhaled his last breath, he said he could see himself in his friend's face. He felt like he was holding himself, dying in his arms. He knew he would be next if he didn't leave that environment. He decided right there that was the end of the life he knew there.

From there he headed to the South Bay Area where we met. He had worked his way up to manager.

A lot of suburban kids in the early 90's had a fascination with the hood. Some people associated being hard and thuggish with bravado and masculinity. You started to see a lot of suburban kids wearing sagging pants and baseball caps turned backwards because it was popular and in style. With no understanding of the deep-seated degradation. Of the poverty, vice and killing associated with it. They wanted the bravado without the accompanying suffering that so many young men had to face.

Jay and I went to see *Menace to Society* in 1993, which addressed some of these things. This movie really helped to expose suburbanites to the reality of inner-city life. The only difference is we had the luxury to turn off the TV. The shootings were not happening on our corners every weekend. It was not until I met Jay that I truly began to understand how blessed I was and how precious my father is and how much he shaped my life. Being an awesome role model. Showing it. Showing what manhood looked like. Jay didn't have that, or the lifestyle my parents' salaries had provided me coming up. I didn't understand low income until I moved out on my own, when the ramen days started.

One of the scenes that really disturbed me in *Menace* was when Cain's cousin got shot. He and his cousin had just left a party and got robbed by several guys in a van. Cain's cousin was killed, and his car was stolen. It was such a graphic scene, hard to watch. You felt like you just actually watched someone get jacked.

But what was even sadder, and more alarming was the reaction of the young men in the movie theater. They were laughing and cheering at what they had just witnessed. A young Black male, killing another young Black male. No empathy, no remorse, no compassion.

This revealed a deeper problem about how Black males see each other:

> We were divided into us and them.
> My block, your block.
> Your gang my gang.
> Police and young Black male.

The only thing that can heal this cycle of violence – empathy. Young people often feel like no one has empathy for them – as others drive around in their fancy cars, live in these big houses, with big screen TVs, refrigerator filled to the max with food. Often young people don't understand why they're in the situation they find themselves in. They are just forced to survive. They may not see a person had to work to have the lifestyle they have. It may be easier to just go steal the TV than to go get a job and buy one. Some feel as if the system is not playing fair, why should they. Plus, when a person feels deprived of things, they put a higher value on those things. The truth is things are not what makes life worth living. It is our relationships and the experiences we share while we are here. You have some people that live in what middle class Americans would consider poverty that are happy. They understand that money brings comfort, not necessarily happiness.

I found myself between jobs and laying on my futon face down in the heat. Sweating into it the fabric, and heard, "Get up today and get your job." I wasn't even looking for a job. Just laying around feeling sorry for myself. So, I got up, put on a pair of slacks, a nice shirt, dress shoes and a sport coat from Goodwill but didn't look like it. Headed out down Campbell Avenue with a pep in my step, with the hope I was given by the Lord's voice. Past the Lucky's grocery store, McFrugals discount store, the high school, to West Gate Mall.

I entered through a department store through the circular and rectangular clothing racks out into the mall. Where it was nice and cool compared to summer at 11am outside. All the way on the other end of the mall I entered the now late Home Express it was kind of like Bed Bath and beyond meets Ross. Behind one of the registers I saw a man that was most likely a manager. He was about 55 or 60, medium build wearing a pair of brown slacks that barely fit him appearing be a couple sizes too small, a light-yellow button-down shirt, no tie with a white undershirt, slightly obscured by a multicolored used car salesman blazer, his hair line had receded back to his ears and he had a well-groomed thick mustache. I approached him with my I'm-the-guy-you-should-hire persona. I said, "Good morning sir, my name is Lance and I'm currently seeking employment, are you hiring now?" He said, "Sure" and went to retrieve a job application. He said, "Fill this out and I will interview you today." So, I did and he said he would call me to let me know if I was hired. I already had the feeling I was. From experience, I usually get the job when I have a good, relaxed comfortable conversation with the person in charge.

I started strong at the Home Express, then headed across the street to Smart & Final grocery store. The manager said the Mountain View store was hiring and I should talk to David. So, I hopped on the bus and headed for Mountain View an hour away. David was a down-to-earth, humble guy. He would be a subtle kind leader, I could tell.

Smart & Final felt like a real job because they had uniforms. Gray work pants, black work boots and a white button-down shirt with vertical thin red lines a couple inches apart. After speaking with him briefly, which went very well, he told me I could start that week and provided me with a schedule. Elated that things went so smoothly and that I now was employed, I headed back to Campbell. Upon arriving home, I received a message on my answering machine. (Yes, the ones that had a cassette tape in them, so it needed to be rewound to play you the message.) It was the manager from Home Express informing me that I had been hired there too. That is the only time I worked two jobs at once.

God was not kidding me when he said, "Get up and get your job" This is how faith in the Lord is built. On experiences with the Lord.

After working for few months on both jobs, I was starting to get irritable and frustrated with the arrangement. Constantly trying to make the schedules from the two jobs work together. And it was difficult not having a car. Having to ride the bus over to Mountain View. So, I decided to leave Home Express which I hated because it felt like a high school job and I was in my early 20s. Which is kind of funny cause I was still young. I guess I was comparing myself to my peers in college pursing degrees that lead to real jobs. Not couch-surfing jobs where you barely have the money to rent a couch in someone's house.

I started to work swing at Smart & Final, unloading the pallets of food, bringing the boxes to their respective isles and loading the product onto the shelves. I would get off at 9 p.m. instead of working until midnight because the bus stopped running early. To speak the truth, I was borderline suicidal, to the point where one of my co-workers asked me if I was going to commit suicide. I was speaking from a dismal place in my heart.

One of the things that got me through – hip-hop. Particularly that P-Diddy and Biggie song "Poppa" that sampled "Between the Sheets" by The Isley Brothers. I can't describe the way those songs made me feel. But I know they gave me hope and a reason to carry on. I think a lot of people felt that way about some of those tracks at the time. Although the subject matter of the songs was often dismal inner-city life of drugs and violence, there was something in those songs that resonated with my spirit. It was like The Isley Brothers with a gritty edge. One day while walking to work, a car went by on the opposite side of the road. But I noticed after he passed me, he turned around then pulled up beside me. He leaned over and rolled down his passenger side window and said, "Hey brother, the Lord told me to stop and talk to you." He proceeded to invite me to his church. I've learned that is the nature of the Lord. He constantly wants to bring you into the fold. He knows you are out there and he doesn't reject you.

As a Christian, I'm usually not comfortable pursuing people too much as far as getting them to come to church. I have felt that different things inspire different people to seek God. Many of us seek God in times of dire need. Loss of a loved one, divorce, loss of a job. He will be there for those times consistently and he has access to all resources. He can send you people to help you and give you hope and sometimes he gives his calming warm presence if we seek it. That was not the first time someone had approached me about coming to the Lord.

What I realize now is he is already there in our hearts. When we connect with the Holy Spirit, God's love is awoken in our hearts. He is living inside us. That is why often after a person has a strong experience with the Holy Spirit, they feel the need to start cleaning house and changing their behavior. God does not want to abide in a dark lawless environment. But he knows all places. He will go down to the deepest depths of your murky morass, to minister to your spirit and pull us out of the darkness of despair. He has done it for me. And he will continue to however many times we need him to until we learn to live in the light.

Sometimes if we ignore God for too long, we fall under judgement. The sin manifests into something you do not want to see, let alone deal with. I love God because he has seen me through everything. Providing me with grace even when I didn't even deserve it. Which was most of the time. There were times when I did things I knew were wrong and when the punishment looked like it was manifesting, I would turn to him and ask for forgiveness and he would get me out of the situation. See the Lord doesn't want to punish us. But even punishment leads us back to him, when we turn back for help. It is God's nature to love us unconditionally. There are some things we may not understand but we don't have God's perspective. Some people's lives are devastated by crushing circumstances and just can't seem to make sense of it or answer their questions about it. But if you have ever been in that situation, you know after the anger and bitterness subsides what you truly need is comfort. The Holy Spirit is the comforter. He wants you to know he is there for you always and you can lean on him. Even when you are in darkness. Even when the faces around you are unfamiliar and you feel you have nothing to cling to.

Anyone who has ever truly turned to God with a sincere heart in meditation or prayer will confirm the nature of God with you. Being the creator of the Universe, he knows you and the entire context you exist within. He knows you down to your most intimate private thoughts and deeds. When I became aware that God was always with me it helped me to change my behavior. The question to ask yourself is, would I be doing this if God were in the room with me? I believe the Lord is omnipresent or everywhere at once.

How do you build faith? Like with science, you look for evidence to support your beliefs. You have experiences that form your beliefs as you go through life. And once a big enough body of evidence is developed, we form a belief system. I believe it is much stronger when built on personal experience. Often when a person is raised in the church from childhood and indoctrinated to believe a certain way, they may need individual experiences to reinforce their belief. They can't go on what was taught alone. They need to put it into practice and see these principles at work for themselves.

In the '90s Biggie and Tupac brought music and the inner-city issues to the forefront. Here were two guys from similar walks of life on opposite sides of the country. Both incredibly gifted. Both voices so distinctive. Both voices immediately resonating with the core of the listener's psyche and heart. Their conflict was a macrocosm of what was going on in the hoods. In the daily skirmishes between rival neighborhoods and gangs. Typical us-and-them dividing the Black community. This conflict perpetuated the division of our neighborhoods and communities. I really wanted to see a world where people like Biggie and Tupac united to show our young Black men that there is no us and them. Just us. One Black community. One humanity.

How is a community supposed to mourn and heal from the last shooting when another is to follow the next day and the next? Once again, a big part of it is education. All Americans deserve access to equal education. School systems are paid for by the taxes of the local communities. A kid in East Oakland is going to get an inferior education than a child in Marin County. Simply due to the surplus of resources the Marin County school has. My mother taught in East Oakland. Many of the children didn't have the money for breakfast or lunch. And the school would try to provide some things they could bring home to their families. But the resources were limited. Studies show improper nourishment during elementary school can affect the development of the brain. But it is not only about equal education. It is about what we teach children about relationships and how to interact with other people. Teaching positive self-esteem and de-escalation during confrontations. It is hard for a middle class or affluent person to understand what daily life is like for a child in a place like East Oakland. They are exposed to some things that some 30-year-olds haven't even seen or heard.

One time I was working selling Kirby vacuum cleaners. We would often go to some of the lowest income places to sell our outrageously expensive vacuum cleaners. Just to be clear, a fully loaded model cost $1,500 and this was in the early '90s. This day we were selling in East Oakland. I am from a suburb in East San Jose. We never heard gunshots. Nor did we have a need to hustle in our early years for survival. Everything was provided by our parents. So, I was extremely wet behind the ears.

My supervisor, who oversaw the van, gave me a nice knife set as a bonus offer. It had about five knives in it, set into a nice black box with velvet lining. As I was walking up to one of the houses, I noticed a group of four or five boys walking toward me, ages 10 to 14.

One broke off from the group and said, "This is my momma's house. She'll be home in a little while."

So I told him, "I'm selling Kirby Vacuum cleaners." He said, "What's that?" looking at the box in my hand. He said, "You can give the knife set to me and come back later to talk to my mom." Without thinking I said, "Ok" and naively handed him the box. He took the box and headed back to his friends, elated he had gotten the knives. The crazy part is I saw nothing wrong with it until I told the story to my fellow sales people. They were shocked at how stupid and naive I was, and frankly thought it was funny. I never heard the end of it.

After working for Smart & Final in Mountain View for a few months, I found out there was an opening in Redwood City. Another 30 minutes or more each way. By this time, I had fixed the '70 Firebird and was driving it to work. That lasted for about a month. The car was leaking oil and I was frequently adding to it. One day I didn't realize all the oil had leaked out and I blew the engine on the way to work. It sounds crazy to me now, but instead of finding a job closer to my house in Campbell, I took public transportation all the way to Redwood City. Then it was about a two-and-a-half-hour trip home. I was literally leaving at 5:30 a.m. and getting home around 8:00 p.m. after stopping to get dinner.

I was so tired when I would get home, sometimes I would fall asleep with my clothes on. Right there on the futon in the garage. After a couple months of the grind of a commute, I got a bit of a reprieve. I started working grave. The buses didn't run that late, so my poor co-workers would come pick me up and take me to work. One of them was Eric. He was a big body builder and T-shirt company owner I met at Kinko's years before. He said when he was heavy into body building, he was eating two chickens a day and he and his wife would buy like a dozen chickens at a time. Eric was funny that way.

One day we stopped at Denny's on the way to work. He cut up his pancakes into squares and proceeded to devour the food on his plate. Chin hovering about 3 inches over it. For Eric, he went to a restaurant to eat. Not socialize. When I tried to make small talk, he said, "Shut up and eat!"

One time, Eric couldn't pick me up, so a new guy recently transferred from Fresno came to pick me up for graveyard shift. We hardly spoke besides me giving him directions to the freeway. From there he appeared to know his way up 680 toward SF to Redwood City. It was quiet in the car.

I thought to myself, "I wonder what he left behind in Fresno?"

A few seconds later he answered as if he had heard the question out loud, "I left my girlfriend of two years behind." I can't remember the other question I asked in my mind, but he answered that aloud too. It was really a trip because we were so tired we were like in a dream state. Some people believe the energy we have in our bodies is vibrating at a certain frequency. Just like a cell phone vibrates at a certain frequency and the other phone picks up that frequency and two people can communicate. If you want to know more about it, check out *The Secret*. I know some will try to say this experience was a coincidence. But like many of the things I've experienced, it has happened more than once.

While I was living with my mom and Dad, I was sleeping upstairs right above their room. As I was laying there semi-conscious I heard something repeating over and over. After it repeated many times, I began to focus in and listen to what it was saying. "Anne will receive smoke inhalation" over and over and over. Realizing my sister may be in danger, I rushed down the stairs into my parents' room and told them what I was hearing. Dad is usually quite skeptical about these types of things. But he immediately said, "Maybe her house is burning down." Mom said, "Anne is in LA right now!" This is before cell phones, so there was no way to call Anne and check on her. So, we had to wait until Monday when she got back. It turned out Anne was at Disneyland during the fireworks display and actually said, "I feel like I am going to get smoke inhalation." She used the exact same phrase.

One thing I learned from this is when you say words with emotions attached to them, the energy can be transmitted to someone you have a deep connection to.

When you compare telepathic communication to a cell phone, it makes more sense. Just think of how magical it is when you just pick up your cell phone. Dial a number. High frequency sound waves are sent out. Those high frequency waves travel to a tower which then directs the signal to a receiving cell phone and then you can speak to the person. But maybe humans come equipped with the ability to communicate with waves telepathically. Perhaps this explains how primitive societies that have no access to one another were using some of the same architectural designs. A collective consciousness. A pool of consciousness from which all individual consciousness draws. Maybe the human brain has a primitive version of a cell phone built in.

While still living in that garage at a friend's house, lying there in my borrowed futon at night, I kept hearing a sound like a marble or ball rolling on a counter. Every couple of minutes, the silence in the darkness was interrupted by this sound. Curious, I reached over and flicked on the light. Against the wall in the garage were wooden makeshift shelves with several knickknacks, photos in frames, empty can of Black Label beer and an open bag of yogurt-covered malt balls from a Casa De Fruta. I noticed one of the malt balls, about the size around of a quarter, was moving a little. When I looked closer, I noticed a little creature that looked like a cotton ball with little pink feet and muzzle. He was too small to grab the malt ball and take a bite of it. Every time he went to take a bite, it would roll forward away from him. Making the rolling sound I had been hearing. He really wanted to take a bite of that malt ball. But every time he moved forward, he pushed it away.

Maybe that is what I'd been doing. Pushing the things, I desired away from me by being overbearing and coming on too strong. At the time, I didn't know any better. Much like the mouse, I just wanted what I wanted and didn't know the right way of pursuing it.

The fact that I had made multiple attempts at music and had not seen the results I expected which was beyond frustrating to say the least.

I had one honest friend ask, "How long have you been doing music?"

I said, "20 years."

She said, "You should just give up and do something else."

But I know in my heart of hearts the promises God made to me. What hurt – I wasn't sure if I totally believed in them, so this really rattled my cage. It made me question the destiny that had been revealed through the voice at Shoreline. I wondered

– does God want me to be happy? does God even love me?

I thought about the countless rejections and disappointments through the years. What I didn't understand is there is no such thing as rejection from God's standpoint. Only open doors and closed doors in this crooked labyrinth of life. My grandfather Osborne Rainford used to say, "How can you lose what you never had?" and "No one can take away what is yours." He read the Bible daily.

We are children to God. Much like our earthly children we have wants and needs. And we tend to want to have them met on our own terms and in our own timing. As parents, we know this is sometimes not possible. Things need to be prioritized and managed properly.

Sometimes when a person doesn't receive what they want from a person with the authority to give it to them, they may feel like it's being withheld because of something they may have done wrong. Some even conclude that this person doesn't want me to be happy. Maybe this person doesn't even love me. Why won't they let me have what I so desperately feel I want or need? We can all sometimes be this way with God.

My mom was from New York and my dad Texas. They both went overseas in their 20s. My mom as a teacher and my dad a sailor. They both ended up in San Mateo, California, on one fateful day that changed both of their lives. They have been together ever since. It was their destiny to meet that day and create me. When my dad was overseas in the Philippines, he met a young beautiful Philippine woman in a bar. They spent a few days together. She took him out to her village which was very organic. No running water, lights or bathrooms. She introduced Dad to her father because she wanted to marry Dad. He was supposed to go back the next day and visit her. But instead went back out to sea, leaving her behind. It was a door God had closed. If he had married her, his life may have been dramatically different. That path would have taken him off the trajectory of meeting my mom. That closed door sent him in another direction, one step closer to the woman he was supposed to have a child with. If I was to exist, they had to both be there. That year, that day, that time, that location.

Those are the same laws that govern my meeting the woman I'm supposed to be with. It doesn't matter how lonely I get, how frustrated I become, how disillusioned I feel.

Life is like this huge equation with billions of unknowns. Every person being a variable in that equation. Every variable effecting the other variables, a ripple effect. As individuals, we only have access to a few of the variables in our personal equation. But there are many variables that effect our daily lives that we have little or no control over. Like the weather, someone else's feelings. And there are other things we usually have control over that can be affected by circumstances beyond our control. Like driving our car and getting in an accident. There are way too many unknowns for any one human to ever be in total control of their own circumstances or anyone else's for that matter.

If a person does not have faith, it can be a scary notion to think they are not in control Especially in our sometimes cynical, negative society. I wonder how much people's perception of Christianity would change if they were told God loves them unconditionally and wants to bless them. Instead what people often hear is legalism. God's love for you depends on your behavior. I believe that it is true that there will be consequences for ones' actions. But this doesn't mean God doesn't love us. We are just being held accountable for our behavior. Just like a parent may discipline their child by grounding them. It doesn't mean they don't love the child. They just want a change in the child's behavior.

Many non-believers feel they are "going to hell" for not conforming to a distinct set of rules. The truth is we all make mistakes. And God was aware of this fact when we were made. We are perfect in our imperfection. Some of the most beautiful things were stumbled upon through making mistakes. Just like in jazz music. The whole band is playing in a certain key, when the sax player drops one note in that is slightly off. The bass player hears that one note in another key and begins to use that as a root note to another scale. That change causes a change in the feel of the part and the drummer slightly changes the beat. Because one person dropped in a note out of key, just off the cuff, the whole direction of the song changed. It's a musical journey.

Even in rock bands there is a lot of jamming during the song writing process. Like jazz you go back and find certain parts you want to use and build the song around. Every person brings a unique voice and cadence to the conversation. I think that is why people tend to play music with like-minded people. In the early days of our band Wood, we were three frustrated, angry, disillusioned people who all had something to say as individual musicians. Three kindred spirits talking about the same topic both lyrically and feel wise. What fueled our anger was seeing all the injustice and suffering in the world around us. And our personal negative experiences only added to that angst. Wood was addressing a lot of these issues head on. And offering some solutions. We were compelled to see a change in the world around us. And we were willing to contribute.

I believe many young people are like that and that energy needs to be harnessed and used to change the world. I have often heard people be cynical about young people saying, "They think they have all the answers and they haven't even lived yet." Instead, elders should see the fire in the young and fuel it with knowledge. So, they can be the change that was once only a dream. A steady source of inspiration, one of the keys to making a positive impact on the world around you. Immerse yourself in the cause. Like the Civil Rights Movement of the '60s. The injustice in the world around us is a constant reminder there is still lots that needs to be done. But we must use that as a motivating force to call us to action and make a positive impact.

By '95 the band was solid and had played many shows in the South Bay. Often multiple times at the same clubs. It was at that club I experienced one of my few Rock Star moments. This was a great bill – Bronson, ItIsEye and Dragonfly, a band Joey the bass player from ItIsEye's brother Bobby was in. Although he played guitar, he kind of reminded me of Ian Gillan '70s Deep Purple singer. For this performance, I made a special trip to the thrift store to purchase a maroon turtleneck sweater, maroon bell bottom slacks and maroon dress shoes. I think I even had a maroon blazer. I was really stylin' '70s all the way. Our friends from Sleep wore bell-bottoms along with most of the rest of the people in the scene.

Usually my ritual before going on stage is washing my hands with warm soapy water. My hands get sweaty and clammy before I go on. And I hate that. The gear was all set up and the guys were ready to go. So, I quickly ducked into the bathroom to pee and wash my hands. When I walked into the bathroom, the urinal was directly to the left on the other side of a dividing wall that separated it from the next urinal over. So, I made that immediate left into the first urinal stall. Sometimes I get what I call nervous pee-pee where I can't begin to pee until I feel comfortable. I once had a friend say, "If you ever have that problem, just sing this portion of an old song ... Close the window, come alive and it will be all right, let it out, let it all begin, learn how to pretend." This always makes me laugh to myself which helps me relax and pee.

However, this time no one walked in until I already had the stream going and was almost done. I didn't really see who it was. I just heard them come in. As I was finishing, I realized the person was standing right behind me. When I turned around, I was nose-to-nose with a thin girl in her mid-20s. She had short hair and strong facial features, pronounced nose and lips. She looked very alluring but also seemed like kind of a druggy. Before I could say a word to her, she pressed her lips against mine and we began to make out right there. I was sucking her bottom lip between my lips and gently biting it. After a minute or so, I realized the guys were out there waiting to start the set. Without saying a word, she took off her light brown, long-sleeve sweater and I took of my maroon turtle neck and we switched. I later found out that girl had quite a reputation in the scene. I never saw her again. But the show went on.

As usual, we started with a stoner bluesy jam. Gary thumping on the bass with smooth grooves, Phil with the heavy beats with the steady ghost strokes every time around and me rifling into my wild solos. Sporadic bursts of notes and steady leads. For some reason, after we performed, I was disappointed with my performance. After we tore down the gear and took it out to the cars, I went back inside to watch Dragonfly. I was telling Tom from ItIsEye how I hated my performance over and over. Rather than babying me, he said it did suck. After I drank a few beers, I started to feel less depressed ironically, after all alcohol is a depressant.

Dragonfly was a unique '70s jam band. The guitarist Bobby reminded me of Stevie Ray Vaughn but he had his own style. Very clean soulful blues playing which was very refreshing to hear live. John boy was on drums. He had a solid handle on stoner groove drumming. The song that stands out most in my mind had a driving groove that sounded like a freight train coming down through town, with the howling wail of an old coyote just as loud as the train.

Then nothing could have prepared the crowd for the headliner of this show – ItIsEye. Whose influences ranged from the industrial sound of Godflesh to the droning riffs of the Melvins. They also had Brian "Terrorizer" in their arsenal. He was one of the most enthusiastic but borderline overbearing people I'd ever met. He was menacing in size and stature. Standing about 6 feet and easily weighing over 300 pounds. He spoke in abrupt loud bursts of sounds that often didn't make sense.

Barking, "Hey Lance! Lance! Lance!!!"

"What Brian?"

"Saw is family" We thought for a while he meant, "I saw his family." Who knows.

One of the funniest things is some of the band names he would come up with. "Dude, Dude, Dude hubcap! Fuckin' bum eating cereal out of a hubcap! Fuckin' tire iron! Highway"

When I first met him, he said, "Hey Lance, Lance. I used to be a racist." Was he trying to start something? I just didn't respond. He changed gears and went on to the next person. Although Brian could be overbearing, sometimes he would turnaround and surprise me with some insight of wisdom beyond his years. I think he spent so much time alone he had plenty of time to go over his thoughts and iron things out. I remember in high school Tom even used to like Ice-T but he had a mellow side too. And a love for another style of music that I didn't expect – country. He and I composed a country song about our friendship. It was about the times we had when I first moved out from Stockton to Sunnyvale. There was a lot of canned green beans and canned generic pork being eaten. I mean the can was plain white and just said pork on it in big black letters. I remember those lyrics:

> "Don't need a job or money to feel free,
> got a quart of wine to keep us company
> and were feeling fiiiine,
> side by side."

We were like two hobos enjoying the freedom of being unemployed.

I also remember when I first met Tom's roommate at the time Matt Pike. He was about my height and thin as a rail like me. Matt was also a guitarist in Asbestos Death, the band incarnation before Sleep. Matt seemed to share the angst so many of the people in the scene at that time were feeling. He had come from Colorado. Aggressive and assertive. He went after what he wanted without hesitation. And he always had a girl. The day that we met I believe we were going across the street to Denny's. At the time, they had a $2.99 Grand Slam. That was a constant stop for us at the time and they were open all night. So, it was perfect to go to after a show. Most of the time we made $50 for the whole band at a show, so we could all eat after on it and have a few bucks each for ourselves. On the way over to Denny's, Matt jumped up in a karate side kick and smacked the stop sign with his foot. Impressive. I knew how limber a person had to be to do that.

In the early days of Sleep, they played places like Pony Express Pizza and Saratoga Lanes. One of my favorites was Saratoga Lanes. At the bowling alley, they had an extra room in the back that held about 50 people standing. There was no stage. In those days, bands were just happy to have a group of people to perform for. It was just as exciting as a bigger venue and from my perspective, it almost meant more. It is kind of like how money is relative it depends on your reference point. The less money you have, the more valuable it becomes. If you have $5 in your pocket and someone gives you $50, that is a lot of money to you. There were times when I only had $5 or $10 dollars for food for the entire week. At the time ramen noodles were about 10 cents apiece. I distinctly recall not eating breakfast, having one of those king-sized Hershey bars for lunch and two ramens for dinner. One of my roommates asked me if I loved ramen. No, it was all I could afford.

We played many shows between '92 and '95 but one venue and show stood out to me. It was a venue on the second floor on First Street in San Jose called the Red Light District. This club was hot in the scene and it was right on the same street as Cactus Club, Marsugi's Night Club and Club FX that bigger bands played.

We were excited to get a gig there. The people in there looked early '90s trendy. A lot of ripped up jeans, Primus T-shirts and flannels tied around waists. There were even some girls there who looked like they were straight out of a Janet Jackson video. Tight shirts, form-fitting bell-bottoms and chokers. It really felt like a club too. The lights were dim red and purple. It was a big space with a raised-up stage.

The first time we were supposed to play there was a wash out. We got bumped off the bill by some band from LA. Often when a band was from out of town they would get preferential treatment and more pay because they had to travel to get to the venue. Especially if it was a head liner that our local scene had heard of. We were supposed to go on one under the headliner which is an awesome slot. Everyone was at the club by then, so the crowd was at its fullest. Having lugged our equipment up the stairs and waited all night to play, we were obviously pissed we were getting bumped. The club owner Manny just stood there with a blank look on his face, tongue hanging out of his mouth. My sister had come to the show to check us out. She was very assertive and knew how to handle the situation. She negotiated a $200 payment – the most we'd ever been paid, and we weren't even performing. Looking back, she should have been our manager. We usually made $50. He assured us we could come back and play a similar slot soon.

So, we arranged to come back. That time we were well prepared and jazzed up. I also had invited a violinist named Benito Cortez to come check us out and see what we were about. It had been such a process trying to find a violinist who would play with a jazz rock fusion band.

The first thing I did was went to the source, to Santa Theresa College and a symphony rehearsal. All the musicians were there. Including a string section. When they were taking a break, I asked the leader if I could ask the musicians a question. He said yeah. So, I stood up, hands clammy, lump in my throat and somehow formed the sentence, "Hi my name is Lance, I am in the jazz rock fusion band Wood. We need a violinist to fill in our sound. Any of you interested?"

I exhaled, relieved I'd gotten the words out. After 5 to 10 seconds, the sobering reality hit me that no one was responding. My heart sank in my chest. I stood there for another 45 seconds that seemed like an eternity and shuffled out the room like *Napoleon Dynamite*. Upset but still determined, I headed over to Starving Musician, a place where all the musicians went to buy, and trade used gear, to ask if they had a violin teacher. They gave me the name of a woman. I called, and she said she wasn't interested but knew someone who might be. That person was Benito.

Benito was unfamiliar with our sound, so he didn't know what to expect. This was new to us too. Playing a place that big and packed. As were started the show with our standard heavy droning jam, the crowd stood there glued to us. Observing our every move. Trying to anticipate our next motion, our next note. For once in my life, I felt like I was being acknowledged by my peers for my gifts on a more professional level. I could see how someone could want to do this every night.

I remember one girl in the front saying, "Scary" between songs.

My face showed I was not feeling that comment.

She quickly added, "In a good way"

We weren't even aware of how dark our music was. And it was coming from a sincere place in my heart. I really felt that way. Frustrated. Angry. Confused. Isolated. Bitter, Disillusioned. Sad. Jealous. I didn't realize how toxic those emotions could be if they were not dealt with at their source, and not constantly vented through this music. I remember thinking "I don't want to feel this way forever."

After we performed, the guys and I off loaded our gear into a space right to the left of the stage. Then, I drank and hung out with everybody. As a rule, I usually didn't drink before playing. Our music was very complex and difficult to play. I couldn't have a clouded mind and perform well. After a while I went back over to check on my gear and realized, my amp was missing. Someone had either stolen it or mistaken it as one of their amps. Many people used Fender Combo amps at that time. Looking back, I feel it may have been a sign. I don't think the Lord wanted me playing music that dark. I didn't have the money for another amp. So, my friend sold me an amp for what I could afford. It was a SUNN head and a 4 x 12 cabinet. What I liked about that SUNN head is it gave me a new more bassy sound. I wrote different parts inspired by the new sounds.

By this time, I was starting to get tired of my arrangement in Campbell. The commute was absolutely killing me. I was not getting enough sleep, enough nutrition, enough anything. One day while lying in my futon half asleep, I heard a sound. I quickly opened my eyes and saw a stark white rat about the size of a small cat up in the rafters in the garage. I grabbed my stuff and headed into the living room. I couldn't live with the idea of what this rat may be doing while I was laying there asleep.

At the time, I had this roommate named Mike. He had a very strong personality and a set routine that he liked to do every morning. He liked to listen to National Public Radio and trudge around the room reviewing his thoughts. He had a lot of energy pent up inside him. You could see it. He was a white guy, but he used to say he had a "ghetto pass." He was not afraid of anyone or anything. I was a little more aggressive at that time, but I tended to be relatively passive and mellow unless stirred. Mike on the other hand welcomed arguments and wouldn't back down. One time we went to a sports bar and almost got into it with some guys. I told him I didn't like that kind of stuff, so it didn't happen much after that.

One-time Mike and I had gone to a show in Downtown San Jose. I had a few drinks earlier in the night, but I was down by the time we were heading home around 1:30 a.m. I was more tired than high. So, we were driving down San Thomas Expressway and right before we got to Campbell Avenue I saw blue and red lights behind us. My stomach was in knots at the idea of going to jail that night, so I tried to play it cool. The officer came over on the left side of my car to speak to me. I can't remember what he said, but it felt like he was trying to see if we were any threat. Mike stayed in the passenger seat of the car. He didn't say much.

The cop had me get out of the car and come back behind the car. It was then I noticed another cop standing in the darkness about 5 feet back, with his gun drawn and at his side. I realized how much potential danger I was really in. How the other cop had clear head shots on us if we so much as moved when we were in the car. Seeing that I was polite and articulate, he let me go. I sometimes wonder if that got me out of many of the stops I've experienced. Just the fact I didn't speak with slang and was respectful. I was pulled over many times by that point in my life and the only ticket I ever got was a fix it ticket, to change my muffler. because my Pontiac purred too smooth. A sound that I loved. That old glass pack wub, wub, wub. I didn't have the typical inner-city experience with the police because I was often pulled over in the suburbs. But it was obvious the police assumed I was a threat until proven otherwise.

This was the profiling so many people have spoken of. Of course, an officer must gauge potential threat, but it is inaccurate to always assume a Black or Latino is guilty until proven innocent. It is demoralizing to be considered a threat just because of the color of your skin. Many white people have never experienced this. They look at the police as people there to protect them. Luckily, I haven't had some of the experiences with police so many other Black men have. I can't imagine how it must have felt being so outnumbered and so over powered.

Then again, I've met Black guys from the inner city who say they were beaten almost daily walking home school by people in their own neighborhood. They had to pick their walk home based on how many fights or beatings they would face. And this was at the hands of other frustrated, angry young Black males. This kind of cruelty and lack of empathy is the cycle perpetuated every day in places like Chicago where dozens of people are shot often in a weekend. There are more murders in Chicago in a month than in an entire year here in Stockton.

This is too often what the military calls collateral damage in these inner-city wars. My mother saw this firsthand at Lockwood Elementary School in East Oakland. East Oakland has a huge low-income area and a severe problem with violent crime. One of my mother's 8-year-old students told my mother she'd been shot in the crossfire. Raising up her little shirt to show the scar where the bullet was removed. Children should not have to face this type of warfare just because they live in low income areas. I know for a fact there were no shootings that involved children the whole time I attended Terrell Elementary School in West San Jose. But West San Jose was an affluent area at the time, a so-called good part of town. It was also predominately white. How does a kid from East Oakland get the same education and safe environment as the kid that lives in Atherton, an affluent suburb in the West Bay Area? We must start looking at ourselves as one humanity. Having empathy for one another. Providing more resources for those who need it most. There are so many wonderful, kind, loving and patient people working tirelessly toward the goal of peace and love for all of humanity. I want to be counted as one of those people, in whatever I do. It really starts with a simple honest inward smile. Giving yourself some slack. Going easy on yourself. Even back then, I was learning to be patient, kind supportive of myself. This is so imperative. The greatest loss is the love of oneself.

6

Mental Challenges Ahead

After some of the experiences I had in the South Bay, it was nice to be back with Mom and Dad in late '95. There was such a sense of familiarity with them. When I was in the South Bay, I met lots of people. Some loved me, some were indifferent, some I had issues with. Thankfully most of them were in the first group. But one nice difference with living with Mom and Dad – I actually had an air-conditioned house, a nice bed, food in the fridge and more financial freedom. I had transferred from Redwood City Smart & Final to the one in Stockton. For a brief time, I worked at the register day shift. But shortly I was moved to graveyard shift to work the load.

I was carless, so my dad would drop me off around midnight. That was when I met Larissa. She was about my height. Thin with broad shoulders. She had long flowing strawberry blonde hair that adorned a round cute face with delicate features. She was one of the coolest down-to-earth women I've ever met but circumstances were against me yet again. She was married. She was only about 25 which struck me as kind of young to get married. She said her dad was so mad when he heard she was getting married he went out back to chop wood. And that was not his normal behavior. We talked about everything. Almost like we were courting. Sometimes she would give me a ride home. One day she came over to my house. I opened the door with shorts on but no shirt. She stood there glowing with excitement. Right behind her I could see the brand new '95 Camaro. She was kind of a rocker/country chick. I thought she and the car were completely bad ass. I was a little reluctant since she was married, and I wanted to maintain my integrity as best I could. So, we went out for a short spin. It was convertible, so we had the wind blowing through our hair as we flew down 5-North toward Sacramento. It was exhilarating, and I wished the feeling would never end. But reality was just sitting there as a back drop, reminding us that we could not be together, she had made her choice. And although we shared similar feelings, it wasn't me. I could see why she got married so young. This is the kind of woman you marry immediately. She was that special.

My manager and I had similar negative senses of humor. We had this machine that was a cross between a forklift and pallet jack to unload pallets from the truck. We would joke about flying out into the parking lot, furious and plunging the forks right into the side of a customer's car and lifting it off the ground. We thought that was hilarious. I still had a lot of angst and negativity in my heart at the time. Things that would be appalling to the average person, I found funny. And I think this really did demonstrate the state of my spirit.

They say you judge a tree by its fruit. The fruit I was producing was not healthy and possibly toxic. See the fruit comes from a seed. In my case, it was a seed of rejection. And it manifested into all this other toxic fruit. Anger, frustration. Interestingly, I was unaware there was anything wrong with my attitude. I surrounded myself with people that reassured those beliefs and enabled those behaviors. Anything can be made to be normal if everyone around you is doing it. But when it is time to face the consequences for your behavior, that's when you start having regrets.

In my case, I was not out there acting on negative ideas, like running the forklift into the car. But there are people out there that really would do that. And the fact I had that train of thought, that was a warning sign that the state and condition of my heart needed to be changed. Every sin starts with a thought. And if we think that thought often enough and for long enough, we may begin to act on those thoughts. And once it goes from a thought to an action, a line is crossed. Once that line is crossed, many times it begins to get ignored as if it is not there and it just becomes a habit. Then you rarely even think about it as wrong or a problem.

The other Juan, a fellow worker, and I had some awesome times joking around through our graveyard shift. Because we started at 12 a.m., our lunch would usually be around 4 a.m. We both loved old '80s songs that we thought were cheesy and we always made fun. One time we went through a nearby Taco Bell drive-through early morning, blasting the Michael Jackson's title track "Thriller." The people inside Taco Bell weren't in on the joke. I think they thought we were just stupid and we didn't care. We were in that moment. It's little things like this I miss when I look back. We didn't know it at the time. No one tapped us on the shoulder and said enjoy these times.

You are going to look back some day and remember how awesome this was. There is a profound lesson in that. The incredible gift of enjoying and truly appreciating the present moment.

Of course, we often don't choose the circumstances that impact our choices. But this is where faith comes in. This is where we begin to trust in God to do his part. He is in control of the circumstances that affect our daily lives. If we can start to work in unison with the Lord, a powerful friendship and partnership can grow over time. I've learned the Lord wants to be our confidant. He wants us to trust him with everything. He is a master craftsman and we are his works of art. He is tirelessly working to mold us into the most useful vessel we can possibly be to humanity around us. I truly believe in my heart of hearts there is no higher calling than humbly serving the Lord and being a manifestation of his greatness.

When I think about the radio music of the late 90's, the work of brilliant singer songwriter Alanis Morissette comes to mind. That was when her first album *Jagged Little Pill* was in heavy rotation on national radio, music videos on MTV. Her angst had the energy of grunge but she also had a sensitive side. She said things the average working 25-year-old could related to.

"I'm broke but I'm happy,
I'm poor but I'm kind."

She had her finger on the pulse of the average young adult, and she was taking note of our vitals. The music, although dark, was raw, honest and definitely rock 'n roll. As a songwriter I noticed that she used a lot of listing in her work. Her song *Thank You* moved me beyond any place I had ever been taken by a pop song. God was all over it. Brilliant.

After a few months working at the Smart & Final, I became restless. I was tiring of working with the public. I wanted to be behind the scenes in a warehouse environment. I was given the opportunity to transfer again, so I took it.

My job was to take audits of the goods in the warehouse. They would give me aisle numbers and I would go there and count how much product was on the pallet. No heavy lifting. Just counting. Sometimes I got to use the cherry picker to go up to the higher up locations. What an adventure. I would put a safety belt around my waist, tethered to the machine which looked like a reverse forklift. I would stand on deck with a pallet behind me to stand on, sometimes going 20 feet up. I also drove the electronic pallet jacks. So fun.

After a few months doing that, I started work in the return section. This was where the partially broken cases of soda and packages been opened by customers went. I worked with a guy who was walleyed, wore thick glasses, blonde with a bowl cut. And his face was always sweaty even though we were doing very little lifting. We just had to load the things on pallets, log the items and send them away. One thing I noticed is he was always eating the candy from the broken cases. He said it didn't matter because the company was writing this candy off anyway as a loss. I didn't know if the supervisor before him told him that but that's what he told me. After a while, I reluctantly started doing the same, here and there, thinking what he said made sense.

One day before work, I saw a guy across the street in the convenience store that looked kind of like an undercover cop, but he had a Smart and Final ID. Later that day I was called in the office by that same man. He told me they had me on tape eating and throwing candy. And how upset the management was because it was already a mess back there. Fearful they were going to press criminal charges for technically stealing candy, I tried my best to be honest. He told me it was going to be all right, to just be honest and put it in writing that I'd eaten and thrown some candy and sign it. I felt it was easier to be honest. Even not knowing if I would face any legal punishment. He fired me and told me I didn't have to worry about criminal charges because I confessed. It was about 10 a.m. Since I lived with my parents, I had to tell Dad first. I knew Mom tended to be more understanding, so Dad was the one who was the disciplinarian, even thought I was 26. I told him what happened, and he was cool about it. He understood I just made a stupid mistake.

After about a week or two, Dad started to really pressure me and give me a hard time. Which was justified as I had been reckless. The pressure became so great I went out to stay with my sister in the Richmond Hills. This was right around Thanksgiving, so it was hard being away during the holidays. I remember speaking to Dad on the phone, and he told me he felt no one was on his side. I told him he was not alone. That I just needed time to get on my feet and the Bay Area was where I wanted to do that. I felt closer to Dad after that conversation. I could tell he loved me because he was hurt by me not being around. Sometimes when things got to be too much, my pressure release valve was to remove myself from the situation.

Anne worked in the City and she had to walk down to BART train and take it through the Transbay tube into SF every day for work. Sometimes, when it was raining or when she was tired she would take a cab back up the hill. It was a long walk descending from the hills. It felt like I had to hold myself back from falling forward, like I was a couple steps ahead of myself all the way down. And back up the hill was an aerobic workout, to say the least. Sweat would be on my brow and my heart would be racing by the time I got home.

Anne was not home much of the time between the long commute and visiting with friends. The house we lived in was small probably about 1,200 square feet and two bedrooms. It had hard wood floors. So, any time someone was walking it would echo through the house. It would sometimes get unbearably cold at night. Since I was unemployed, my days usually started around 11 a.m. I would usually walk down the hill to El Camino Real to get groceries or just hang out. Then I would trudge back up the hill, often with heavy bags in hand.

When night would fall, I would find myself alone. I was really into the Dark Progressive Rock band, King Crimson at the time and would often play their dreary dark tunes on my old record player I'd bought in a thrift store in the early '90s. Amazing it still worked. I had read a lot about religions when I was in college in '90s. It is a topic that had always intrigued me. A few years prior I had met a guy that turned me onto another spiritual doctrine, so I was reading it at the time. I was about half way through it.

One night I was alone in the cold house, reading the doctrine when something sexual popped into my mind. Which really stood out, like it was almost not my coming from me. Immediately following that, I heard a disembodied voice coming from the doorway of the room which was to my left. It sounded as if there was a person there, the voice was not in my head. It said something very threatening to me. Assuming it was God talking to me I said, "No! Don't turn your back on me." I was sorry for the impure thought and felt I'd provoked God to anger. The voice told me to "suffer so you may learn humility" and believe me this incident was to cause a lot of suffering. It was a seed of fear planted into my psyche. It put me in immediate emotional and spiritual bondage. I didn't question the voices source, I just assumed it was the Lord. Which looking back was very naive.

Terrified, I jumped up and begin to pace around the house. Looking through the cracked curtain feeling totally unsettled about what I had just experienced. I didn't know if it was going to happen again. To give me something to ground me, something to cling to in this time of complete and utter duress and chaos, I called Gary my best friend since high school. I spoke to Gary from around 11 a.m. until 3 a.m., mostly just me ranting about my fears and newly found paranoia. Gary didn't speak much as it was really late and I'm sure he had work that morning. But he listened and listened.

Inserting words of support and encouragement. I went all the way down the line with my fear. Being a very creative person, I was imagining all kinds of terrible things that could befall me. In the end, Gary agreed to pick me up at BART in Fremont the next day because Anne was going to be away for the whole weekend. Which would leave me alone another night to face this entity, spirit, God, my own mind … whatever it was.

The next morning, I headed down the hill looking for a church and someone I could speak to. I walked down San Pablo and encountered several closed churches since it was still early on a Saturday. After about 30 minutes of walking, I found a Catholic church open and spoke with a priest. I told him about what had transpired and what I encountered. I can't remember what he said, but he implied it most likely was not God. Which at that moment, I refused to believe. I was convinced of the doom hanging over my head. That I was choosing to believe in. He prayed for me and gave me a Bible.

When Gary picked me up in Fremont, I was super relieved to see someone I knew had my back and cared about me. He said not to worry, it was just my mind. What we see here in our physical environment is all that's here. I listened but still was reluctant to believe that. We had a pretty good weekend where I could get my mind off my fears a bit and enjoy being around my friend. On Sunday, he took me back to BART. I was finally able to tell Anne what happened too, and she was totally supportive. Telling me not to worry, that God was with me. But the fear was still lurking, like an ominous backdrop to every scene I entered. Being alone during the day and into the night at the same house this had happened in was almost unbearable. One day I walked down to Safeway and on my way back up, I saw a guy driving real slow by me. I assumed he was out to get me, to the point where I drew a photo of him and hid it under some papers on my sister's nightstand. In case something happened to me, they would have a clue as to who may have hurt me. Now I was reacting in the physical world to something going on in my mind.

This was right around Thanksgiving, so my dad and Mom had arranged to meet at a Chinese restaurant for dinner. Which is something we are known to do. A couple times we even had pizza on Thanksgiving. At dinner, Anne and I went to the buffet counters at the same time. My mind was starting to change. I thought I was supposed to show Anne how to choose her food. I took a little of everything as my mind was telling me, "This is your last supper!" By the time the dinner was over, I was convinced of my impending doom even more. So, Anne and I went back to Richmond. Mom came back during the day that week because I was having a meltdown.

I was so wound up that I knew I needed professional help. So, I called a good friend of mine from Kinko's a few years prior. Robinmarie told me to go to Herrick Hospital. At the time, I didn't know that Herrick was a Sutter Affiliate, not Kaiser which I had. And that it most likely wouldn't be covered. So, Mom picked me up and went to see a doctor. They decided to admit me because my paranoia and delusions were becoming debilitating.

By this time, my mom had called Dad and insisted he come to my bedside. I was really in dire need of emotional support that only a family could give. When Dad arrived, he laughed when he saw I was just sitting there on the exam table.

"You're ok, there's nothing wrong with you." I think he didn't want to see me so vulnerable. He wanted me to be strong. By this time Anne had arrived too. They took Anne and me into a little room. The police had to come in and verify I was a potential danger to myself. I told them how I was feeling, and they agreed to admit me.

Once I was in, I felt like I was in a fish bowl. It was night time and I paced back and forth, back and forth up the hall. I was beginning to feel like a hamster in a cage. I had endless energy. My mind was going around and around just like when I was on mushrooms. After a little while of pacing, a male nurse took me into my room to take my vitals and give me my meds. I tried to say something to him as he was taking my blood pressure.

He interrupted me saying, "This is my horse, let me ride it." I was immediately intimidated and felt threatened by him. Which didn't help with my current situation at all.

They gave me Risperdal for voices, Lithium for balance and Klonopin to help me sleep. Little did I know it was going to be more difficult to sleep than I thought. I had not met my roommate yet. He was about 5 feet 6 inches and about 100 pounds. Feminine elven features, high cheekbones, wild sandy blonde hair framing his face. He didn't speak at all for the first 10 or 15 minutes.

Suddenly the silence was broken by a soft unassuming voice that said eight simple words, "They won't let us have razors in here." This too was not helping with my paranoia, so I didn't respond. After a few more minutes, he began to describe how he would defend himself against me if I attacked. I quickly realized he was probably more afraid of me than I was him. I continued to lay there in silence. I was just starting to fall asleep when I felt a presence like someone standing too close to me. When I opened my eyes, he was standing there naked. I didn't say a word or change my demeanor. After about a minute, he went and got back in his bed.

Then I noticed the staff comes in like every 15 minutes. It was almost impossible for me to get a good night sleep. Now I realize we were on suicide watch, so they had to check on us frequently. When the morning came, I was exhausted, having gotten almost no sleep. Around 7 a.m. I heard a big commotion. They were wheeling a guy through tied to a gurney yelling, "Why can't I punch people? I don't understand why I can't punch people?!" His face contorted with unquenchable rage. Drool swinging off his bottom lip, like the muzzle of a Basset Hound. Sprawling upper body out of control, tethered at the waist, his upper arms pinned to his waist at his lap. His booming voice quieter with distance as they headed down to the end of the hall. Finally, almost silent as they closed the room door behind him. Hopefully on the opposite side of the building.

I concluded that the mental ward is no place for a paranoid person. It exacerbated my symptoms, amplifying them to almost a fever pitch that first day. The second day after breakfast I was moved to my own room. Which was just big enough for a twin bed to fit, with barely enough room to stand on either side. They said I was a good patient. Because I was not causing any problems like that other not so gentle man. Shortly after my mom and Anne came to visit, I learned from a provided pamphlet that I could not leave until they deemed me safe to go out into the world.

Suddenly it occurred to me this is like jail. They may not let me leave. Thankfully it turned out that they just wanted to stabilize me on my medicine to their satisfaction. So, I was discharged to go home with my parents.

Shortly after I returned to Stockton with my parents, I entered the IOP program at Kaiser (Intensive Outpatient Program) as suggested by my therapist Dr. Meade. An interesting guy. A quiet wise man. His presence was comforting as was his pleasant demeanor. On his wall, he had one of those Native American dream weavers, like a God's eye. Along with the walking stick of a seasoned long trail hiker. It was about five-feet long. It looked like a crooked yet sturdy stick that could bear his weight or more. At the end of it were feathers and what looked like leather twine wrapped around. Larry's approach was holistic. He asked me things and how those things made me feel. But most importantly, he listened intently. And it was genuine. Not just his job. He truly cared.

I spent quite a bit of time sitting across from him in that comfortable chair. Walking him through my delusional world, as new to me as it was to him. I am sure he had dealt with people like me many times, but no one with my exact story. He helped me sort fantasy from reality. I told him about my dream/goal to be a Rock Star. He may have considered that another delusion, I don't know. But a side of me felt like he may have thought it was possible.

IOP was basically a group therapy for those who were still somewhat "at risk" due to their instability. It taught us ways to cope with our problems. Plus, it gave us a chance to voice our heart to our peers and get feedback. The people in there ranged from 20 to 40 in age. They first taught us about depression. How clinical depression is beyond just being a little down. How often the person is depressed for no reason. In my case, it was triggered by a bought of paranoia.

But it was more than that. It turned out – I was diagnosed as bipolar, so out of control I'd started to hallucinate.

The diagnosis was tough to accept because the voice had told me things earlier in my life that had inspired me, given me hope and a direction as to what my destiny may be. I was convinced and still am that there are different sources of voices. Sometimes it is hallucination, sometimes a spirit, sometimes a relative trying to communicate with you and sometimes God and faith. Being bipolar, it is harder to differentiate but I truly believe in sorting through the sources of these voices. I believe there is a spirit realm that exists that we simply don't fully understand.

They taught us that depressed people engage in all or nothing thinking that if indulged in too much could lead to suicide if it goes unchallenged. They gave us tools to cope. Much of which I had read in Psych 101, only now it was for survival and not a grade. There were about 10 of us in the sessions. All of us had terribly low self-esteem and acting out in one way or another. These were people from all nationalities, religious backgrounds and walks of life. When I got to my story, I shared how I felt unloved by my dad which I still somewhat did and how I had so much trouble finding a woman to express myself with. Many of the people in the class were empathetic. Many of the girls in the class couldn't understand how a guy as young and decent looking as me could have trouble in this area. One Black guy in the class who was around 40 offered me a ride home which saved me over an hour walk. On the way to my house, he told me he was like my dad. That he was taught the man was supposed to provide for the family. He was not a very sensitive person to his children. And I'd made him realize he may have had a similar effect on his kids.

Lance West

13-year-old Lance West proudly displaying highest rank achieved Red Belt

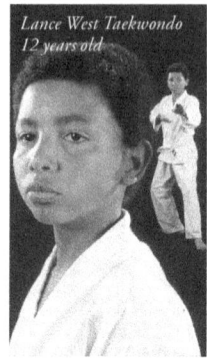

Lance West Taekwondo 12 years old

Lance West Taekwondo always in my own head

My Grandfather on my fathers' side Curtis Hudson Sr.

My Grandfather on my mothers' side Gibson Rainerd

Me and my little brother James Toldeo early days

My Father Curtis receiving Award from UDLP for outstanding performance 1999

My Father Curtis next to tank he designed parts for UDLP

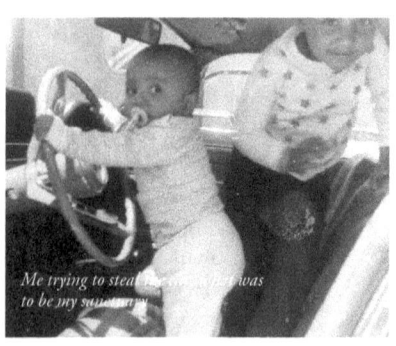

Me trying to steal the car that was to be my someday

Lance West at the Pinnacles CA 18 years old

Momentum

My Uncle Cardell in front of Grandma Mattie's house

My Sister Anne and cousin Christine

My Grandmother on my fathers' side Mattie Dawson2

My Mother Mable with the cotton candy afro I spoke of

My mother Mable in New York about 20 years old

My Sister Anne, our cousin Lisa from NY, and young Lance West

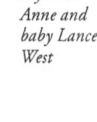
My Sister Anne and baby Lance West

My Grandmother on my mother Mables' side Minnie Rainford2

Phil Romero - Drums, Gary Niederhoff - Bass, Lance West - Guitar, Vox

My short stint as a PAL football player Go Rams!

Outside of IOP, which lasted about three weeks, I was walking for hours. I had endless energy. I would walk from our house, sometimes past the mall about an hour and a half walk one way. I could easily walk for four hours without stopping. My legs would get tired, but my mind kept going in circles. I don't know if it was the medicine or the illness, but I had boundless energy.

In the mornings Dad left around 3 a.m. and Mom shortly after to commute to the Bay Area. When Mom left, it was still dark outside. I was so paranoid someone was going to break in and assault me. I would get up when she left and stay up until well after the sun came up in the living room. It was so creepy being alone in such a big house like that. Plus, that was how I was preyed upon before by the sinister voice. Alone in a house.

Then one day I just woke up and it was gone. Just lifted off me. After IOP, I enrolled in Delta College for early classes. Mom would drop me off at Denny's and I would have breakfast there and then go to class. I really didn't like Delta College but just felt I needed to do something productive, so I wouldn't get a lot of pressure from my parents. After a couple months at Delta, I began to grow increasingly more and more disinterested in attending. It was a chore. I didn't enjoy anything about it. I didn't even want to be around people at all. I just wanted to play music again.

I moved back with Anne in Richmond. This time with the intent of moving back to the South Bay where I could get back to rehearsing with the band. In those days, I was not even using the internet although I think it was starting to become available. I got a San Jose paper at the store in Richmond and found an ad for a laundry delivery driver. The place was called Nelson's Cleaners. I got a ride down there to the interview with my mom. I got along well with the owner Ron and his wife Sally. They hired me on the spot and I started that next Monday.

I contacted a friend of mine who used to shoot videos for our band. David agreed I could live in the garage below him at a house in Los Altos that his Dad had designed and built. It was a Spanish-style house with a lot of archways and big wooden doors with vertical slats of wood. The design was perfect for a horror story, almost creepy there. The garage had a padlock on it. I would enter through there. It was like I had my own apartment, kind of. If I needed to shower, I would go upstairs where he and his two daughters lived. His brother also lived on the bottom floor with his three children. It was a two-car garage divided down the center with the frame of a wall.

It didn't occur to me I could just buy a bed, so I took two fence boards and nailed them together. And propped them up on either end of an old toilet and an ottoman to form a makeshift cot. And I would lay my sleeping bag on top of that. I just didn't want to be on the floor with bugs and rats. I slept with the lights on because I was afraid of what would be crawling around in the darkness. At least I could see what was going on if I woke up and heard or felt something moving. Also, there was a window on the other side of the garage and I often felt someone might look through it at night. That is the only thing I didn't like about having the lights on.

For my job, I had a regular route in the morning where I would pick up people's laundry at their houses. Sometimes fancy places like in the Saratoga Hills. I would just take the bag of clothes and bring the clean ones back on hangers and well folded, bound little packages for certain items. I also went to another cleaner in Palo Alto, where I had a lot of clothes to deliver. The guy at that cleaners didn't have a lot of the machines to do the work, so we would do it and deliver to him. Also, I would sometimes go to apartments and residences to pick up drapes. Take them down and deliver them back the next day and put them back up. A tough job, sometimes hanging 7 to 10 sets of drapes in just one apartment. And I would sometimes do two or three apartments at a time.

One day when I got off work, I decided to walk to the bus stop rather than wait for the bus to get a ride there. Bus fare was a dollar and ten cents. I had a couple dollars in my pocket and didn't want to have to go into the store for change, so I said to myself, "I am going to find a dime somewhere between here and the bus stop."

I didn't even hesitate, looking as I began to walk. I was certain I would find one. I had chosen to take a different street over to the bus stop. After about five minutes of walking, head down staring at the ground beneath my feet. In the gutter, I noticed something shiny and silver. It was not a nickel, not a quarter, not a Susan B. Anthony – it was a DIME! I reached down and picked it up totally reassured I was supposed to find that dime. Whatever the case, I found it just as I had thought I would.

I think faith is kind of like that. You know what you want, and you know you are going to get it to the point where you are anticipating it. But it must be God's will. Some will say you can manifest anything you want. I personally believe you cannot take God out of it. My underlying belief is in destiny. I believe whether we perceive things as good, bad or indifferent it's all part of the story. And I truly believe it is all working toward a higher good for mankind. At least I hope this is the case.

Nelson's Cleaners also had a sister store. That is where I met Sister Rose. An unassuming woman with long straight hair, with a broach hair pin tying it back, an untucked button-up dress shirt and a jean skirt to the ground almost totally covering her sensible shoes. You could see just the toe of the shoe poking out at the base of the dress. I could tell she was a devout Christian by her attire. She began to invite me to church every time I stopped by to pick-up and deliver clothes. After about the tenth invite I agreed. I was open minded, and at the time I was in desperate need of a spiritual direction, purpose and most importantly love and acceptance from my peers.

The first service as most consisted of singing at the beginning, a short sermon and a long prayer session at the altar as it was a Pentecostal Charismatic Church. The cornerstone of our belief was that people just like in the days of the Bible could receive the Holy Spirit, speak in tongues with stammering lips.

At the end of service, the pastor would always encourage us to come to the front of the church and connect with God's Holy Ghost directly. I was desperate to have a break from my discontentment with everything I had been experiencing up to then. So, I went to the altar, praying at the front on my knees and leaning my head down next to the altar – when a loud sound boomed from my mouth much like a bark – my body lunged to my left side. I began to convulse and gyrate on the floor next to the pews, uncontrollably. The barking sound continued as I kicked my feet against the floor pushing myself from in front of the pews up against the adjacent wall, out toward the back of the church. Several of the brothers were attempting to get my heaving body under control with no success.

After about five minutes of what seemed like an eternity, the barking voice subsided, and they raised me up to my feet in victory. By now the terrified occupants of the building had all but left except for the few who had seen me through the ordeal. It was hard for me and possibly some of the others there to believe I had that lurking in my spirit. Aside from having a lot of disappointments, I was all but normal and friendly in most people's eyes. What we witnessed that day was something biblical. (Mark 1:26, 27).

After everything settled down, some of the people filed back in and I spoke to some of them with a soft quiet voice. A gentle voice. The opposite of what I had just uttered minutes before. I have never felt that light in my life. I felt like I was hovering a couple inches off the ground. The burden of 27 years of insecurity, doubt, fear, anger, frustration, resentment, bitterness, jealousy, envy, sadness had been lifted off my shoulders in five minutes. I had been given an incredible gift. A new spiritual lease on life. The Lord had cast a spirit out of me that had kept me in bondage for so long.

This experience made me aware that a human spirit can be kept in bondage by dark spirits without the host even being aware of it. Maybe this could explain my life-longed battle with negative self-worth. And my deep-seated feeling of being unloved and or unworthy of love.

After service, I was given a ride to the bus stop saving me about a half-hour walk. Then I took the bus up El Monte where I began walking up the dark road to where I lived. It was dark as a moonless night. No street lights but I felt like the Lord was illuminating my way home.

When I got to Dave's house, I paced back and forth for what seemed like a couple hours in front of his house. In awe of the move God had made in my life and my spirit. I had never been so certain there was a God that loved me, I felt like an infant with his mother looking down upon him. I just replayed repeatedly in my mind what I had experienced. It was the ultimate affirmation of God's existence.

After this experience, I was totally open to the Lord and United Pentecost Church. I would do anything to feel the Lord's presence. I was like a lightning rod for the Lord. When I would pray, and someone would lay hands on my forehead, my legs would buckle beneath me and I would crumble down to the ground. It got to the point where I would get knocked down, jump right back up and get knocked down again multiple times. Prayer at the end of service was also a wonderful time for healing and rejuvenation. One of the services I just sat in the pews a few rows back soul crying. Crying from the core of my being. Like my heart was being cleansed of the guilt I felt for all those years I'd sinned with no regard for the Lord. Reckless, thoughtless sin. Trying to make atonement for all that I had done. I finally understood what it meant to lay my burdens to rest at the altar before the Lord.

There were about five or six guys my age in the church who were single. One time we got together after church as a group to talk about what it is like to be Apostolic and single male. We went to Carl's Junior. One of the guys was telling the rest of us how Pastor Lawrence said we could only date and marry an Apostolic woman. Which means a woman of our denomination. I immediately addressed my concerns. "It's difficult finding a wife, imagine how hard it is going be limiting ourselves to a certain denomination of Christian." Looking back, I think he just wanted to build on our church which was so small. About 25 people. Of which only 10 to 12 were adults.

One time my sister Anne came to service and met Sister Rose. Sister Rose told Anne not to worry, we are not a cult or anything. We just believe in the Holy Ghost. Anne did not really attend church much at the time. She may have been a little skeptical about the choice I'd made in church, but I told her how great a connection I had made to the Lord there. She told me after that she felt the Pastor was a bit controlling. She did not totally feel right there but she supported my choice.

What I have learned is God is everywhere and he will use anything and or anybody to get to you when he wants to reach you and teach you his message of love. He has all the resources he needs. But I did not realize the Lord had been in pursuit of my heart for years. Wanting to love me and free me from my mostly self-imposed burdens. He had to get that spirit of bondage out of me and continue to work his healing and restoration in my heart. I truly believe we are vessels just like clay pots to the Lord. He is a master craftsman and will never stop working until he feels he has completed us and we have served our purpose.

Having received the Holy Spirit in my heart, I was sensitive when it came to spiritual matters. I was really starting to have some interesting experiences. One time I was lying face down on my makeshift cot. I was in between sleep and awake. I heard what sounded like people praying in tongues out in the driveway in front of the house, which was all dirt and rocks. It even sounded like there were footsteps out there. It was late, around 2 a.m. As I lay there, I started to feel the presence of what felt like a spirit hovering over my body. Close, like two feet above me. It felt dark and creepy. So, I shook myself out of the between consciousness state and jumped up more alert. Spun around, my bare feet on the cold concrete floor of the garage. I don't know how or if I fell back to sleep, but it was a touchy situation for sure. Being there all night with the lights on I often felt once again like a fish in a fish bowl. Like someone was looking into my room and observing my every move.

In the services at church, I was starting to feel more and more anxious. One time I felt like I knew who the Lord wanted to bless with the Holy Spirit next and I called out his name in prayer to let him know the Lord wanted to bless him. The pastor later said in the sermon, "Some people think they know who is going to be blessed next but only God knows that." Of course, he was right, but I felt so heightened spiritually, so connected. I felt the Lord was guiding me that way. I don't know if I was still taking my medicine at that time, but it seemed that I was having an intense religious experience along with some of the symptoms of the illness I was being treated for. But these experiences I was having transcended all experiences I had with my mental illness until this day. It was a very difficult situation to be in.

I was starting to feel as if the life I was living with my job was not the path I wanted to go down. I felt like my bosses were taking me for granted. I was making a half way decent salary and they'd given me a job when I really needed it. One day I felt this compelling desire to tell them how I felt and that I no longer wanted to work for them. It came as a shock to them, but they told me they understood. As I walked out, feeling as if I had done the right thing, I wasn't aware of the effect it was going to have on my life.

When I got up the next few days after leaving the job, I had tons of energy. I felt like I could walk all day. And for the most part I did. I was questioning if the music

I did with the band was Christian and if it was all right with God. On my way down El Camino, I stopped by Burger King and called my friend from childhood Chuck, whose number I had gotten from a mutual friend. I talked to him about the dilemma, about the music.

He said, "You can still do the same music. You are just coming from a different place as far as where your heart is. If your heart has changed, that's all that matters to God."

I felt there was a lot of truth to that. That kind of music would not even resonate with my spirit in its new evolved state. A person that has truly evolved spiritually would not be wasting time with negative emotions and getting bogged down with that. I think the music I played reflected the condition of my spirit. Before I experienced a connection with the Holy Spirit I didn't know what it felt like to have love in my heart. After that experience, I finally did. I just needed to nurture and grow from that seed of love.

After I got off the phone with Chuck, I started to think a recording artist I liked at the time was in San Francisco. So, my twisted logic told me it is quicker to walk down the freeway to SF than to take the city streets, so I did just that. I walked out to the freeway and went down the circular entrance out to the open freeway, right alongside the cars whizzing by. I walked for quite a while all the way from Mountain View to the University exit in Palo Alto.

Suddenly, I heard a car pull up behind me and someone getting out blasting in a booming voice, "Stop … Stop!" My mind told me to keep walking, so I did. Within seconds, I felt someone grab me from behind and swing me around by my waist. Almost immediately, I felt a terrible burning sensation in my eyes. Unbearable. The next thing I know, I was on the ground totally subdued by what I then knew to be police officers.

As they got me up and handcuffed me I said, 'I am sorry, Officer, I'm sorry!'

One of the back-up officers said, 'This is the nicest guy I have ever met!' They could tell I was no real threat to them. They just were playing it safe. Not knowing if I was on PCP or something.

I quietly rode in the back of the car not knowing what was going to happen. When we got there, I was fine until we got to the building where I began to realize I was being taken into custody and may not get out. For some reason, my mind said, "This is Grandma helping. We are going to get you out of here."

Comforted, I didn't resist as they took my picture, checked me in and put me in a private cell. After hours of just lying on the bench, unable to sleep, the door opened, and they released me. It was still night time, probably about 2 a.m. I had never been outside all night alone before, so it was a little creepy. I hung around by a train station where there was a security guard nearby, because it made me feel safer. Once the sun came up, I headed down El Camino to Los Altos, opened the garage door and went to sleep. I didn't even tell Dave what happened.

Later that evening, I headed down to El Camino on foot to downtown Mountain View. My mind was still cycling. They were having a live performance in the Mountain View Arts Center. I somehow roamed into the center without paying. I can't remember what I did or said, but I know I got on stage in front of the whole crowd.

I was ushered out into the lobby where I sat down on a bench. An irate man from the show came over to me. My mind told me he was the devil. About 10 minutes later, Mountain View PD arrived. I mentioned 5150 to them, which I now know now is the code when someone is a danger to themselves or others. I don't know how I knew to tell them that, but I avoided going to regular jail that way. They took me to the Psyche Ward at Valley Medical.

It was night. About 12 of us were in there. Just as with Herrick, the room was glass from about the waist up so that the nurses could see us. I had a lot of energy. I didn't want to sit in the room with everyone. I went out into the hallway area and began to roll my body down the wall, as if I was a child rolling down a hill but standing. I also tried the handle on a nearby door. I was rambunctious.

They took me in a small room where they had what looked like an exam table, laid flat with two pieces that stretched out like arms. They strapped me down to this apparatus.

They administered some sort of sedative and I lay there for about an hour.

After, they put me back with everyone in the room again.

There was a white guy in there with a baseball cap. He had all kinds of cuts near his wrist, on his forearms. I told him it is just like being on acid. The way I was feeling. He smiled. He never spoke and seemed pleasant under the circumstances. My mind told me he was a friend too. After a while, they let me out. It was still night. I called Gary to come get me. He later said he had no idea there was anything wrong with me. I acted like I always did.

That evening I walked down El Camino, all the way down to Sunnyvale, over to Fremont Street to United Pentecost. It was dark when I got there. Service was going as usual, only this time I was really starting to unravel.

Pastor found out I quit my job. After service, he pulled me aside and asked me, 'Are you independently wealthy?'

"No."

He said, "Well, how can you afford to quit your job?'

"I know what I want to do and it's music."

Being a voice of reason, "But you need an income while you're pursuing your goal."

He'd also expressed to me how he felt about worldly music when I jammed one with this awesome 16-year-old drummer in the church. That kid played some solid beats and I played bass. He said we shouldn't play that kind of music in church. I'd broke a string and thought it was a sign.

At the time, I hadn't heard of God not approving of an artist to the point of telling them they need to quit. I am sure I knew how he felt about evil music. But I honestly didn't consider the music I played with the band evil or bad.

I remember my Mom used to ask, "Why are you guys playing such angry music when you are such happy people?" I think the truth is we were nice guys with deep-seated anger inside that was unresolved and we needed to vent. I remember telling the guys, "I don't want to be angry for the rest of my life. I want to find the source of my anger and overcome it." Well, I had finally found the source of my anger. It was that spirit.

On the way to service, I started to feel like throwing things away in the garbage. I don't know why. I was thinking about the Phil Collin's song "Throwing It All Away." It reminded me of cleansing. Getting rid of anything and everything tying me down. I threw all my cash in the garbage.

A lady saw me and said, "What are you doing?"

I got the money out of the garbage, walked over to her and said, "Do you want this?"

She looked shocked, realizing there was something wrong with me.

I was starting to see what it was like to be one of those random lost people you see on the street.

I still had enough wherewithal to make it to service somehow. The service went as it always did until toward the end of the sermon. Pastor Lawrence didn't like that Sister Rose had walked out of service because the words 'the devil' were used in a song in the last service. It was her belief that you should never say those words in a holy place like a church. That was just her personal belief she had the right to. He told her to stand up. So, she did. He then he began to scold her like a child about how she shouldn't have left service and how it was disrespectful to the congregation and she should apologize to everyone.

Suddenly I heard a voice say. 'Stand Up!' At first, I didn't respond. But as he went on scolding her. I heard it again, 'Stand Up!'

So, I stood up.

Pastor Lawrence barked, 'Sit down, Lance!!'

I continued to stand.

'Sit down, Lance, or you can walk out of here and never come back!'

I tried to say, "I just … " He barked the order again. Before I could say what I had intended, one of the bigger guys in the church rushed over to my side, cupping his hand tightly under my right arm. They forcefully ejected me from the building. As I saw Pastor Lawrence as a representative of God, I felt as if I had been ejected and rejected from God's kingdom.

As soon as I got out into the night air, I raced across the street out onto Fremont Avenue. I felt like someone was chasing me when no one was there. Proverbs 28:1 "The wicked flee though no one pursues, but the righteous are as bold as a lion."

I ran down the street near Mike and Christina's house. I encountered a couple taking a walk and ran past them. They looked scared. I ran to the left on West street where I used to live. I ran up to the old house and touched the garage. I think I needed the comfort of feeling connected to my past. After that, I went out to El Camino. I was extremely wound up about what had just happened at Pentecost. So much so that I needed to talk to someone I loved and trusted. I called Anne and told her what transpired. Anne is always loving and supportive. I am sure she told me not to worry and she loved me. She had her doubts about the church anyway. Once I got off the phone I walked all the way down El Camino, up to El Monte and up the dark road as I had done so many times before. When I got to Dave's, I asked if I could borrow his car. Not seeing anything outwardly wrong with me, he agreed. Once I got in that car, my mind was going in circles like the gears of a locomotive. I now had energy and momentum that could keep me going for hours and days.

I was convinced that after I left, Pastor Lawrence had a heart attack. So, I went to El Camino Hospital to go see him. Not only was I delusional, I was acting on those delusions. I got on Highway 85 and headed out of Mountain View.

There was no thought process in my head.

I was on autopilot.

If someone were to ask me my name, I couldn't have told them.

I headed north, going all the way to Lodi. It was like I was retracing my steps back into my past. A place where I was comfortable. Where I had so many laughs and beers with friends. It was as if I was clinging to the last vestiges of my identity, yet not consciously knowing who I was. My psychological autopilot led me to 417 N. School Street in Lodi. Where I had lived with Dave, Bob and Dina. I didn't get out of the car. I just drove by. Having reached my second ex-residence, I had nowhere else to go in the database of my mind, so I just got on 99 South and headed out into the night aimlessly.

Headlights cutting through the darkness, reaching out ahead of the car. The peace I had known, the love I had known and the hope I had known. I felt lost, but God had taken over. He was carrying me and protecting me, despite the fact I thought he'd abandoned me. He was there to guide me through the darkness. I drove for what felt like an eternity.

I was even going back to old Star Wars fantasies. I thought if I pushed a certain combination of buttons on the dashboard I could make the jump to light speed, just like the Millennium Falcon.

I was flying down the freeway until suddenly the car began to drag gradually to a stop. I just sat there in the car, for what felt like another hour until a car pulled up behind me. I had already thrown the keys under the car. I have no idea why. Within a minute or two, I heard a sharp tap on the window and I could see the flashlight.

"What's your name?"

I told him it was, "Jesus Jeremiah."

He knew I was having a mental breakdown. He took me to the Merced County Jail. When they went to check me in, I didn't have anything to tell them. They didn't know who I was. They ran the plates and found out the car belonged to Dave. That is why they took me into custody. They thought I had stolen the car.

I was in a low security block. There was about 50 of us that would sit in a main room and watch TV. The room I was in was about 15 feet deep. It consisted of little stalls on the left and right of an aisle way. No pillow, no mattress, just a concrete bench. The first time they served us meals, I began to throw the meals in the garbage. They didn't take too kindly to my throwing meals away. I was just bent on throwing things away and moving things around. So, they locked me in one of the bathrooms to keep me out of trouble. I noticed that if I ran the water fountain, water would be all over the floor. So, I did just that and made a big mess. When the guard came to check on me, he was pissed and made me clean it up.

When I was watching TV, I saw a middle-aged Black guy and my mind told me he was my grandpa. So, I talked to him a little bit.

No one in there was friendly. They just wanted to do their 30 days or whatever and get out of there. That night I couldn't sleep at all. So, I just laid there until the sun started to come up. I couldn't contain my energy any longer, so I got up and began to pace up and down the short hall from over by the bathroom to the window. Over and over. When everybody woke up, they would play cards in one of the guy's stalls. He was Filipino. I felt comfortable around him, so I went and sat over there against the wall.

After a few hours, they came and got me. It appeared as if I was getting released. I sat in a little cubicle with a lady on the other side of the desk. She filled out some paperwork and I headed out of the building. A guy in a pick-up truck drove me to the Greyhound Bus Station. I didn't get a ticket or anything. I just got on one of the buses, having no clue where it went. I don't think the authorities in Merced cared where I went. They were just glad I was out of their hair.

As the bus drove down Highway 5, I noticed the sign said Wesley on it. Which is my middle name, so I thought it was a sign that God guiding me where I was supposed to go. Even though I was delusional, I'm sure he was on some level. I ended up in Gilroy. I walked to a nearby grocery where a cute brunette was sitting outside on the edge of the building having her lunch. I asked her if she had ever been to Reno? I had a totally unrealistic crush on her.

I went across the street to Orchard Supply to the lighting department. I told the guy that worked in that section I was getting married. My woman was across the street shopping and I was looking for lighting for the event. He was convinced I was telling the truth. It was hard to tell something was wrong with me, I thought. He showed me some lighting ideas. I went back across the street to talk to the girl again and it appeared she'd called the cops. Her mother was there too. Which surprised me because I hadn't done anything aggressive. But I didn't realize how intimidating it could be to women when I keep talking despite her lack of interest. Two cops came and talked to me. My mind told me the one on the right was Gary, my longtime friend. So, I calmed down and was not worried by them.

They put me in the back of the car. During our ride, my mom and dad's phone number just popped into my mind. Knowing I was having some sort of mental breakdown, they called my parents instead of having me deal with the authorities any further. Little did they know, they were saving me. It was a huge blessing I ran into these awesome public servants. They truly cared about my safety and well-being. I could have ended up in LA not knowing who I was, and my family may have never found me. Once again, this was the Lord protecting me and saving me from hardship. I was fortunate.

Many people who are mentally ill suffer all kinds of abuse on the streets. I believe those cops were like guardian angels. They didn't even put me in a cell with other prisoners. They put me in a police lobby.

When Mom and Dad arrived, I found the love and familiarity I'd been searching for out in the world for the last few days. I don't think they had a clue what I had been through.

I was quiet on the way home. I counted the tail lights on the trucks. One had three groups of three lights on each side. I thought white cars were saints of God.

When we got home, I was sluggish, lethargic and depressed. I had almost no energy. One thing I liked to do was move things around and hide things. It may have been my way of trying to control things when I felt so helpless and needy.

Once I took the remote control and put it on the counter in my Dad's bathroom, next to the toilet. Dad got mad because he thought I was trying to make him associate going to the bathroom with watching TV. He also gave me a hard time about "walking around like a zombie." One thing I noticed about Dad is he didn't want to think there was really a problem with me. He wanted to deny it. I think he just wanted me to be strong and he associated this mental problem with weakness in me.

Soon I started to feel myself being stabilized by the meds. So, I decided to go out and look for a job. One of the easiest jobs to get was as a security guard. Which was kind of ironic because I had problems with paranoia in the past. The first site I worked on was Red Roof Inn. I didn't have a car, so I would take the bus over there. Now that I was more stable I was starting to really want to play with the band again. But it was hard with limited transportation.

One of the signs of me being healthy is songwriting. If I am songwriting, I am healthier. I came up with a few songs I recorded on my 4-track cassette recorder. I would think about my songs all the way over to the job. Every chance, I got I would be listening to my ideas and trying to improve the songs. I loved this process. It made me feel alive and still does.

The job was boring, and it was graveyard shift. But sometimes we had spare tires stolen. Usually off SUVs and trucks. I would walk around and around the circular parking lot, which was much like how my mind worked even on meds. There was a little breakroom I would spend a little time in, here and there.

The next site I worked at was the Radisson Hotel. It was one of the biggest hotels in Stockton and sometimes celebrities came through when they were playing in town. Radisson was a huge eight-story hotel and once again I worked graveyard. Working grave is so unnatural. I don't think we are meant to be up all night every night, five days a week. It seemed like no matter how much I tried to sleep when I got home, I never felt rested. I felt trapped on the security job. Sometimes I would be so depressed I could hardly bring myself to get going.

One time I was riding home from work, totally wound up having a whirlwind of emotions. I felt so frustrated and hopeless. When a quiet calm voice said to me, "You have nothing to prove son." God was speaking to me as a heavenly father. I have never felt so reassured. I knew God was with me and he didn't want me to worry about the daily grind. Maybe I did feel I had something to prove. Like I had to play Shoreline to prove that I was worth something. What I didn't understand is that God loved me, and I didn't have to achieve something to earn his love. He just loved me unconditionally. Not that it may not be my destiny to play Shoreline, just that I needed to put Shoreline in perspective. Playing venues that big was to connect with a larger group of people so I could spread God's message and wisdom. It wasn't required for me to have value to God.

One of the other sites I worked at was the PG&E electric plant in Central Stockton. It was in a rough area. So, the walls around the property were about 10 feet high. The back of the property was fenced-in with the regular wire fencing. I could see someone had breached the fences in the back from the graffiti on the building inside. I wondered what would happen if I were to encounter these graffiti artist in real time. Because of my insecurity about facing them, I would climb up this 15-foot ladder alongside of the building. I figured there was only one way up there and I could keep them from coming up if need be. I always feel safer being above and looking down. I was a huge Jewel fan at the time and was always listening to her beautiful, angelic and soothing voice up on that roof.

Many nights Jewel kept me company. The tone of her voice was the sound of hope. Hope that there are kind, caring and loving people in the world. Not just ones looking to breach the perimeter of my life with bad intensions.

Not knowing what people's intensions can be scary and intimidating. I had the tendency to just assume someone's intensions were bad, without having any actual evidence that this was the case. One could just as easily assume kids jumping the fence were relatively harmless and just seeking to pass time with a little adventure in their otherwise boring small-town life. I am sure the reality most likely was somewhere in between.

I wasn't thinking about it at the time, but there were people outside the confines of the walls with no protection. Vulnerable people who roamed the streets all night with nowhere to lay their heads. No sense of safety and security. Out in a world where anything could happen at any time. While I would go home and sleep in comfort every morning when I got off shift, their struggle persisted. It is impossible to have gratitude without something to use as a reference point.

One of my assignments was at the Del Monte plant in central Stockton. It was a huge fruit and vegetable processing operation. Most of the year it was quiet with hardly any employees. There were half a dozen employees back in the grapes section of the plant where they made vitamins. It was a dark and dreary plant on graveyard. And the plant had two parts one on either side of a street that ran through them. The plant across the street was for cherries. That is where the would process them and make them into maraschino cherries. I hardly ever went out to cherries unless it was picking season. It was so dark and deserted in the back. I was imagining all kinds of horrible things that could befall me and no one would even know.

One night during picking season, I received a call from another guard. He said something I couldn't quite make out. I asked him to repeat himself and he said, 'I have a guy over here by cherries bleeding!' I said, 'Bleeding!?' I told him to bring the guy over to the guard shack. It was a Mexican man who could hardly speak English. He was about 5 feet 10 inches with a short sleeve button up dress shirt. Tucked into a tight pair of straight legged stone washed jeans. He was wearing worn cowboy boots and an oval shaped metal belt buckle, about the size of the palm of a hand. I could see through his hand clenched around his nose. Blood was splattered all over his shirt. He told us two Black guys had done it.

I later found out that was common in Stockton. Two or three guys jumping and overpowering one guy for fun. One guy I used to work with even told me they would play a game to see who could knock out some poor unsuspecting person with one punch. They called it a 'one hitter quitter' and were proud of themselves if they could do it. I wondered what would make someone want to prey on someone they didn't even know like that. Maybe at one point they were preyed upon in the same manner and are looking at it as someone else getting their turn?

My supervisor and the police came out to interview the victim and the other guard. They only stayed for a few minutes. I think they took the victim home. One thing I found interesting was the perpetrators were two Black males and the guards who helped him were two Black males. So, he could see some guys will hurt and some will help. It's bigger than a racial thing.

Stockton was a really dangerous place in the '90s, a lot of gang violence. I was somehow able to survive as a Black male in his 20s without getting in fights or shot at. Some of the guys I met from other cities actually considered Stockton a sanctuary compared to where they had come from. Where everything was way faster paced.

Overall the time I spent in security was one of the most hopelessly depressing times of my life. I was in the midst of my sorrow and discontent. I couldn't even deal. One of the only highlights was getting my car and being able to rehearse with the guys at Loud Cloud on the weekend when no one was there. The band was life to me at that time. It was my reason to carry on through the lethargy and oppressive times. Looking back, it may have also been all the meds I was taking that cause drowsiness and malaise. But I had the mindset to match. A dreary listless mindset.

On my birthday weekend in 1998, I went to visit my sister. She lived in Hayward then. We went to a nice restaurant by the water in Oakland's Jack London Square. That night they had a house band. It was an R & B cover band. They were really tight and playing some awesome songs that were popular at that time. Anne got up to go to the bathroom. When she returned she, had a look on her face like she was up to something, but I didn't know what. I know one time at Chevy's she had them put a sombrero on my head and sing happy birthday to me.

Suddenly the female singer said, "Give me an upbeat." They fell right into a slightly reggae groove. After a few bars, she started, 'I heard he sang a good song … ' I instantly knew it was 'Killing Me Softly' by Roberta Flack. But she was singing the Lauren Hill version popular at the time. I liked that version, but I love Roberta Flack's. When she sings, it feels like you are an infant in your mom's arms. Gently soothed by a heartfelt lullaby. It reaches deep into the heart on a spiritual level. Comforting you to the core of who you are.

The singer came over to my table and got me up to dance with her. Embarrassing but super fun. I learned from Anne – don't avoid experiences. There may be something awesome you'll miss out on.

By the end of the night, I was starting to wake up to the sobering reality I had to go back to a job that was holding me down like a childhood bully. Not letting me up for a breath. I told Anne how I was feeling. She told me I could just quit and come and stay with her. I had some money in the bank and a credit card with a $1,000 limit. I basically had no bills other than my car which hardly ran anymore. So, I did just that. It felt so good to be able to sleep at night again.

Now I had the freedom to do what I really wanted. We lived right across the street from a Safeway. I used to love to go into the deli section and get the mini corn dogs and wedge fries. Sometimes I would get the chicken strips too. The deli section was perfect for a bachelor who didn't want to cook. Anne didn't cook that much either. She wouldn't get home until later and she loved to talk on the phone with her friends until the wee hours of the night.

After a few months of basically doing nothing, I started to get bored and was running out of money in the bank. Plus, my card was almost maxed out. So, I decided to look for a job. It was right around Christmas, so a lot of the retail stores were hiring. I don't know what possessed me, but I decided to apply at Toys-R-Us. I would mark that as one of the biggest mistakes I ever made in my life.

Before we started in the store, about 10 of us sat in the little room about the size of a public restroom and watched training videos. I have never seen such an assortment of uninspired, uninterested people in my life. It was like sitting in the pews at a funeral. Like the first and last day of our lives. I don't remember anyone saying a word in the little training session.

I was going to be a cashier. The next thing I know, I was ringing up people one by one, like a conveyor belt going by with me getting every question and complaint I could imagine thrown at me. It always seemed the less a job payed the less training.

One of the things that really frustrated me was people coming to the front with the tag for an item. I would have to ring them up and then call to the back for them to get the item. This would hold up the line. I could see the impatience welling up in people's faces as I tried not to make eye contact. I have never felt so overwhelmed in my life. It was the opposite of security. When I had all the time in the world, my opponent was boredom. Now my opponent was upset customers. What I didn't understand is I should have been patient and kind to myself if no one else would. I could have been my own support network in real time and stopped myself from falling into the frustration of the moment. I didn't know how to do that then. It was like a pressure cooker, with no escape. No release valve to vent those feelings. I didn't even have the band to blow off steam or any healthy sexual outlet. All I had was porn, coming up with parts and recording alone.

After about three weeks at Toys-R-Us, I just didn't go back one day. I had only received one check for two weeks. I didn't even go pick up the check for the last week. I figured we were even for me quitting without notice. I wondered if there was anyone who enjoyed that job. Looking back, I only saw the negative in these jobs. I didn't really appreciate them. I felt like I was wasting my time doing something I didn't want to do. What I didn't realize is I chose these jobs. There were other jobs that I could have done to make me more fulfilled. I was just being complacent. I wanted Plan A to blow up, but Plan B seemed to be my reality. I didn't know how to take the big leap of faith. I was too fearful. And I felt like I wasn't even getting an opportunity to excel at Plan A.

By summer of '99 I was getting bored living unemployed with my sister. So, I decided to head down to the South Bay which is where I really wanted to be. This time I didn't have a job lined up. Gary was living with roommates in Cupertino. One of these roommates was Stacee. When I first called over there, she picked up a few times and I spoke to her before we met in person. She sounded cute. Gary described her as tall and thin and looked like an elf with high cheek bones.

Nothing could have prepared me for not just how she looked but the energy she gave off. She was very alluring. She was about 5 feet 10 inches and had what has become my favorite body type. Broad squared shoulders proportional to the hips which curved slightly on either side. Her face was super cute, like Christie Brinkley when she was young.

I loved that when she smiled, the corners of her mouth extended out past her pearly white teeth. She had light brown hair she wore kind of like a hippie. Hanging down with a little curl on the sides. She always wore those pullover sweaters with a college logo on it. With worn jeans and her favorite Ugg boots. She drove an older Jeep Cherokee and had a dog that looked like a wolf. The kind of dog that sizes you up when you walk in the room.

In one of our early conversations she said she was just going to keep dating guys until she finds the right one. I was so prudish at the time I took this as her being too reckless. Most every 20 something at the time was living with that as their reference point. I had so little experience I had no clue what people were doing.

She and I were playful around each other. We liked to wrestle together in the living room. One of the roommates sarcastically said, "Why don't you guys just do it already?" But I was working out of town at the time and could only see her on weekends. After about the third weekend, another guy came into the picture. He made a move on her right while we were starting to build something. He got into my head and told me she had a lot of boyfriends. Which wasn't true. He simply saw that it was either going to be me or him that was going to be her boyfriend. And he didn't want it to be me. He knew how squeaky clean I was and knew I would be turned off with the idea of it. Once they started to see each other exclusively, I got pushed to the side burner. Where everything would cool down.

In '99 I actually moved into the house where Stacee and her boyfriend lived. Her boyfriend was really cool. Him and I got along pretty well, even though sometimes I would flirt with her when he wasn't around. Which is not something I am not proud of. I just had intense feelings I wanted to express and couldn't. Stacee told me that if I was going to live there, I had to get a job and pay rent.

Although I agreed I spent at least three weeks just living in the fun room, which was like a greenhouse/living room. Stacee was really into crafts. She would do stain glass and other cool stuff in there. It was a room where everyone hung out. It was a little creepy sleeping out there at night because the entrance was a screen door with no lock, so anyone could come in the back yard and walk right in. The first week I got drunk every night to cope with my insecurity back there. She also grew sunflowers on the opposite side of the entrance.

I wrote a song for her called "Sunflower" on *Art of Solitude*, my first full-length solo album as Lance West. Every morning Stacee would get up around 7:30 or 8:00 and make herself an espresso.

She absolutely loved espressos. Then into the fun room to hang out before going to work.

One morning she asked me, "Why did you stop calling me?"

"I don't know." The truth was I'd believed what her boyfriend had told me in the beginning.

A few days later, she came into the fun room. I was sitting up on the sectional couch with sheets covering my lap and legs. When she came by the table and stood there I could feel the tension between us. As I looked into her eyes, I began to feel a sensation I'd never felt. I have been turned on before, but this was different. My heart was racing, and I could feel tingling through my whole body. It got so intense for her too that her left knee buckled like she was having trouble standing straight up. I had no idea what she was feeling. But if it was anything like what I was, I understood that buckling knee. Her and I could communicate without speaking. Looking back, I realize how wrong I was for lusting after a woman with a live-in boyfriend. But at the time I was really frustrated beyond words. Not just sexually but by the circumstances. I think her boyfriend knew I liked her but thought I was pretty much harmless, so he wasn't intimidated by me. One time I put my dukes up to him and he said he didn't want to hurt me. I had seen him sock her ex in the face right in front of everyone and her ex didn't even fight back. So, I knew he was capable of throwing blows. But like I said, I honestly thought he was a cool guy. The whole situation was weird.

At some point Stacee started to get pissed that I was not keeping my word about finding a job. And she began to relentlessly pressure me to get a job. Totally calling me out on it. So, I went pounding the pavement. I was offered a job as a security guard. Before I started the job, I saw in the newspaper that Nelson's Cleaners was hiring again. Shortly after the last time I left I had called Kevin and told them I had a mental illness that caused the whole thing last time. Knowing this he said he would hire me back when I called. He said he would never speak to me again if it happened a second time.

So, I started at Nelson's. This time I was living on Stevens Creek, so I would take the 23 Bus down to the mall and walk the rest of the way. which was like a 30-minute walk. I didn't mind because the air was nice and cool in the morning, like Tahoe in the spring. It was so easy to breathe. I felt so alive. What a great way to start a day. What was cool is that my friend Matt from Sleep was the person I was replacing as a driver.

At the time, his band High on Fire was starting to take-off in the Bay Area. I remember them on the cover of *Bay Area Music* magazine. So, everything just resumed like I had never left. I was getting out of the house every day and doing my part, so Stacee let up and was chill with me.

One thing I learned about Stacee is she liked me to put things together for her. She wanted a guy that was handy. I never learned these things from my dad. One time she bought a metal bookcase to organize things in the fun room and told me to put it together. I did put the basic structure together, but at the bottom was a little lopsided. No matter how I tried to fix it, I just could seem to get it right. Seeing that I was doing the best I could she said her boyfriend could help me when he gets home. Which was totally humiliating. I wanted to be the one to put it together. Maybe that was just it. The best man won. He came home and had no trouble fixing it.

After about two months, I began to get a little stir crazy with the job and the frustration at the house. Oh, and Gary was on tour with Noothgrush, so I didn't have our friendship to lean on. I slowly started to feel as if things were falling apart again.

Instead of making my stops, I started just aimlessly driving around. One of the places I would deliver to was in Menlo Park to a guy who required our services for his business to run. Instead of delivering, I drove past Menlo Park up 101 into San Francisco. My mind was going into cyclical land again. I stopped at a park. I had no clue where I was in San Francisco, but I got out of the van. There was a little lake with ducks. I found a book of matches on the ground, opened it and began to light them one by one. Shake them out and throw them on the asphalt next to the van.

An Asian guy about 30 years old walked by. I had a Phil Collins song playing in my mind.

So, I said to the guy, "Do you remember ... do you remember ... we were friends." Like I had known him from a past life or something.

When I headed back down 101 South, I got off at Brokaw Road where my dad worked. I went up to the security and told them I wanted to speak to him. When Dad came out, I told him I wanted to propose to a girl named Stacee. I had asked her already and she said she was too young to get married. She was in her late 20s. Somehow, I thought I still needed to tell my dad about it. I was getting off kilter for sure. I told him she was white. He said he was ok with her being white and just wanted me to be happy.

When I got back to the shop, there was almost no one there. Including the manager. Just his assistant. Who immediately informed me I was fired. I was fine with that. I left on foot. Feeling a little lighter as I didn't have to go there anymore or be tied to something that wasn't my true calling.

From there I slowly started to descend back into mental illness. My mind was telling me I had an army of spirits with me as I walked into the mall and up the escalator onto the second floor. The mall was the perfect environment for my state of mind. It was like everyone going every which way in different directions. All with individual destinations. Despite how scattered my brain was, it was like I was still on a general mission. After walking through the mall, up and down between department stores, I walked out to Stevens Creek Boulevard and headed back up toward Cupertino. As I was walking by a coffee shop in a strip mall, I noticed a guy sitting outside. Made very brief eye contact and continued to walk. He jumped up and walked up right in front of me blocking my way. This was in the day time. It was kind of like he was jamming me up. He was a white guy, a little taller than me, dressed pretty much like the times with semi-hip-hop attire. I stopped and just stood there starring him right in the eye. I honestly wasn't scared or intimidated by him. I knew I had my army with me. We just stood there for about a minute without saying a word. Then he moved to the right as if opening a door for me and I continued past him.

When I got back to the house in Cupertino, I started behaving weird with my roommates. I almost felt like a cat hanging around a house. Stacee told Gary she saw me in the neighbor's yard, kneeling, watching her go by. At the time, I had bought a couple disposable cameras and was taking a lot of pictures. One of the things I took pictures of was Stacee's sunflowers. Someone must have seen me take the pictures. Because when I went out there later, someone had cut some of the blooming flowers down as if they'd slashed it with a knife. And they had taken a bite out of one of the flowers with it still on the stem growing. My mind said this was the devil. Like someone saying these are my sunflowers and I will partake of them any time I want.

Over the next few days I walked around aimlessly for hours every day. Coming home in the evenings with barely enough energy to stand from incessant walking. When I was walking down the streets and into stores, I felt as if my path was marking things off and dividing spaces.

One time I went into the living room where there was a big mirror right over the fireplace. It was there that I saw my first major hallucination. As I stood looking in the mirror, my face started off as normal. Then it began to change form, shape and color. My nose got bigger. I had big protruding pimples and my head increased in size and was more circular than oblong. My skin turned a deep purple color. The skin on my face moved in an undulating motion. I stood there for probably five minutes, but it seemed like forever telling myself, "This is not my face" in my mind. Perhaps I was seeing a distorted version of myself, just as I was having emotional distortion.

One night I was interfering in a conversation with two of my roommates who felt I'd crossed the line and they told Gary I had to go. Gary informed me and called my parents to come get me. I hugged him for the second time since I have known him. My mom came and got me. On the way home, I called my friend and our drummer Phil's house and got his brother Joe on the line who had known me since high school. I told him people thought I was crazy and I had to go prove to them that I wasn't. He said, "You're not crazy. The world is crazy." That was somewhat true. I was not where I needed to be as far as my mental stability.

The first night I got to Mom and Dad's, I called Stacee who'd moved to Reno. I told her I was sorry and not crazy. She said she knew I was not crazy, I just needed help. I find it interesting how people use the word crazy as a blanket statement. I have bipolar depression along with 5.7 million other people in America. I just need medication to stabilize me and keep me balanced.

Crazy almost implies someone is a lost cause and will always be. The ironic thing is I remember when I used to say the words "clinical depression" like it was some outrageous thing I could never have. Same with hallucination.

My friend and I used to watch this video about a schizophrenic named Bob. He lived with his parents and they would take him to Kmart for exercise. He heard voices and medication didn't decrease his symptoms. He continued to struggle to tell the difference between reality and fantasy. We would make fun of the video. Not realizing how much of a prison mental illness can be for a person. I learned never to make fun of people. These things can happen to anyone, including me.

The next morning, I tried to call Stacee again. I really felt I needed her support. But she wasn't available. When she finally answered, I heard her voice blurt out, 'Leave me alone!!!' and she hung up. Heartbroken, I did just that. That was the last thing she said to me.

I was so depressed I could hardly eat. I lingered in the state of spiritual and emotional limbo for quite a while before I began to see any light at the end of the tunnel.

7

A New Millennium

It was hard to believe the year 2000 had finally arrived. And that I hadn't received my jet pack yet. Or all those private vehicles flying every which way. I guess they hadn't worked out the air traffic control issues. There were a lot of things I was expecting to see. Like robots walking down the street with us. And I mean humanoid looking robots that serve similar functions to what humans do. I think the technology was there it was just that everything was too expensive to start rolling it out. Another thing I had fantasized about as I am sure many had was civilian passenger space flight, travel and possible colonizing the moon or even another planet. The interesting thing is all though these things hadn't come to mainstream fruition. We were on that trajectory. I think the childhood fantasy was that of the Jetson's or Lost in Space. Ok, now I am giving away my age. And of course, Star Wars that captured the creative minds of so many children and young adults. Even when I was seven, I remember crying because I couldn't be up there with Chewbacca, R2-D2 and Han Solo. Movies like that really brought robots to life as mechanical beings that could learn and interact with humans.

My aspirations were in the stars, as much as mankind's hope for colonizing Mars. Me wanting to play Shoreline and all. At least that is how the goal felt. Like a gazillion miles away. I had to find a job, so I could have money to pay the few bills and to spend. One of the places I applied was Community Integrated Work Program (CIWP). The program allowed developmentally disabled adults to go out and work two hours a day and go out into the community and interact with the world. This was the only truly altruistic job I had ever applied for. And I am a caring person. So, it was a good fit. The management agreed. I was going to be driving a van with five clients and another co-worker, a petite Mexican lady named Theresa. She was about 4 feet 10 inches with long wavy black hair and caramel-colored highlights. She wore bright red lipstick and was about six-months pregnant. She didn't speak much and when she did, she was kind and soft spoken. Sometimes she would re-direct me if I was handling a client wrong.

Most of our clients were very high functioning at the level of a 10 to 12-year-old.

If they weren't violent, it was just like dealing with watching kids that age. One of the clients was Leamon. By that time, I had a large belly. Leamon shared my body type but his hairline had receded almost to total baldness. He spoke with a slight lisp and was sharp with a good memory. Often, we would listen to hip-hop in the van. Artists like Dr. Dre and Eminem but his favorite song was "The Thong Song" by Cisco. The whole song is about women wearing thong bathing suits on the beach. In one part of the song he says, "Baby move your butt, butt, butt, sugar say it again." One of the funniest things in the world was Leamon repeating "Butt, butt, butt," then he would pause for a few seconds and say it again. We would laugh so hard. But people at his care home didn't think it was funny. Maybe it wasn't, and I just had an inappropriate sense of humor at the time. I don't know but it sure made the day more pleasant.

Another client had a reputation before I even met him. His name was Dominic. I was told he would have fits of rage and get angry and be violent toward clients and staff. That was all I was told about him the day we went to pick him up. Of course, the first thing I wondered was, "How big is this guy? Am I going to be fighting with this guy every day?" When we pulled up I saw him emerge from the house with his home aide. He was about 5 feet 7 inches and 150 pounds. Normal stature but you could tell by his face something wasn't quite right. His face would contort in different ways as he spoke. He looked very distraught and uncomfortable most of the time. The first thing I learned about him is whatever I would say he would repeat. He would even repeat me telling him, "Try not to repeat yourself Dominic" with 'Try not to repeat myself Lance?'

Every day we would go to Outback Steakhouse, where we would clean the silverware and fold them in the napkins. Most of the clients were fine, but it was hard to keep Dominic focused on the task at hand. Sometimes his eyes would dart left and right, and I wondered why. I think he may have been hallucinating because he said, "I don't want my eyes out of the socket. I want them in the socket." He said the people outside the window were going to do it. There was no one outside the window. I felt so bad for Dominic because he was trapped in a scary world he couldn't get out of. I knew the feeling.

Sometimes he would bite and dig deep in his hand between the thumb and pointing finger. And even punch himself in the face hard with a closed fist. He even lashed out at his fellow clients. One-time punching Leamon and others. Leamon didn't hit him back and he was lucky because Leamon was big. I had a special empathy for Dominic and the clients because I knew what it was like to be lost in a world between reality and fantasy. And I was blessed I made it through and the medicine worked for me. Some people take meds and continue to struggle with severe depression and hearing voices. The more fortunate stabilize on meds and integrate back into society.

In my case it was meds, therapy and having a safe comfortable environment to rehabilitate in. This taught me how important gratitude was. It is so easy to take for granted the blessings, comforts and luxuries we have.

One of the things I regret with Dominic is that unlike the other clients, he had a specific occupation that fascinated him – construction. We would often go to downtown Stockton and pass by a Mexican restaurant undergoing some renovations.

He would specifically ask for me to drive by that place, so that he could see the progress being made during the construction. It was his passion. I could tell that's what he would be doing if he could stabilize. But that seemed almost impossible. I wish I could have given him that. A chance to do what he dreamed of doing. I am sure he wouldn't be able to use tools without supervision, but we could have gone to the construction site and cleaned up scraps of wood or swept up. We all should be able to find a place of dignity and respect in this world.

After working at CIWP for a few months, I got called into the office by the manager. It seemed that I had gotten too far behind on my paperwork. Having not done it at all almost since I started. I told the manager I didn't have time, but he wasn't having it. He told me come back to the office a half hour early and stay a half hour late until you finish. So, Echo (who had replaced Theresa during her pregnancy leave) and I did just that. The whole thing seemed kind of stupid as we had to try to remember what we'd been doing and check all these boxes and fill out all this paperwork.

One day after work a woman walked into the room we always did our paperwork in. The first thing I noticed about Nichole was her sweet feminine, almost sensual voice. She asked, "What are you guys doing?" We told her boring paperwork and she decided to help us every day after work. She wore the same color clothes every day except for the shirt. It was always black pants or leggings, a black jacket and black shoes. The shirt was sometimes more vibrant and wild. It was much like her personality. She was sophisticated when it came to work but she had a very passionate extroverted side too.

One day after doing our paperwork, she followed me out to my car where we could talk in private. I remember trying to talk to her like I had game. Which was funny because I had so little experience. What I didn't get is game is not required when a woman just likes you. Looking back that makes the most sense. I think if you must talk a woman into something it is the wrong woman. A woman knows when she is attracted to a man. And they often know right away. Guys that have game know what to say and when to sway the woman's opinion of them in their favor. What some guys don't realize is getting the girl is just the beginning. Look them up a year later and see if they are still with her. It's easier for some guys to hustle women with lies to get them into bed than it is to build a relationship based on mutual respect and unconditional love.

At first, I met her children. First Cicily, who was the cutest little girl on the planet. I call her Dora the Explorer from the cartoon. She stood just above Nicole's knee. With her arm around her leg, looking up at me with the wonder of the world in her eyes. And her son Joseph who was about 7 years old. I remember his legs were so short they couldn't touch the floor in the car. They stuck straight out.

I held off on getting romantically involved with Nicole while I worked at CIWP. I ended up getting a job at her brother-in-law's shoe store in the mall. Which was the furthest from my dream job as I could possibly go. Of all the jobs, I had I just never saw myself working in a shoe store. They carried every kind of shoe. My boss Federico who we called Fed, was a huge fan of Madonna. And "Ray of Light" had just come out. So, I must have heard that record 100 times. I actually liked some of the songs off that record. Madonna had been a household name for almost 20 years by the time that record came out. Fed ran a tight ship when it came to business, but he was easy to work with and played good music.

Nicole and I both lived with our parents. So, we had nowhere to go if we wanted to make out. It was funny. It was almost like we were high school kids. And that was almost the case for me, being I hadn't done much other than make out up until that point. I remember sitting in the car in front of her parents' house after dates, talking for hours. Or in front of my house looking into each-other's eyes. Her skin which was caramel colored but looked light blue in the moonlight. The curves of her full lips were so alluring and her warm deep eyes. She was pulling me into her world like an imploding sun. Taking in a huge part of me. She ironically accused me of hypnotizing her. Feeling her bottom lip between my lips was mesmerizing and extremely arousing. It was late in the game, but she was my first real girlfriend. We spent so much time together. I could plan any activity and she would go with me without question.

As we drove, I loved to hold her soft left hand in my right. This was something that calmed me. It didn't matter how upset I was or what the situation. It literally soothed the savage beast. This was the first time I was really seeing the effect a woman can have on a man. I felt like I had a purpose and something to live for. It was the opposite of depression where I wanted to die. I wanted to live forever. So, I could continue to enjoy what we were building.

I don't know why but after a while I started to not feel right about our relationship. Maybe it was too new to me. I wasn't used to it. But I felt like I wanted to run from it. One day I did just that. I had about 12k in the bank, so I decided to quit my job and go back to the South Bay. I packed up a backpack and grabbed my Strat guitar. Walked down to the bus stop around the corner. I took the city bus to downtown Stockton, were I hopped on the Greyhound bus. Yeah, this is when people actually took the bus to nearby cities because they didn't have a car or Uber.

I took the bus to downtown San Jose. Planned on moving in with my hippy friend Robinmarie I'd met at Kinko's years prior. I thought she would take me in. When I arrived in San Jose, I took a taxi cab to the nearest hotel. I checked in at the front and they gave me a room in the upper left-hand corner upstairs. It was a little bit creepy sleeping up there at night by myself. There was gang writing in the closet, and the furniture looked like it had been picked up at a flea market. Which in no way am I putting down, I was a proud thrift store shopper for years when my money was tight. I just didn't think a hotel should be like that inside.

In the morning, I went down to the hotel café and ate a bacon cheeseburger and fries with a root beer as that's my favorite. That night I contacted Robinmarie and she informed me she couldn't take me on. She had her own stuff going on and it would be too overwhelming trying to take care of me at that time.

I had left a note with my parents but by now my sister knew about it too. I am sure they were worried it was another mental thing. But little did any of us know this was to be my renaissance. I remember the date. I left Stockton on Wednesday, November 15, 2000. I called Gary next and he said come on over. Which was timely because a couple months prior he told me he was getting lonely at his apartment in Berkeley. My sister arranged to pick me up on Friday to take me to Gary's.

Gary lived in a one-bedroom apartment with two connected apartments that shared one driveway. Upon arrival, I saw what was to be my new digs. A black futon in his living room. Which was cool. It was like I had my own room as Gary would spend a lot of time in his room. At the time, I was getting a check of $600 a month from the government. Gary informed me rent was $400, my Kaiser health coverage premiums were $200, and I had 12k in the bank. Amazingly, those were the only two bills I had. So, now I could just take some time off to chill and regroup in an environment where I wasn't pressured and could just be myself. The ground rules were simple. Gary didn't care what I did with my time if I just paid my $400 a month. That was super cool of him. I think he knew that I needed a break from everything. Mom and Dad later told me they called Gary and told him that I was on the way. I am so grateful and blessed once again that I have a friend like Gary who selflessly helped me out giving me a place to stay. He is the only person other than my sister and parents that had taken me in more than once. And he had seen me through high school and the '90s. Friends like that don't come around often.

My life was pretty simple there at the apartment. During the week, Gary would get up and go to work in the morning a couple hours before I got up. Which I know could be hard. Knowing he had to go to work while I just chilled at home. The thing that is awesome is he never mentioned it as being a problem and didn't give me a hard time. When Gary would get home, we would talk for a little while, then he would go to his room and hang out watching the TV shows he liked – The Daily Show with Jon Stewart and Adult Swim which was adult cartoons. It was cool. We both had our space, but we knew a friend was in the next room to joke around with too.

On the weekends, we had a routine where we would go do our chores in Gary's Blue cargo van that his band Noothgrush used for touring. We would go to the neighborhood laundromat and put our clothes in the washers. Then to the post office if need be and sometimes the cheese store 10 minutes away. They had so many kinds of cheeses it was crazy. This is where I got turned on to some cheeses I'd never tried like Muenster, Havarti and one of my favorites Smoked Gouda.

Then we would go back to the laundry to put our clothes in the dryer. After that, off to the grocery store. Usually Berkeley Bowl which was a local family-owned store with the hugest vegetable and fruit section I've ever seen. There were all sorts of exotic things I had never seen until then. Sometimes we would go to Trader Joe's, which was my introduction to the store. There were so many awesome yummy things there. I loved their frozen cheese enchiladas, apricot yogurt and mochi balls, which were tea-flavored ice cream surrounded with a rice-based coating and dipped in powdered sugar. It was kind of an adventure learning about these new stores Gary was turning me on to. The other store we would go to was Safeway. I would always get my breakfast burrito ingredients there. Tortillas, eggs, breakfast sausage, jack cheese, frozen hash browns and my favorite – Herdez mild salsa verde. After a month or two, I was an expert at making those burritos. I could have opened my own burrito shop. I remember my grocery budget was about $60 a week. I used to keep a journal of how much money I had left in the bank. I didn't have a cell phone at the time, so it wasn't as easy to check the balance whenever I felt like it. I knew the amount was just going to dwindle and dwindle as I had no job and eventually I had to go back to work.

After a few months of doing basically nothing, I decided to take advantage of some of the free time I had to be creative. At the time, I was working on poetry, solo music and band music. So, I broke things down into time slots and began to practice these things like disciplines. I had guitar scale study, song writing for the band, song writing for the solo project and writing poetry. For a total of four hours a day of work. Over a six-month period, I wrote a lot of music for the band and solo project. Up until that point in my life, I'd always considered the solo project something I did privately. Not as something I would share with the public. I kind of looked at it like selling out on the band.

But as I began to think about it, things began to change. I started to think the music was an expression of my true feelings. And that as an artist, I should be honest with the people I share with. I also noticed there was a lot of sadness in my solo music. Because many of the songs were about relationships that had fallen through and unreciprocated love. What I realized was under all the anger and frustration I felt with the band was a deep-seated sadness. I felt that by connecting with the deeper feelings and expressing them could be the path to transcending them. The next natural question is what is the source of the sadness that sits under the anger and frustration. Being ejected from that church had hurt me deeply and I was questioning if I was worthy of God's love. One day a friend of mine from the band Sleep had his wife call me and told me they had a friend who wanted to take guitar lessons. She was wondering if I was interested in teaching her. She said her name was Shannon, she was an airplane mechanic and busy, so I would have to be flexible as far as time goes. When I spoke to her on the phone she sounded really cute. We arranged a time for our first lesson.

When the time came, I heard her footsteps coming up the driveway. When I opened the door, I was shocked and stunned at how cute she was. I almost couldn't talk. She was just under 5 feet tall with short black hair. The features of her face were so chiseled which I love about women in their 30s. They lose that baby look for a more mature look. Her plump lips really stood out. It almost looked like she was puckering them with her face at rest. She was wearing a tight form fitting shirt that clung to her hourglass little body along with black jeans that accentuated every curve of her hips and thighs. And to top it off she had the '90s combat boots. Seeing how overwhelmed I was by her, she couldn't take the smile off her face. It took me a few minutes to settle down and get into first lesson mode.

One of the first things I do with a student is assess their level of ability. Shannon was definitely a novice. So, it was cool. I was going to get to shape a guitarist from the ground up. I really have a passion for grooming someone to be an artist. She wanted to learn a few songs to play around the campfire with her friends. She was the perfect first student. It took her a while to pick things up, but she was so tenacious that she would keep going no matter what. That was a good character trait. She was so cute that if anyone was around they would get sucked into her energy and attracted to her.

We had even more connections when we talked on the phone. I told her how life was like gears. Everything affects everything. If you turn one gear, it turns the next which affects the next thing and so on. She said it was interesting because she has a tattoo of gears on her shoulder.

I was still a huge fan of Charlie's Angels at the time and recorded numerous episodes on VHS tape, then mixed out the commercials with another VCR. Cheryl Ladd's birthday is July 12, same as Shannon's. Also, her last name was the same as one of the companies who made the medicine I was taking. She was unique. She even drove a motorcycle.

When I first started giving her guitar lessons, we would talk at length on the phone. She is one of the people who inspired me to play my solo music. She agreed it was better to be true and express the full range of emotions I was experiencing, not just anger. I was really enamored with her. I even wrote her a poem. When she read it at home, she called me and told me it had really touched her deeply.

Inspired, I decided to write and produce a song for my solo project album *Art of Solitude* titled is "This Night." I really haven't thought about the impact she had on me until right now. I think she was supposed to come into my life. But not as a girlfriend. To inspire me. That is the main push artists need – inspiration.

It turned out that Matt, one my old friends from Sleep, and Tom from ItIsEye were hanging out at a nearby house in Oakland back in 2001. Shannon invited me over there to chill. I hadn't accepted that we were just going to be friends at the time. And I hadn't revealed the song to her yet. When I got over to the house, lots of my old friends were there. Including Matt's girlfriend Kelly, who'd lived with me in Campbell back in '95. We learned Matt and his band were playing a house party at another house in Oakland. My friend Tom had a yellow school bus he'd converted into an RV. So, we could drink in there just like we were home. This whole situation was awesome.

I hadn't hung out with people in quite a while. So, a bunch of us piled into the bus and headed over to the party, which I probably wouldn't have attended otherwise. I had turned down going to parties in Oakland Shannon had invited me to before because I was uncomfortable. Not knowing my way around. As we drove over there, I noticed a young woman sitting across from me. She was just under six feet with light brown hair and a kind inviting demeanor. I immediately began to joke around with her and she was very receptive. I was telling her how we gotta watch out for Canada. Guys up there might try to cross the border into Montana wearing hockey gear and attack civilians. She thought that was funny because she was from Montana. We joked around the rest of the way over there.

When we got there, the first thing I still wanted to do was find Shannon. She'd gotten there in a separate car. I found her in a large group of people in the backyard of one of Oakland's big Victorian homes. There was about 60 to 70 people back there. It was like a mini show. Matt said when he saw me he was going to pull out all the stops. Which is how musicians show each other respect – playing extra hard and blowing things out. I was still enamored with Shannon. So, I gave her the tape and stood beside her for about 15 minutes of the performance, like I was her man protecting her.

Then suddenly, all I wanted was out of there. I had so many mixed emotions regarding Shannon and the somewhat awkward environment. I was just feeling weird socially. I didn't realize it at the time, but I think it was anxiety.

One of my other friends had to leave early, so he gave me a ride home. I felt bad later cause it was like I had abandoned Matt when he was going to pull out all the stops. But my anxiety outweighed everything. The next day Shannon called and thanked me for the song but said she didn't think it was going to work out for her and I. Looking back, I can see that a love song was a little too much at the time. It takes maturity to understand that different people come into our lives for many reasons. And there is some lesson God is trying to impart to you.

Shannon continued to take lessons from me for quite some time after, even though we weren't going to date. That was really cool of her. Many people would have stopped thinking it would be awkward. The best moment of all was when she started to comfortably play a few of the progressions we had worked on. I learned that fretting the notes without muffing them with nearby fingers can really be difficult for a novice. And the importance of newbies learning to curl their fingers on the fretboard instead of keeping them flat. Also, getting their fingers to contort to all the various positions for the chords can be hard. But with practice and patience all these things can be overcome.

As the end of 2000 began to approach, I decided to make a few big and necessary purchases for my next phase of musical development. A Martin D10 acoustic guitar and a Roland JC 120. The guitar is used by top musicians like Bob Dylan and the amp has an incredible solid, loud clean tone. I was planning on using a Fender amp for distortion and the JC for clean. And the acoustic guitar would be my primary instrument for the solo project. These were pivotal purchases that affected both projects dramatically. And the guitar was a first step in the direction of the solo project.

One day I was watching TV and saw a commercial about Bryman College, a trade school that specialized in the medical field. As I sat there it reminded me of this commercial they used to play on TV when I was a kid – I used to laugh because the guy looked like a loser. The company was called Control Data Institute. It was a guy sitting in a bar, staring down into his drink. And he was saying in his head, "I'll go to school for that good paying job tomorrow, tomorrow, tomorrow … " an ode to procrastination. Which I had indulged in many times. I realized that when I started working, I was going to be taken off my government assistance. And I didn't want to go back to making $7 an hour. I don't even think I looked at how much a Medical assistant (MA) made. I just knew it would be much more than 7 bucks an hour and pay benefits.

I hadn't spoken to my dad since I left a year prior. For Christmas, I decided to go back and share the news with my parents. I'd already been to see the enrollment counselor and they told me I could get the loan through Sallie Mae. I would just have to pay about $200 for 10 months while I was attending the school and I could finance the remaining $6,000. When I told Dad the numbers, he told me that he would pay it. My dad was a huge advocate of education. His Dad had forced him to quit high school to work a month before graduation. So, Dad knew the value of school.

He had been to two different trade schools. One to service two-way radios in cabs and air planes and another for drafting. He got his certificate for the two-way radios but when he went to look for a job, race was a barrier. It was a good job but there were no Blacks or other minorities in the field. So, he decided to pursue an education in drafting, a government job with equal opportunity hiring practices. He also helped my sister when she went to UC Berkeley. He wanted his children to get the highest education they could. The sky was the limit because he didn't have the opportunities we did coming up.

Turns out, going to Bryman College in San Francisco was one of the best decisions I ever made. Dad was right about it all along. And it was perfect for me because I never liked taking classes I wasn't interested in. I was really interested in the medical field. I owned a *Gray's Anatomy* book just because I was interested in the different organs and body parts and how they function. It is interesting because my cousin Jenny that was born the same day and year as me also liked the medical field. In fact, she wanted to be a brain surgeon. She ended up going into medical management which she really excelled in.

I hadn't been to college in years. And I had never gone to college while living with a roommate rather than my parents. I had to take the BART train into the city as I didn't have a car. And even if I did, parking is so terrible there it would be way more difficult to commute by car. I was not a huge fan of San Francisco in general. The only time I would go there was if there was a band playing I really wanted to see. Otherwise, I would avoid it like it had the plague. Which is interesting because that was where my dad lived for 10 years after he got out of the Navy.

My dad loved SF compared to the South because there was no segregation. There was still some racism and prejudice when it came to housing. Black people could not live outside of the Black neighborhoods. But you could come and go as you pleased and date whomever you wanted.

Being raised in the suburbs, I was not used to the pace of big cities. I always feel like a sitting duck in big cities and large crowds. Like prey to the sharks that know that environment. I've even seen some dangerous situations in SF when I would go to shows. A man with wild eyes wielding a knife as people filed around him like he wasn't even there. It was difficult for me to feel so nonchalant about it.

The BART would drop me off right at Market Street in the heart of downtown. When I walked into my first day of class, I was a little nervous, not knowing what to expect. When I swung the door open, I immediately heard someone blurt out, 'A MAN! Turns out it was a woman about 25 years old who said it. I immediately felt embarrassed, not knowing what to say.

After a while, once everyone accepted I was the only guy in the class, I settled in. Our program was broken up into one-month mods and classes started every month. So, we had a graduating class every month. The first month I was the only guy, in the second month I was joined by Hefflin, a Filipino guy with a heavy accent. We had so much fun in class joking around.

We had several classes. First was computer lab, then lecture and lab. And I was lucky or blessed enough I didn't have to work while I attended school. I have never been so broke in my life. My mom would send me a 20-dollar bill by mail twice a week to supplement me while I went to school. BART fare was 5 dollars roundtrip, so my total weekly expense was $25. I would buy $15 BART ticket that would last me through Wednesday. Then I would take the remaining $5 and buy my one real meal a day – a Jumbo Jack with cheese at Jack in the Box, which cost exactly $1.62 and a water. That would last me thru Wednesday which is when the next $20 would usually arrive in the mail. And I would do the same to get through the rest of the week and the weekend.

Friday nights were my party nights. Sometimes all I had was $5 for the festivities. So, I would buy a $2 half pint of rot gut vodka and a can of soda, usually grape or orange, to take the edge off the horrible vodka I was drinking and a bag of chips. The truth was I was just glad I had any money to do anything. I don't think I understood what a privilege it was to go to school and not have to work. Many of the women in my class had a child or more, working full time and going to school four hours a day. I was willing to take my broke grind over that any day.

I don't even remember what we accomplished in computer class. I think they just wanted us to know basic Microsoft Office. I don't remember learning the medical software used by medical firms I think that was learned on the job. It was early 2002 and Destiny's Child was hot at the time. One of the women who sat in front of me was always singing that song "I'm A Survivor" with her great Filipino accent. I have always had Filipino friends and loved their accent. Such friendly and kind people. When I was a stranger, they treated me like a long-lost friend. They had my back in high school and my ex Nicole was Filipino and Mexican and I loved her family. There were a lot of Filipino women in the program.

I quickly learned how to study and get A's on the tests. Unlike regular college, trade schools want you to learn, pass the program and retain that knowledge to get a job. It seemed in junior college, they would make it harder. They would tell you to read the whole chapter and wouldn't tell you exactly what was going to be on the test. You just had to know the whole chapter. And when you had questions, the classes were huge. It was like theater seating in there. Asking a question was not only embarrassing but the instructor didn't have enough time to address all the questions. And often that would affect your grade dramatically. Plus, I really didn't like the social aspect of junior college. I felt like I didn't have a face. Like I was just in a sea of lost pimple-faced kids who were just going through the motions of preparing to be productive citizens.

But now I understand the value of education more than I did in high school and junior college. I have been out in the world and saw how hard things can be. Working all those random shifts. Swing, grave and day for minimum or just above minimum wage with no benefits. Bryman was perfect for me. They spelled out what was going to be on each test, all I had to figure out was a successful study method. I found flash cards were the best way for me to study. I would put medical word parts on one side and their definitions on the other. I would even put conceptual things on flash cards. Then I would go through the flash cards at home and on BART on the way to school. In the lecture part of the class I was on Honor Roll seven mods out of eight. And I had perfect attendance for the entire program.

For once, I was excelling and getting good grades. I found a method that worked for me. In high school, I would get so bored sitting there reading all that stuff I didn't care about that I'd nod off and fight to keep my eyes open. And I wasn't learning anything. I felt as if it was something I didn't want to do that was being crammed down my throat. In Bryman, I learned when you are interested in something, learning can be fun, inspiring even exciting.

In the third segment of my courses at Bryman I had the most fun of all in lab. This is where I learned the actual skills needed to do the daily job of an MA. Injections, phlebotomy (drawing blood), taking vital signs, weight and height, we even had a class on massage. Which was obviously my favorite. Let's just say I was the patient a lot more than I was the one giving the massage. But I did learn some good massage techniques. Pressing down and going in circles with my thumbs. That is the one I have got the best responses for. Every day we did those things. By the end of each day, I'd been given injections in both deltoids and had my blood drawn on both arms. I felt like a pin cushion. We also had to learn the other sites injections were given, what gauge needle to use for what site and the type of medicine being drawn up.

One of our mods, we learned to do EKGs. But I really goofed off quite a bit and just like the massage, I was always the patient. Little did I know this knowledge was going to be an integral part of my job and could even cost me a job if I didn't know how to do it fast and correct. Some of the ladies in class would say Lance is never going to make it if he plays too much. And Mrs. Moreno, our awesomely cool teacher said, "He'll be fine. There's a place for everyone." She was such a patient teacher and so honest with us about the reality of being a MA and what was going to be expected of us.

There were two Jennifer's in my class and both liked me. One of them was single and cute but a little dorky. She was from Ohio. I have found women from Ohio love me for some reason or at least the ones I've met. The other one as usual had a boyfriend. But she was my favorite. There was another girl named Jeanne I liked too and reminded me of Nicole, who I'd so abruptly left behind.

The single Jennifer came on real strong with me. She let me know straight up she liked me and was available. Looking back, I probably should have just dated her. It is easier to just date someone that likes you than to try to talk someone into something. But at the time I was more into Jeanne and the second Jennifer. I liked Jennifer #2, so much I looked online to see if I could find out her last name and send her a friend request on Facebook. Jeanne also had a boyfriend I'd seen her with before. He drove a motorcycle and looked like a popular type guy.

One time I sat with Jeanne on BART back to the East Bay. I was trying to spit some game. She called me out, "Are you hitting on me?" I immediately said, 'No, no!' backing down, knowing she had a boyfriend. I think the truth is she may have wanted me to say yes. She wasn't married and was still not serious about things. She was about 25. One time she called me and invited me to go with her and friends to a dance club. I had danced for her in class and I think she liked my moves. At the time, I was socially insecure and said no. I missed out on so many opportunities just shooting myself in the foot with doubt and insecurity.

One thing I've learned with relationships – there's a short window of opportunity to ask a woman out. If you let that window close, the chances are slim you'll get another opportunity. It's the guy that steps up, that gets a shot. Many times, I took myself out of the game. But there is no place for regret in the story that is my destiny.

All the doors that opened or closed were meant to open and close. That is how God guides us. Timing is key. It isn't just hitting that perfect note on the fretboard of the guitar. It is hitting it at the perfect time and in the right context. The perfect note can change the whole direction of the song. Or perfectly emphasize that right note that raises the hairs on the back of people's necks.

By the time I was in Bryman, Nichole was starting to write me love letters all the time. Sometimes long ones, like 15 pages handwritten. I still have them somewhere in my storage. It felt good to have a woman who cared for me that much and wasn't afraid to let me know. One time she came to visit me in Berkeley at the apartment. I was totally broke. I had nothing but love to give her. With things so tight while going to school financially. She showed up with $300 to last for the weekend. I was used to eating ramen and a Jumbo Jack a day. Sometimes having to borrow the money from Hefflin. We had more than enough resources to have a good time. We went to Safeway in Albany and bought everything our hearts desired, which for me centered around a 12 pack of Dos Equis lager. Along with every kind of treat from the frozen section, chips and treats of all sorts. It was nice having her over for the most part. But I began to realize and remember I didn't feel she was the right woman for me when I left Stockton. And I knew that had hurt her deeply. I should have put the brakes on her writing me all those letters, but a side of me liked it. As I said it felt good.

That night we fooled around a little. But I am a very private person and felt uncomfortable doing too much with my friend in the next room. So, we were limited in what we could do. By the end of the weekend, I decided to tell her I still stood on my original decision, which was to just be friends. It really hurt me because I could tell how much it hurt her, and I sincerely cared for her. I just didn't feel right in my spirit. I think I knew in my heart of hearts that she wasn't my woman. God has this way of closing doors and guiding me to close the wrong doors. At the time, we may not know what is going to happen relationship wise. When I closed that door, I had no idea when I was going to get another chance to have the companionship and connection we had.

She went back to Stockton and soon met Donald, an author of poetry and books. He also published his own projects. Nicole loved books. She said she loved the way a new book smelled and just holding it in her hand. She likes passionate authors like Pablo Neruda. I didn't know it or think of it at the time, but some women love authors as much as some women love musicians. I had a college teacher who loved my writing, but I never really considered it a way to connect with women like music. Now I know otherwise.

Nicole and Donald published poetry compilations of local Stockton Poets and some from abroad that would submit to them. I have some poetry in one of their first compilations, *Sun, Shadow, Mountain*. With Donald, she could get immersed in the craft of publishing books and she loved that. She was very creative and a poet herself. She used a lot of water themes in her writing, which could be abstract and beautiful. I didn't find out until later, but she wrote some poetry about the experiences she had with me at that time. She also made me a compilation cassette of songs that expressed how I made her feel. One of the songs was "You Made a Fool of Me" from the film *Love and Basketball*. And another had the words, "Fly away sweet bird of prey, fly away." Listening to that tape cut me down to the bone. It forced me to face how my actions had affected her. After that weekend, Nicole and I didn't communicate much.

The next thing I knew it was finals at Bryman. It was like our normal tests but on steroids. Tons of word parts, definitions and concepts. It was a 200-question test. They were good about letting us know what we needed to study, so I grinded out with my flash cards and got 86% on the written test. I passed the lab and computer tests too. Our formal graduation was planned for almost a year later. And just like that, I no longer had to go to the city or scrounge for BART money. For once in my life, I accomplished something I could truly be proud of. I had proven to myself I could excel in school, if I was interested in the material and had the freedom to study in my own way. I saw firsthand why it's a good idea to go off to college where you can start building an independent life for yourself. It is really character building.

It was late 2002 and I was back to just being home at Gary's. Now all I needed was just a little income for food. My rent and medical were covered. My routine was now like 2001, except I didn't have that big nest egg in the bank. I decided to seriously start giving guitar lessons to put food on the table. I started with friends and friends of friends. I even expanded to putting ads in the paper and welcoming in the general-public. I came up with a curriculum based on a theory book I'd bought. This way I could hand out the next lesson to the student and they could slowly build a knowledge base to look back on at any time. Most of the students were novices, and I'd occasionally get a student that was from the metal scene that just wanted to jam. Just like before, my specialty was grooming students to write their own songs.

One of my friends from the old San Jose scene sent me three students. The first was a rocker chick from the Oakland scene named Jenna. She was the total stoner type and she just wanted to jam. We'd only got together once because she was moving way up north. She was a rad woman. Really strong and solid.

The next was Rabiah. What I liked most about her was how straight up and genuine she was. The kind of woman I could have married. We talked about all the aspects of the human experience. She was from Chicago and I was from the suburbs. Although she was tough, she was very kind and down to earth. Sometimes I would walk her back to BART after our lesson with my bike and ride back. We talked about how she was raised and how important it was to her that a man keep his word as men in the past had let her down. One of the times we walked home, we talked about Kama Sutra. This was something I had heard of regarding sex. I wasn't that familiar with it. But I was too naïve to see she may had been interested in me? I'm not sure. But if that was the case I missed the cue and I think she thought I wasn't interested. I had met a lot of women in my life. But she was one of the most well rounded and stable people I had known.

The next student was Liana. Who was in a band with Rabiah. Liana always had this infectious cute smile from ear to ear. She had such full lips that stood out on her face. Plus, bright open eyes that could just suck a person right into her aura. She was attractive on so many levels. What was funny is how she talked dirty all the time. You would never expect it to come from such a sweet woman, which gave her another dimension I found alluring. One time, I wanted to make a move on her but didn't have the confidence to and she said, "It makes me feel bad when a guy doesn't make a move on me." Liana went on to marry and move away. Like I said, I truly believe in destiny and we aren't supposed to interfere with another person's destiny. She's was an incredible woman, she just wasn't my woman.

I had another student named Kinto. He showed up to the lesson on a motorcycle with his guitar in a soft case strapped over his back. My sister said she thought it was funny, like something from a commercial. He was a fast learner and fun to teach.

For about a month or so Gary was hardly ever home because he was at girlfriend's in Castro Valley. It was like I had my own apartment. It was just quiet at night. I was used to joking with Gary after work. It looked like Gary was going to eventually move in with Lisa.

One day he told me I could come and rent a room at his and Lisa's place. Which was awesome for me because I would have my own room and we would no longer be on a street where people sold crack. Also, around that time, I went to the office where I had done my externship with Bryman and spoke to Linda. She was my friend who had trained me. She said she would ask her supervisor if they could make a position for me. I was hired as a floater for that office and an adjacent one.

That was a major change in my life. I was about to see the fruits of education my dad had spoken so much about when I was coming up. When I first started as a floater, I had no car and had just moved to Castro Valley up in the hills. So, I would leave home when it was dark and walk all the way down to the BART station. About a 30-minute walk. Then I would take it all the way to the El Cerrito BART and walk about 10 minutes to my job from there. This commute was really a grind, but I had to do it. It was kind of an adventure, traveling so much every day. On Fridays, I would go to Sizzler and have my Malibu chicken with fries and a root beer as a treat. Then I would stop and get a half pint of something, usually whiskey. Sometimes I would even sip it on BART.

I was able to save some money over those first four or five months. One weekend I went with my mom and dad to the Honda dealer in Stockton. I put down a grand on a 2002 Honda. That was the newest car I'd ever bought. And only four months into my new job. This was the beginning of my renaissance. It felt so good to be able to come and go as I pleased. If I ever wanted to get away for a while, I could.

Another milestone – I finally went into a studio for the first time as a solo artist. I found a cheap recording studio called Assesso in Fremont. I only recorded four songs, just acoustic guitar and vocal no overdubs. I called the record *From Me to You*. One of the songs on that record was called "Carmel." When my mom heard that song, she actually said, "Oh my God!!' She absolutely loved that song. And that meant so much to me that Mom loved it so much. I have done several revisions of that song. The final version is the title track of my 2013 record "Proof" – I sincerely think it is one of the best songs I've ever done. I think it could find its home on the soundtrack of a romantic comedy or something. At least that's my vision for it. "Robin" is a solid song that was also re-recorded and available on *Art of Solitude*.

Shortly after getting my car, I was laid off from my position floating between the two doctors' offices. I remember sitting in front of Gary and Lisa's house in my damn near brand-new car that I had only had for a month. Unemployed. Pint of whiskey in hand. I had no idea what I was going to do. I knew I needed to find a job, so I could make the car note. I just didn't know if I was going to be able to find one fast enough to keep the car. I didn't even look for a job. I just waited on God. I don't know why I always do this. But 9 times out of 10 it has worked. Just simply trusting in God to make a way. I find when there are circumstances I can't control, that is the best thing to do. It allows me peace of mind while the details are being worked out. I am not saying don't be proactive. You should be. But waiting seems to work for me.

After about a month, I got a call from Brenda, the manager of the Berkeley medical office. There was a job available for a medical records/ medical assistant position. I would work primarily in records and room patients here and there, if someone called in sick. Without hesitation, I took the job. Turns out God had a great plan. This job was kick back. I was mostly in records and did a lot of filing. My co-worker Nicholas did a lot of the more involved work.

Dealing with paper charts was a pain. Instead of just being able to look up the patients' chart in the computer and answer the question on the phone. You had to locate the chart. Nicholas had a damn near photographic memory. Sometimes when Nick wasn't there it would take us a half an hour to find a chart, with three or four of us running around like banshees looking. And sometimes it was a serious matter where the doctor needed the chart urgently. And once you had the chart in your hand, you had to thumb through all the previous labs and reports to find the one you were looking for.

Working with different doctors was a unique experience. I got to see all the different temperaments and personalities and learn to deal with them all. Doctors have an enormous amount of responsibility and little time to get it all done. Seeing patients, returning calls, signing off on medication requests to name a few. Some doctors handle stress better than others. And they're going through different things in life, just like the rest of us. I found that once you knew the doctor's basic temperament and learned to accommodate it, you were fine. They are analytical by nature. So, lead with facts pertinent to the situation at hand or you are of no use to them.

Once I finished recording my first demo as Lance West, I wanted to get out and perform a bit as a solo artist. For my first show, Lisa suggested I play the Bistro in Hayward. I considered it and set up a show. The venue was basically a small little bar on the corner of B street. It was a little area where there were other shops and restaurants. I also decided in advance that if things went south and I couldn't remember the words to the song or something, I would just play "Little Wing" by Jimi Hendrix which I knew like breathing.

It was a really cool first show because Gary, Lisa, Anne and her boyfriend and my mom came. It was always nice having the moral support of people who really cared for me. The bar had a slightly raised stage that took up about a third of the room. When I got up there, the bar was on the right. The first thing I noticed was people were not interested at all in my singing or the performance. They were just talking really loudly, almost as loud as I was, and I was being amplified through the speakers. I decided I was going to sing loud, hoping maybe I could get their attention by the end of the half hour.

After the first couple songs, the people in the seating area were just watching me and clapped and gave their support. Which felt good. I felt like it was an honor that people had come out of their way to see me even, if it was primarily my click.

I think it was about the third song in when I forgot the second verse of lyrics. Which was about eight lines. In those days, my songs had a lot of lyrics like the David Foster songs from the late '80s. (I learned later that less is more and that being concise wins over being verbose.) When I forgot, I just repeated the same verse I'd already sung. One good thing about doing originals is no one knows how the song goes yet. Especially when it has just been recorded and unreleased. No one even noticed. I tried not to be hard on myself, but I felt like I had messed up.

So, I went into my go-to song when everything is going south. It is funny cause I had told Gary about my plan, so he knew I felt like I canned it. People loved "Little

Wing" and I got substantially more applause than with my songs. Probably because people knew it and like Jimi I have a nice voice. Once I finished the set, I got the final applause and left the stage.

The people by the bar which was about 8 to 10 people were still talking loudly. But I think they may have had a little more respect for me for singing all those mellow songs in a bar. Something tells me a Rolling Stones cover band would have done exponentially better with that crowd than I had.

After I put away my guitar, I went over to the bar. Without even saying a word, the bartender tapped a beer and pushed it across the counter. I went to take out my wallet and he put his hand out like no. I think he knew I had earned it. The whole thing was super embarrassing but exhilarating. Looking back, I probably could have gotten a few drinks for free. Often when you play a venue they give you drink tickets and a little money for playing. I don't remember getting paid though. I was just relieved that I had made it through. Little did I know this was the first and last time I was going to get to play a set in the Bay Area.

The next venue I played was Freight & Salvage in Berkeley, a folk coffee house with seating like a venue. It had a real raised stage and around since the '60s. On Friday and Saturday nights old school famous artists like Sean Mullins and Joan Baez would come through and tickets would range from $30 to $60 dollars. On Monday nights, they would have open mics. If I came alone, I could play one song. With two or more people, I could play two songs. And I had to pay to get in.

This environment was a way for musicians to grow and nurture each other. Often it would be primarily musicians and singers, but sometimes local people would just come and watch. It was easy preparing for the open mics because I just had to rehearse one or two songs. I would bring my guitar to work and practice during breaks and lunch. There would be many more performances there between 2004 and mid-2005.

One show that stands out to me was the one my Aunt Dorothy and Uncle Neville attended along with my mom, sister and one of her friends from work. There was about 100 people there that night. The venue only held about 200. Usually when I played there, the crowd was about 20 to 30. That was the biggest crowd I ever played for as a solo artist. It was awesome. It was a different kind of rush than playing with a band. Everything was on me. I couldn't look to the left or the right and see anybody up there with me that night. That night I had a unique experience. A calm came over me I'd never felt playing live before. I felt like I was playing in my living room for my mom. Or just sitting on the edge of my bed, playing and singing along. I think that peace of mind came from God. It felt so good playing that big of a crowd, with my family from New York there. I wish I could have told them that was the norm.

I experienced that same peace on a public access show in San Francisco once. One of my friend's girlfriends worked for that station and they held open mics that would get televised and provided you with a tape after with good audio and video. The day that it happened it was me and several other acts. I played there a few times but the time when that new peaceful feeling came over me stood out. A calm I can't describe. Like I was serving my purpose. It almost felt how I would imagine flying would feel. Sometimes it takes courage to put yourself out there and be in that space. I know some athletes mention focusing so hard they can block out all distraction, sometimes even blocking some of the sound from their minds.

One thing I learned, especially when performing alone is practice is your best friend. I realized that I am the one that is going to be up there. I must have my own back by practicing until it gels. To where I no longer had to think about the lyrics. It must get to the point where you can focus on the performance being top notch, not just trying to remember words and chord changes. Once things gel, it can become pure expression. It gives you the freedom to sing from the heart, without worrying about the scales. You have already practiced the vocal runs until they are in your core. Otherwise, you are in for a lot of uncomfortable performances.

I also learned you must be kind and empathetic with yourself in real time onstage. You must let yourself make mistakes and carry on without being too hard on yourself. My guitar teacher used to say. "Whatever happens, keep smiling."

I remember one time I was on the list to perform at Hotel Utah in San Francisco. I was by myself and getting more and more nervous at the thought of having to play. It is a small intimate venue with the ground floor about the size of a living room in a small house and there was a loft up above about the same size. I was about tenth on the list and we were at number 2. I felt the longer I waited and the closer and closer my number got, the greater my anxiety became. Restlessness, heart jumping out of my chest, sweating. And to make everything worse, I had no one to talk to about how I was feeling. The pressure got so bad I just turned around, walked out, jumped in my car and drove away. I felt relieved, but I also felt like a failure for bowing out on my performance. But it didn't really matter. No one knew who I was anyway, and they had not paid to see me. I guess this is where empathy for yourself really needs to kick in.

Another time at Hotel Utah, I picked a number – almost last on the list of about 15 performers. That time I said to myself, "I 'm going to play tonight. I am not driving all the way home without playing."

I waited through all the acts. By the time my number was up it was 1 a.m. and just me, the sound guy and a drunk guy who had passed out on a bench in booth seating. I followed through and sang like it was an arena to the two people there. Sometimes it is about integrity, not just packing a house. It is about paying your dues.

One time, Al and his girlfriend Tina came out to see me at Hotel Utah. It was so nice to see him. Him and I had talked many times about the Lord and attempting to walk in wisdom as much as possible. We helped each other through many challenges. He was always an inspiration to me because he was living his purpose as a bassist in bands. He told me that he felt something good was going to come to pass regarding my solo project and I should carry on. When it came time for me to perform, everything went well. Later that night they asked if a banjo player, a violinist and I wanted to jam. I was tuned down a half step. When you play things open, almost everything is sharp. The banjo player didn't seem to care but the violinist was kind of huffy. I told him, "I'm tuned a half step down to D#." I began to play a simple A minor progression with alternate finger picking. I just held down a solid rhythm as the banjo player plucked and the violin played beautifully bowed melodies and runs. By the end of it, we were all happy. It was so fun. I had never played with two people I didn't know like that before. Especially with different instruments. Most of the people I knew played guitar, bass or drums.

Another place I played in Berkeley was Blakes on Telegraph which also had been there for years. Blake's was a dark, shadowy basement-like setting. It could only be accessed by going down stairs. My mom and sister attended that time too. When we walked in a guy said something crazy to my mom. My mom said it didn't bother her because she was from New York and had heard everything. I thought that was funny. Even though she is a sweetheart, she'd seen her share of nonsensical people. It had a bar and a pool table too. Much like the Bistro in Hayward it had kind of a bar feel. Not really the kind of place you'd expect to hear the warm voice of a balladeer like I was back then. I found once they heard my voice come out of those speakers and fill the room, they were captivated and totally silent. All and all that was one of my favorite shows. The crowd quickly and fully responded to my voice, despite it being a bar setting. I think this was one of the only other venues that let me do more than one song.

I recently ran across an old photo from that performance. It was a photo copy print. Blurry and dark. So much so my dad couldn't even Photoshop it to make it clearer. But I cherish it. It is one of the few reminders of the 30+ open mic/show stretch I did between 2004 and mid-2005. I honestly feel there is nothing more confidence and character building than taking the stage alone and facing your fears. When you come out on the other side you are a changed person. You know what you are capable of. And when another challenge comes along, you will be more apt to take it on rather than run the other way.

After about a year and a half of working in medical records in the Bay Area, I started to feel like I wanted to have my own independent life. I began to think about moving back to the Central Valley. It would be less expensive to live out there and I could probably get my own apartment. I decided to take some time off work and look for a job in Stockton where my parents lived. Shortly I got a response from a place I applied. It was United Cerebral Palsy. They told me to come out and check out the work environment to see if I would be interested.

When I got there, I saw the clients with cerebral palsy. They ranged from able bodied to what looked like babies laying on their back, only about the size of a one-year old. Those ones were totally helpless and would be for their entire life. It would be my job to care for these clients. Changing them, feeding them. I wasn't sure how I felt about working there, but the job paid about what I made as an MA in Berkeley, so I accepted the job. The next step was passing the government FBI fingerprint test. That was not the normal background check where they just check the local databases. It was everything going all the way back to teenage years. Well, they found out I'd been arrested in Palo Alto for resisting arrest in 1996. I told them I didn't feel I needed to tell them because it was so long ago. I told him I had a mental illness, and this happened before I had been stabilized on my medication. He told me he couldn't hire me. The only thing was I had already quit my job and moved into my parents thinking everything was going to go through. So, suddenly I was unemployed.

I went out and looked for another job right away. One of the places I applied was DHL, a package delivery service like UPS or FedEx. The interview went well, and I was basically hired on the spot. The weekend before I started, I went with Nicole to see the area where I'd be working. Up Highway 4 to Angels Camp, Murphys, Arnold and sometimes all the way up to Bear Valley, a ski resort town. So beautiful up there. Tall trees and huge forests as far as the eyes could see. I never knew there was that much lush country out east like that.

I quickly noticed I didn't have enough time to deliver all the packages. Some of my stops were way off the main road. Sometimes 15 minutes each way. I sometimes had over a hundred packages to deliver.

I did get to see some nice terrain out there. That was one of my favorite aspects of the job. For the most part, the people I encountered were very friendly. But I didn't see any Black people out there and almost no Latino people. When I was training, Kenny told me, "If I see houses with a confederate flag in front, don't even go up to the door. Just throw the package out the window in the driveway." Kenny was a white guy from the South who'd been discriminated against because of his lifestyle choices, so he related to being on the other end of racism.

One time I drove up to a house and went down a little hill to the front of their house. Dropped the package at the door and proceeded to attempt to drive off to no avail. My van was stuck in the gravel of the driveway. I was a little nervous. I'd seen some confederate flags out there before. I was almost certain some people would not be welcoming to me. I called back to dispatch to tell them I was stuck. And he said he would send a truck to pull me out. So, I waited and waited. It was probably late afternoon, so people would be home soon. After about an hour, I went to his neighbors' house to ask when he would be home. He said about an hour, but he had a tractor to pull me out. He seemed standoffish with me and couldn't wait to have me off his property. But he pulled me out and even drove my van back up the little hill, so I could just drive off

I went to shake his hand and thank him, and he reluctantly put his hand out to mine. I drove off. One thing I've learned about racism and prejudice – every time you encounter a person you feel may have preconceived notions about you based on race, it's an opportunity to contradict their prejudice. It is an opportunity to build a bridge, not another wall.

Walls come down one person at a time, one encounter at a time. To slowly chip away the wall that the person has built around themselves and even the one you have built around yourself. I must say I met some people out there that lived way off the beaten track that were so kind to me I couldn't believe it. I believe that when it comes to race relations, hope is so important. We must not give up. I like to be an ambassador for change. With hope, empathy, compassion and kindness as my tools to mold the situation as much as I can to favor the good of all parties. The illusion of division must be dispelled.

We are all breathing the same air. And governed by the same natural laws. We all have the same human blood running through our veins. We must learn to stop practices that perpetuate division. Someday we will be a healthy balanced humanity. I have that hope for humanity. I know the Bible speaks of the end, but the Lord is extremely merciful to anyone who turns back and mends their ways. There are many characters in the Bible that changed their ways and were embraced by the Lord. One of them even persecuted Christians and changed his ways and was redeemed by God.

After about four months of working for DHL, I decided to quit because it was starting to snow in Murphys and Arnold. I knew the off-roading was going to be a nightmare. Some of those roads were dirt and had so many potholes. The last week when I was training the kid who was going to take over for me, we went up to Bear Valley one day and it began to snow. So surreal seeing the delicate flakes float down through the air covering the road, the tall pine trees. It looked so calm and serene like a Christmas postcard come to life. I felt like sitting by a fire with a warm cup of coffee with plenty of cream and sugar. When we got up there and I got out of the car, the reality of the winter hit me. I stepped down into about five inches of slushy freezing cold water. Totally waterlogging my shoe and sock, sending a shockwave of chill up my spine.

Around the time I left DHL, I decided to take Nicole up to Tahoe for a quick overnight mini vacation. On the way, leaves were changing with fall. Yellows, oranges, reds – it looked like we were driving through an oil painting. Only this masterpiece was crafted by God himself. When I got to a certain junction I thought I should take, Nicole said we should take the pretty one. Having a weakness for her cute voice, I did it. The next thing I knew we were in a valley and I could see the snowcapped mountains to our left. I knew something was wrong and I had gone too far. I didn't have GPS, so I went in my trunk and got out a good old-fashioned atlas. I was redirected to Tahoe that way. It was a real adventure.

I must say this was an instance where I was glad to get lost. It was an awesome detour with great scenery. We decided to stay at a mom-and-pop hotel. The kind where your door is right on the balcony where anyone off the streets could access it. When we got out of the car, we saw two black cats standing there looking right at us. They were like a welcoming committee as we were wearing all black too. The hotel felt a little creepy when I was trying to sleep. As I laid there, I imagined all the people who'd rented this room before us. All the good, bad and indifferent energy that had occupied this space. They say rooms have a memory. That is what I was tripping on that night. I was really desiring Nicole that night. But the energy there didn't seem right, so I didn't go there. On our way back, we listened to David Gray:

"This year's love better last,
heaven knows its high time,
I've been waiting on my own too long."

This song captured exactly where Nicole and I were in our relationship. We wanted it to work out. It almost felt like there was no Plan B at that moment. But there was still uncertainty. I held her soft hand as we listened to this song over and over on loop. It felt like we were healing each other. Like we were both getting something spiritual from each other we desperately needed at the time. It felt like a transition in a song. A time of change.

After leaving DHL, as always, I wasn't worried too much about being unemployed. I just chilled and relaxed for about a month. Then after checking the paper, I found there was a home health agency called Real Care that placed home health aides with work. Being an MA, I was immediately qualified for the work. They hired me and asked me if I was ok working with a cancer patient who was terminal. I said sure, never thinking I'd be asked that. I didn't know home health had to do with hospice.

The only drawback was the job only paid about $7 an hour, dramatically less than what I was used to making.

On the way to the client, she explained to me the details of the case. He was newly married with twins, a boy and a girl who were two years old. This added a whole different dimension to the story. I knew this was something I had to do, something that was put on my path. After he and his wife interviewed me, they agreed to hire me. The first day of work, at the beginning of the shift, I took him for a walk in his wheelchair down his street Glenbriar and around the corner. One of the first things he said to me was that I was his new best friend. I wondered what it would be like to be in his position as I pushed him down that sidewalk. I knew there would come a day when I would need someone to help me. I honestly would have done this for free. I was honored they would let me into their lives at such a sensitive time on their journey.

One time a person came over the house and I said I was Lance from Real Care, just to qualify myself as being fit to work with him. He took it as if I was considering it business instead of friendship, which hurt his feelings.

I went everywhere with him while I was there. I was like an extension to his body. Where he was limited, I could take over from there. He was paralyzed on one side, so I would have to move him from the couch to the wheelchair. I also helped him exercise his leg, around in circles and forward and back like a kicking motion. One day I took him to see his oncologist. He asked the doctor if there was a chance for him to live. The doctor said he didn't want to give him false hope. I kept thinking that must be the hardest job in the world, to desperately want to help someone but there is nothing you can do. He had been given so much chemo there was nothing else they could do.

One day when I was with him, his wife and kids at the mall, I got a call from Sutter Gould. They offered me a full-time job at $5.50 more than what I was making at the time. The only problem was I would not be able to work with Elias due to conflicting hours. I spoke to his wife. She understood this was a great opportunity I couldn't pass up on and it was in my field of training.

The timing was terrible as we had grown attached to the idea of me being around until the end. I had met his whole family, including his mother and brother. I felt so bad. Like I was letting him down. I didn't want him to feel like it was only business, as he'd feared. I truly did care for him, his family and the situation he was in. I just had to do what was best for me at the time. I didn't know when another opportunity like that was going to come around.

8

An Equal and Opposite Reaction

The weekend before I started the job with Gould, I heard an old friend was coming to Sacramento with his band The Black Jets to play a show. I hadn't seen Tom in years, so I was definitely going. I took Nicole with me, driving up Highway 5 to Sacramento.

When I saw Tom, we hugged and talked about music. His band was cool. He played bass instead of guitar like he did back in the day and another old friend Roy played guitar. Their singer was a real front man. He put on a show, dancing and gyrating on the floor. He had a good voice. He had swagger like Mick Jagger. Their music was like good time rock 'n roll. Party music.

Nicole and I kissed a little at the show, a little unusual for us. We usually did those things in private. All in all, it was a great show and nice to see the guys I had such a history with.

I got to thinking how I'd gotten so caught up in my own world I'd neglected some of the most special people I'd ever met in my life. I truly regret that. I never intended to hurt those I was closest to. I was just lost and fighting for emotional and spiritual survival. Little did I know that's what friendships are for – to help us through rough times.

I held myself back from reaching out to friends. I didn't want to burden them with the darkness I was in and drag them into it. Instead, I tried to just standalone to the best of my ability. Friends leaning on each other can really strengthen the friendship. But when it starts to be one sided, carrying the other year after year, the person may become bitter that they're always doing the carrying. But if we're lucky, we have at least one friend who will be there for us through thick and thin. Giving us a place to stay when we are broke, listening to us offload for hours on the phone, laughing with us when times are good. For me that person has been and still is Gary. It is almost like we're assigned a person like a guardian angel to stand by us through life. I never had a biological brother, but Gary is like a brother to me.

Phil is also like a brother that really had my back too in the early 90's when Gary was in school, we used to go to the Sleep shows all over the Bay Area together. Phil was like my dad, he wouldn't back down. And he would ride with me no matter what. We even took El Camino all the way from Santa Clara to San Francisco. Talk about serious cruising. There must be 100 lights or more on that stretch of road. I remember we were listening to King Crimson's "Red" all the way there. By the time we got to the City, I had a headache. The music was so aggressive, pounding and dark it affected our mood. We got lost up there and got so frustrated. We actually had to turn the music off. It's ok to listen to music that connects you to your negative feelings for a time. But at some point, you have to stop venting negative feelings, discover the source of those feelings and address them.

I decided years ago I don't want to be angry and frustrated for the rest of my life. It is suffering, and I don't want to suffer indefinitely. I struggled for years with the music the band was playing because of this. Wondering if playing this heavy stuff was just perpetuating my problem. I wanted to make a positive contribution to the world of music also. And I had taken a step in that direction with the 2003 debut solo record *From Me to You*.

I understand the allure of heavy music. Some of the riffs just sound cool and there is a power derived from those loud amps and power chords. Perhaps that is why they call them power chords. For years I used heavy music to medicate and cope with my negative feelings, only to find the feelings were not going away. I think the holy seed planted in my heart then has grown substantially and it's affected my musical vision considerably.

After Tom and Roy's gig in Sacramento, Nicole and I headed South on I-5 back to Stockton. There is something so calming about a late-night drive back on that stretch of road. And having Nicole's soft hand in mine really drove that feeling home. I know that was the weekend before I started my new job with Sutter on January 16, 2006.

I had to go through and orientation that took a week. Visiting all the different sites to discover what all the different departments do. Just to acclimatize me to the new company and environment.

After going around to all the departments, it was time for my first day of work as a full-time MA. I could not anticipate how much more responsibility I was going to have. Dr.Swisher was a good doctor. He wanted things a certain way and would continue to pressure you about it until you got it right. A stressful environment for me.

I'm not supposed be under a lot of pressure with my bipolar diagnosis. I can spiral out of control. The job was too demanding for me and I was drowning with all the extra responsibility. I had things piling up on my desk, appointments I was supposed to arrange for MRIs and PEG-Intron Hep C treatments I was supposed to set up. None of which I had ever done. There was a lady that helped me along the way, but she only had so much time she could spend with me. She had to take care of her doctor too.

After a few weeks, they started to notice the work piling up on my desk that I had no idea how to do. They started to write me up and make moves in the direction of firing me. They were unaware of my disabilities and the limitations I need help with. The truth is the job just wasn't for a person like me. After the second write-up, I went to my doctor and told him the stress I was under and how it was making me feel trapped. He decided to change my schedule, so I only had work six hours a day. When I presented this to HR, they said the job title I have is full time and the hours could not be modified, so they would put me on leave for one month until we could make another arrangement. After about two or three weeks, I got a call from HR offering me a full-time job in Utilization Management in Ceres where I would be doing clerical type work, phones, mail. So, I took it. I was relieved because it looked like I was going to lose my job. Sutter is a great company because they accommodated my disability rather than firing me.

When I headed out to Ceres for the first time, I was nervous meeting a whole new staff. When I got there, I was going to be about 15 minutes early and decided to go up the street in the opposite direction to kill that 15 minutes. The department was located next to a clinic in a secret location due to potentially disgruntled patients. That first day was overwhelming. There were so many people to meet. I believe the department had about 24 employees when I started. There were about 10 to 12 offices and most of them had two people sharing an office. At first, I was going to be trained by the lady I was replacing. So, it was obviously awkward. She was short with me and negative. She made me feel like I was dumb if I asked a question. After the two weeks, she finally left, and I was stoked knowing I didn't have to deal with her any more. The lady that I was going to work with directly name was Annie Heffley. I thought it was cool because she had the same first name and initials as my sister. I'll never forget what she told me when I started:

"No question is dumb. I don't care how many times you ask me eventually you will know it and you will never ask me again."

That was Annie's nature, always accommodating and wanting people to get along.

When I first started at Sutter, everything was on paper. It either got mailed or interofficed and I had to answer phones. I would start off the morning getting this huge print job off the printer, more than a ream of 500 pages. I had to sort through and separate the ones that needed to be interofficed and the ones to be mailed to patients and providers. I often had some that I couldn't finish and had to do the next day. This was stressful in its own way, but it was a different stressful. It was time crunch stressful, rather than lack of knowledge or inability to perform task stressful. Several of the workers said if I had any other doctor I could have done the job.

After about a month there, I got a call from my hospice clients wife, she said he had passed away and I was invited to the funeral. I had never been to a funeral before. I didn't know what it was going to entail. It was in Tracy where he and his family lived. It was a church service where the pastor read scripture regarding death and dealing with death.

I began to look at my own mortality. It is just something we don't think about until something like a funeral comes along. We are reminded how precious and fragile we are. There came a time in the program where the pastor allowed family and friends to talk about him and the impact he had on their lives. He owned a limousine business which he told me was highly competitive and required you to hustle to get customers. Also, he and his brother had a contract with Trader Joe's to make breads. He told me it took them forever revising the recipe for Trader Joe's to accept their product. Through these two businesses He had made a lot of deep heartfelt friendships.

One guy got up in front and said he was not just saying this because it is a funeral, he was genuinely a nice and great guy. He choked back tears at the end of his short speech. There was an intense aura of deep seated sadness in the room. It sat thick in the air. Almost suffocating. It felt difficult to breath. Maybe breathing patterns change in stressful emotional situations.

At the end of the service, a song rang out in the church. It was James Blunt:

> "Goodbye my friend,
> you have been the one,
> you have been the one for me."

Suddenly the tension that had been welling up in the room was released, through the tears of those that had loved him the most. As people went up to view the body, I tried to approach where his wife was, but it felt like an atom bomb of sadness had dropped in that area and the concussion from the blast kept me away. As tears welled up in my heart all the way up through my eyes, I attempted to head out the door to the left. When I heard someone say something and one of the ushers was pointing to my left at his mother and brother in the front of the pews. Faces blank with sorrow, hearts visibly broken. I held his Mom's hand and bowed to her. I remembered she had told me she was going to teach me Arabic and how she had so lovingly, kindly and graciously cared for her son in his final days as only a mother can do.

Then I stepped to the left and faced his brother, who was considerably taller than Elias. At least 2 inches taller than me and I'm 6 feet. I looked him in the eyes. I can't remember what I said, but I could see the story of his brotherhood with Elias in his eyes. The empire they had built together, that he was going to have to carry on without him. I didn't have the strength to stand there and face him for more than a minute or two, which seemed like an eternity. I think he understood I truly cared for his brother. I wish I could have told him it was never a job. I would have done it for free. In fact, I wish I would have done it for free and I could have cared for him to the end. But life had taken me in a different direction.

I barely made it to the car before I began to sob from the core of my being. I had no idea the effect a funeral could have on a person. I had never been to one. My only other experience with death had been my dog Blackie. There is an old Native American saying, "Keep death on your shoulder" as a reminder to always appreciate life.

As I drove off, I tried to imagine the journey ahead for his wife. I knew the process of grieving was to be a difficult journey for the family. I don't think the children even attended the funeral. I don't believe they would have fully understood what was going on.

A chapter in my life had closed as my good friend left this world. That was a special experience sharing with his family in the final days. I honestly can't imagine anyone doing hospice over an extended period. I would imagine it is like losing a part of yourself every time but also gaining the love of a family you helped. It seems like real rewarding work but a real challenge for the emotions.

No matter what someone's calling, or passion is, it all requires a healthy dose of faith and hard work. Most people fall short, not because they don't have talent, vision or the ability to do the work. They simply don't have the discipline to do the work consistently until the project comes to fruition. I brought multiple projects to fruition. My challenge is following through and hyping my music, resisting self-doubt.

When I really decided to go check out apartments, I was immediately drawn to Greenbriar Apartments because my hospice client had lived on Glenbriar Road. I like to follow signs like that. At the time, my credit was really good, and I didn't have that many bills. When the lady showed me the apartment, I was like, 'I can have this?'

It was 770 square feet, quite a bit of room for one person. I could walk from one end of the apartment to the other and feel like it wasn't claustrophobic. It consisted of a big living room which took up most of the square footage, a kitchen/dining area, a decent size bedroom in the back and a small bathroom with a shower. Anxious to move in, I did without furniture for the first week or so. I just laid on a comforter with a sheet and another comforter on the floor in the corner of the living room. That first night I accidently cut my pointing finger almost to the bone with a knife. I'd underestimated its sharpness. Being an MA, I knew I had to stop the bleeding. I took napkins and wrapped it around it until I could see the blood coming through, saturating it until I had to roll up another makeshift bandage. I knew I had to apply pressure. After about 15 minutes, I was really starting to get worried I may not be able to stop the bleeding. A few minutes later I found a rubber band and made a thick solid makeshift bandage and got the bleeding under control. Maybe this was a sign there was going to be some discomfort living there.

I had never lived alone, so it was a little bit creepy without roommates. If anything happened I was on my own and had to handle it. At the time, I didn't even have a gun to defend myself if something serious went down. So, for the first few weeks I drank almost every night to cope with my anxiety of being alone in the apartment. It would help me to mellow out and go to sleep. I felt like I was living in a hotel. The apartments were laid out similar. Also, my apartment didn't have a deck like some of the others and I liked it that way. No one could climb up there and get in that way. There was only one way in and one way out. All I had to do was keep someone from getting in that door, and I had three immediate neighbors who I shared a porch with. I discovered the bedroom in the back was not comfortable temperature wise year-round. So, I decided to live in the living room like a little studio apartment and use the bedroom as my recording studio/lounge area when friends come over. About a few months prior to moving into the Coffee Rd apartment I purchased a digital Tascam 8 track. The same kind I used back in the day. Only with this one I could burn a CD when I was done producing songs.

After about a month, I made the decision to embark on a new journey – producing a full length solo album on my new 8-track. I started by revising the four songs from the demo *From Me to You* with full instrumentation. What was extra unique about this record is what I used for percussion. I am pretty good with my hands when it comes to percussion with a good sense of meter and time, having played a lot of jazz fusion with a lot of metery odd-timing signatures. I knew how to count things out and find the one.

The first drummer I played with used to do something that intrigued and inspired me. He would put an acoustic guitar in his lap and tap on the surface of it back by the bridge to make percussive beats. Since I didn't have a drum kit and was unable to play one proficiently anyway, I decided to use this method for percussion throughout the whole record which was to eventually consist of 15 songs. When I went to record the beats, I would sit the guitar up on my left leg up on a chair. Put the mic under the bottom of the guitar and tap out the beats down into the mic below. I don't even think I used a metronome on many of the songs because there were tempo changes in many of them. (I later found a metronome is better because it makes the beats sound steady and even when you play over a set meter.) I was super excited when I finished producing that first song. I added a few parts and tweaked the songwriting a bit on the four songs I was re-recording. I believe the first song I did was 'Robin.'

As I produced the songs, I would burn CDs and include the newest song each time and hide it. This would archive my work and keep it safe. In case someone broke in and stole my equipment, I would still have my finished songs.

The day job was a little crazy in the first year or two because we were using such outdated methods to process the documents. But I liked that it gave me plenty of busy work. The kind of work where you can listen to music and it doesn't affect your job performance. Just mindless work.

One thing I noticed about working with women is I had to be careful about how I interacted with them as it could be interpreted as harassment. One lady that I worked with was cute, petite and had a boyfriend. She took the job the boss had offered me. It would have used my MA skill set. But I wasn't that confident in my capability. Looking back, I should have taken that job. One day she was at the copy machine and I wanted to pick up the papers off the fax machine. She misinterpreted what I had said as me coming on to her and went and told the management I was harassing her. I probably should have phrased it different but sincerely had no intention of coming on to her. We had an assistant manager on duty, and she said to stay out of her personal space and don't tell her she looks nice or anything like that. Which I hadn't done. I just remember feeling hurt and embarrassed. I know that harassment is a real problem and women need to be treated with the upmost of respect. It was a challenge for me at times because I was a single guy and several of the women in the office were attractive.

There was another lady in the office I really liked. She sat in the same office as a friend of mine that would tell me what was going on. I did flirt with her not knowing she had a boyfriend. She hadn't told me, and I hadn't heard from anyone yet. She really made a huge funk about it and just came down on me like a ton of lead. Everyone in the office got called in by the manager to ask what their take on hers and my relationship was. Annie and many of the other people said they didn't see me really bothering her, so the whole thing blew over.

Once again, these things were hurtful to me, but I learned it's not fair for the woman to have to feel uncomfortable, feeling like she is getting unwanted advances. Annie told me to stay away from her because she is trouble.

I had no agenda about being in control of women. I was raised with an absolute rock star sister. The Black Wonder Woman. I actually have her in my phone as Wonder

Woman. (I don't think there are a lot of people that have a superhero on speed dial!)

Anne would say, "You deserve a woman who will love you and have respect for you."

The troublemaker my co-worker mentioned was going through a lot in her personal life that was affecting her at work. Her situation was complicated with the boyfriend. He was taking her for granted and she was chasing him despite his problems. So many people are liking the wrong person or in a relationship with the wrong person and miserable. I think people put up with a lot out of fear of being alone.

Being alone can be liberating. Having a chance to find yourself and grow as a person. But it can become lonely and one can get set in unhealthy habits and self-medicating.

That is what I was doing. Disappointment after disappointment, I was getting more and more disillusioned. I was using a triangle of vices to cope with my loneliness, both self-imposed and circumstantial isolation. All were self-destructive and unhealthy, to say the least – alcohol, fatty food and porn. Alcohol was something that I had used for years on and off. But I had to be more discreet when around family and friends. At my place, I could drink whenever I wanted, and no one was there to judge or condemn my lifestyle. It wasn't a good thing. There were times when I would get wasted. I remember a few times when it affected my work. I had to call in sick. Alcohol brings down my inhibitions, causing me to make some bad, misguided decisions.

My main party night was Friday. When I was alone, it would consist of having one of those super burritos from Guadalajara, my favorite nearby taqueria. Or on a special weekend, a rack of pork back ribs with potato salad and I would wash things down with a soda. I think fast, and fatty food is one of the worst habits I have ever had. I don't think I was ever able to stay away from it more than a couple months. Plus, the long-term effects of drinking can be devastating, especially to a person like me diagnosed with fatty liver disease. That should have stopped me and changed my behavior, but it didn't.

Every time I did those things I was reinforcing the idea that I wasn't worth taking care of. The truth was I just liked the buzz of feeling high. That desire to have a buzz had taken my uncle and grandfather on my father's side with cirrhosis of the liver. My grandfather also had a stroke at the end of his life.

And the third vice is porn. By the time I was 36, I started to feel like that was a little weird. I asked myself, 'would you go into people's bedrooms and watch them have sex?' My answer was definitely no. So, why would I watch a video of it?

Porn is another potentially unhealthy thing that has been normalized to a significant extent in our culture. In the '90s when the internet really started to take off, porn was just sitting there poised to take off into the stratosphere. I remember when I was a kid listening to people have sex while the screen was scrambled by cable. Wondering what it looked like. Now anyone that has internet access has access to a sea of sexual content. Google the word sex and hit images and millions of photos will appear that they can just scroll through.

Despite the widespread acceptance of porn by so many, I'm including this as one of my vices because it shouldn't be used due to social ineptitude and not being able to find a woman. It simply does not solve the problem if you are a person who doesn't possess the confidence to go out in the world and find a healthy, meaningful relationship in which sex is a means of expressing love and nurturing the relationship.

It is a dilemma because it can be frustrating never having a healthy sexual outlet and then having to feel guilty when you need to relieve that tension. One thing I learned through the Lord is you must be careful about who you connect with sexually. I truly believe when a man and a woman have sex, they become one flesh. You are intertwining with them physically, emotionally and spiritually. You are welcoming them into your temple. The problem is not everyone you let in the temple can be trusted. If it is a violent or destructive person, you are letting that energy into your heart.

In 2006, I was invited to my old friend Joey's wedding. He was the bassist for ItIsEye, the band my close friend Tom was in. I went with Gary and Lisa. It was at a place in downtown San Jose. When I got to the venue and stepped in, it was like a reunion of so many faces from back in the day – Angie, Al, Marlon, Ed, Tom, Bobby, Natalie. I had forgotten how dynamic and awesome these people were. Marlon was spinning some awesome old school. At one-point Parliament's funk song "Flash Light" came on and we were teleported back to the mid '70s. I felt like I should have been wearing bell-bottoms. It felt so good to dance and have a good time.

My sister used to watch *Soul Train* on TV to pick up on the latest dances. I loved watching my people letting it all hang out on the screen like that. Some of the funkiest acts in the history of music were on *Soul Train*, everyone from James Brown to David Bowie.

I felt that same love here, surrounded by nothing but friends. Some of them I hadn't seen in a long time. It was awesome seeing everyone dance. At one point, they were all in a row like a party train, winding around through the dance floor. There was also an open bar. A lot of us took full advantage of that. I didn't have to drive, but I only got somewhat lit. All and all it was so much fun.

I was all wound up after the wedding. I still had a ton of energy and momentum. I wasn't used to that much stimulus. Once we got back to Gary and Lisa's, I still had to drive over to Anne's in Oakland, which gave me about a half hour drive to wind down. Once I got to Anne's, I went upstairs and stared at the ceiling for what felt like three or four hours before I fell asleep. It was nice. I really felt alive. I saw why people like to go to events like weddings.

In 2007 my sister asked me a question I never anticipated. She said, "If you could go anywhere in the world, where would you go?'

Without hesitation I said, 'Greece!' Mind you, this is something I never even thought about. It was as if I hadn't even chosen, like it was meant to be, the way I just said it without a thought. The crazy thing is two months or so later, I was standing in a hotel room in Athens, Greece. Something I never even thought of as a possibility. On my salary, a trip like this would have been impossible with the bills I had at the time. Anne had a great job, so she was able to do it.

As I stood there in the hotel, I realized everything is written. I don't know if it was a voice in my head or just a quiet understanding. I think it was most likely the latter. It occurred to me I was exactly where I was supposed to be. I also understood destiny was not a destination, it's a journey. A series of choices we make guided by the spirit that leads us down a path. It is awesome to think that everything I do is part of my destiny. Even the mistakes I've made. God uses everything for good in the long run.

There are so many lessons in the mistakes that I made. Sometimes I had to make the same mistake many times before I could generate the resolve to change my behavior. The idea of destiny is biblical. God is the alpha and the omega. He knew what I was going to do before I was born. I have a role in an elaborate play written by God. There are billions of roles in this real-time play and each role impacts the next. I have an aunt Dorothy who is like my spiritual advisor and also believes everything is written.

This may explain why some things are just easy and work out effortlessly and others, no matter how hard you try, just never seem to work out. One of the things I have learned is you shouldn't force things. When things are forced, they tend to break. If a door is difficult to open, try another door. That may not be your door. Or come back later and see if it is open or easier to open. I have never had such a deep-seated and solid understanding of a principle more than I did standing in that hotel in Athens.

That night, Anne and I went to a nice restaurant across the street from the Acropolis. One thing I noticed about Greece is the cab drivers would curse each other out and flip each other off but the traffic didn't seem dangerous like a big city in America. It felt safer to me.

When we got to the restaurant, we had to climb up stairs to get to the roof where the tables were. It was nightfall and the Acropolis was all lit up with beautiful lights. As the new flavors of authentic Greek food exploded in our palates, we heard the powerful operatic voices of outdoor singers. I think it was a play. We couldn't have had a more surreal and amazing first night in Greece. I really didn't want to go out because I had not slept at all on either of the planes, domestically or internationally. But what I quickly was learning from Anne was if you don't have an experience at all, you miss the chance to enjoy the awesome parts of that experience. This got me out of my comfort zone.

As we went on the bus tour the next day visiting all the sights, I would say I enjoyed about 70 percent of it. If I had stayed home, I would have missed out on that. That night we ate at the hotel restaurant. What we quickly learned about Greece is that eating is a social time. They do not rush you away from the table, so the next party can come in to make more money. You can sit at the table for three hours if you want. And there is such an abundance of restaurants there usually isn't much of a wait. I loved Greek food for its strong flavors. We had coconut shrimp that we dipped in a cherry sauce – unforgettable.

After a couple days in Athens, we boarded a plane to our second destination, San Torini Greece which was an island out in the Aegean Sea. I noticed on the flights the stewardesses looked like high fashion models. They were all between 20 and 25 and looked incredible. It was so obvious that was the criteria for getting hired, it seemed discriminatory.

When we arrived on the island, a guide was waiting for us. We boarded the shuttle she drove and headed to our hotel Alessandra, which was about 20 minutes away. The shuttle pulled up to a busy 4-way intersection and just dropped us off right on the corner. We were just standing there with our bags and it felt like we were in the middle of the street. After a few minutes, a golf-cart sized vehicle winded down the hill and picked us up. The lady at check in was awesome. No matter what we asked she would say, "Of course." Our joke was you could tell her I want to paraglide being pulled behind a school of dolphins while eating a 4-star lunch on a hovering dining table and she would say, "Of course."

I had never felt like royalty before San Torini. I remember at one of our meals the waiter brought out bread, olive oil, olives and water as an appetizer. And before he brought the main course, he brought out what looked like a butter knife to get all the crumbs off the table before he brought the next course. He got all the crumbs! I remember feeling strange. Here I am sitting in khaki shorts and a button-down short-sleeve shirt with tennis shoes and I'm getting 5-star treatment. I never knew what a vacation was or why people really take them until that moment. That was the first time I had ever been out of the country on a real destination vacation.

Our first excursion was taking a boat to an island and climbing a volcano. I was going to learn very quickly that when Anne choses an excursion, listen closely to what she says. I didn't hear the part clearly about "climbing a volcano!"

After we ate breakfast, we had to catch the boat by a certain time. There was a pulley car that went down the hill we could have taken down. But there was a long line and we wouldn't have made it down in time. So, we had to walk down to the boat. Little did we know that was going to take almost an hour. At the top of the hill, there were mules you could ride down. But it was so steep you felt like you were holding yourself back from falling forward, even walking. I couldn't imagine trusting the donkey to do it. But Anne and I quickly saw why people chose the donkey option. It was a series of steep downhill drops that went diagonally down the hill, left and right, until it got to the bottom. By the time we got down there, we were so relieved it was over.

Next, we boarded what looked like a pirate ship. It was about 80 to 100 feet long and it even had a bar on it. The water was rough heading over to the volcano. So much so I had to catch Anne from falling once just from the centrifugal force of the boat going up and down. I learned rocking from front to back I didn't mind. But side to side could be terrifying. Especially to someone like me who couldn't swim.

One of our stops was at a hot spring, which turned out to be basically just pulling up beside some rocks in the ocean and diving into the Aegean Sea. I definitely wasn't going in and Anne was like, "Oh hell no. I'm not that good of a swimmer."

After a little while we went to the volcano, where we climbed and climbed and climbed. It was exhausting to someone like me that never exercised at the time. When we got to the top, we could see San Torini in the distance, the trail we'd climbed, and the beautiful stark white buildings San Torini is known for. There was a cute woman by herself. I was interested in her but figured what is the chance of us having anything, why bother? Looking back, I should have talked to her. I've heard plenty of stories how people from different areas met on a trip and ended up moving near each other and getting married. But once again, my lack of faith hindered me. Even if it was just going to be a two-day romance, it would have been nice to have that experience.

On the way back to San Torini, the water calmed down so much that the surface of the sea was like glass, with an occasional ripple. A man played a trumpet for a while and after that was silence. Everyone was tired and just taking in the water and the sky as we headed toward sunset. Suddenly one of my favorite songs began to play. So subtle and smooth. Perfect for this moment. In fact, it was the defining moment of the trip for me. Sade's "Like a Tattoo":

> "He told me sweet lies of sweet loves,
> heavy with the burden of the truth,
> and he spoke of his dreams,
> broken by the burden.
> broken by the burden of his youth."

This song embodied the way I felt as the sun slowly dropped down over the horizon. Waves quietly lapping at the bow of the ship. Filling my senses with reverie. There is a feeling that defies description, that I rarely feel. It is so perfect, words cannot be uttered. Words would stand in the way and the feeling would be lost. I think that is where God is. He is a feeling and truth too deep for words. He sits there like the backdrop of the sky, consistent but ever changing. He is available always. Not just during a sunset, but on your way home from work, while listening to music. I had discovered the secret place where God dwells both in my heart and in the natural world around me.

As the sky was beginning to turn lavender, violet and blue, I ate one of the biggest shrimp I'd ever seen in my life. About an inch and a half thick and about the size around the top of a pasta jar lid. So good and so filling. As I sat there with Anne, I wanted to pinch myself. It felt like a dream. I closed my eyes and opened them back up, to make sure it was happening. Anne felt the same way. It was so special sharing those experiences with her. Once-in-a-lifetime experiences. I just hope maybe I have the chance for twice-in-a-lifetime or three-times-in-a-lifetime experiences too. We'll see.

The next day Anne and I went to a winery on the other side of the island, about a half-hour drive. I think the island was probably only about an hour end to end. We both got to taste four wines. There was only a little bit in each glass, but it was extremely strong. By the third glass, I had a considerable buzz. There was a super cute calico cat at the winery. She was absolutely wild. To the point, my sister was almost scared of her. She would try to climb up our legs for food, love and attention. All we had to feed her was cheese and olives, but she loved it. I took a picture of her that I keep on my keyboard stand in my studio. She was one of my favorite things on the trip. I have never seen an animal that aggressive and passionate. She was probably totally dependent on tourists and the winery taking care of her.

The next day we flew back to Athens and then Mikonos. They don't allow you to fly from one island to another. We were taking so many flights, we became experts. Because of 9/11, we had to keep liquids and things in a transparent plastic bag and we had to take off our shoes at every stop.

In Mykonos, we had the most stunning hotel room imaginable. It looked like the quarters of Greek Gods. The floor was white marble, walls stark white just like the outsides of the buildings, beds white with canopies over them. Straight out of one of those travel magazines. Absolutely immaculate. Every detail was taken into consideration. They even had a little vial of clear liquor that came with the room. When Anne went to check out the area, I drank that and headed off the property to a nearby store. Anne told me it was 7 Euros for one can of soda in the hotel. Which was about 15 American dollars at the time. When I got to the little store, I bought a can of Heineken, a little bottle of wine, a candy bar and a bag of chips for 7 Euros. Lesson learned – leave the hotel and find a grocery store. I even found a McDonald's and kept the menu with Greek writing.

Mykonos was a quiet little island. They had the old cobblestone roads that winded between old buildings and shops that looked like they had been there for eons.

Our hotel room overlooked a cove where you could see the wonderful turquoise-colored water. I could see the people frolicking in the water and heard their unbridled laughter and enjoyment. At that moment, I wished to my core I knew how to swim. I wondered what I was missing and how it must feel to be that free. Enjoying the water instead of being afraid if its murky depths. In the cove, you could see the bottom of the water. It looked like a swimming pool. There was no unknown. Everything could be seen from the surface. I wish everything was like that. Genuine – what you see is what you get. Nothing hidden. But I just don't trust open water, that I won't go under when I try to swim on the surface. Oddly, I really like going under water in a pool. I still don't know how to swim but promise myself I'll learn. I don't want to miss out on another opportunity to connect with nature.

After Mykonos, we flew back to Athens again, then to Atlanta, Georgia – one of the largest airports I've ever seen. They had a train to take you from one terminal to another. It was too far to walk. After that, to LA and then SF. All and all, we made around 10 fights in 10 days. That was one of the most amazing experiences. Once again, I found the value of stepping out of my comfort zone. So many experiences await when you open yourself up to them.

Around that time, Gary and I produced what was to be our only record as Human Anomaly to date, *Blind Juggler* (although we are currently writing one due out in late 2018.) I played guitar and sang, Gary played bass, Fender Rhoades/electric piano and drums. I was amazed Gary decided to take on playing the drums. I noticed a change in him after finding love with Lisa. He seemed to have the confidence to take on anything – drums, building shelves (not always easy!) It was awesome to see that boost in confidence. It showed me what love could do to a person's life.

To prepare for the record, Gary and I rehearsed tirelessly for months and months. It was nice working with just him because we have a similar work ethic and get along really well. Sometimes it's hard to motivate other musicians. Especially when they are not being paid and need so much time rehearsing. The songs were really challenging and fun to play, so it was exciting to produce the record. When we got into the studio, Gary and I played a live take that everything else would be recorded over. We went to a recording engineer named Bart Thurber. He had been recording bands since the early '90s. I think he told me he has recorded over 2,000 bands. He was experienced and easy to work with affordable rates.

I remember being nervous on the first few live takes. There is this one clean part on the song "Tire Iron" that used alternate picking that was difficult to play but we had rehearsed so many times. While we were playing that part, I suddenly felt comfortable and the nerves went away. After that, I felt at home recording the rest of the album. I felt kind of bad cause all I had to do is play guitar. Gary had so much overdubbing to do. I spent most of my time just listening in the control room with Bart and in the side lounge room with a random framed velvet poster of Kenny Rogers.

Another highlight was a song I was going to overdub with this guitar solo. I had a lot of pent up energy and frustration up until that moment, and I took those 30 seconds to release it all. I felt like I was standing beside myself as my hand picked up and down sporadically, as bursts of notes resonated through the live room. It was a first-take keeper solo that I'm still proud of till this day.

A song or a guitar solo is like an audio snapshot of where you were spiritually and emotionally at a given time in your life. It is precious and brings you back to those feelings each time you listen to it. You lived that life and experienced those feelings firsthand. It couldn't be more real.

When I look back, I now feel more empathy for myself. I was so cruel to myself at that time. Fixating on all those negative emotions and amplifying them. I didn't realize it all was self-destructive and part of a negative cycle keeping me in bondage to my negative feelings.

It was such a good feeling when the record was done. It was our first record since 1996 with Livestock. A lot had changed since then but it was still in our jazz metal fusion progressive style. Plus, this was also our first record to be released on a label called *Life Is Abuse*.

An artist friend of ours named Davy did the artwork for the CD. We got so many compliments on that artwork. Davy's gone on to become a successful artist doing work for and touring with various metal bands.

Having finished the record, we had to find a drummer to book live shows and we found one named Bil. Yes, with one L. And he was unique just like his name. His wife was an Oakland police officer and he was a musician for hire and a record collector/dealer. He was funny, almost like a used car salesman. You didn't know what to believe with him. I drove him home after practice once and he kept doing this character, talking about those hush puppies from Long John Silver's, "Get over here in my mouth, you little bugger." Ok, maybe you had to be there.

We rehearsed with Bil for a few months, just long enough for us to learn to play the songs together. I don't know if it was enough time for it to really gel. Just enough so we could play the songs all the way through without making many mistakes. I personally like to play to the point where I am not thinking about how many times things go around. To where it just comes naturally. It gives you the freedom to just enjoy the experience of performing live.

Around this time, Hank came along and joined the band as our Rhodes piano player. He quickly learned the parts and fell in. Being well rehearsed, we booked a show at Annie's Social Club in San Francisco, the same club I'd seen High on Fire in the late '90s. This was the first time Gary and I had played in the city. I even ran into Rabiah, my old guitar student at the show. My old friend Robinmarie and her friend Dee also showed up. So, it felt nice to have some familiar faces.

The thing about the city, I always had this feeling I wasn't hip or cool enough to be playing there. I felt kind of like a dork in disguise. Not exactly. I felt like a dork period. Which is ok because that's really me.

The show went pretty well with only a few mistakes. I did break a string at that show, which was embarrassing because I didn't have a second guitar. Right in the middle of the show, I was trying to string my guitar before the crowd started getting antsy. After we finished, we waited around for a while outside the club, joking around and just generally having fun. We had to wait until they tallied the money from the door and bar to get paid. Gary went in and got the money – I think I got $40. Which was a raise compared to the mid '90s when we used to get $50 for the whole band. I wondered if there would ever be a day where we would get paid what we were worth. I wasn't that hopeful then. But I am now. About a week after the show, Bil informed us he was going to be touring with another band for a few months. So, he wouldn't be able to play with us. It was a well-paying gig, unlike ours. So, I can understand why he took it. The truth was we needed a more stable musician, who would choose us and really commit to the long haul with us.

Determined to continue, we sought another drummer. And quickly found one named Nick. Nick is one of the most professional and genuine people I have ever met. He is a stand-up guy and a true human with character. Nick had a lot of experience with drums and toured extensively with the stage show *Stomp*. His drum playing was beyond that of most drummers I've played with. He was a very active and busy player. Taking full advantage of the wide range of techniques in his repertoire. He told me one of the best experiences he had in *Stomp* was a huge drum circle of over a 100 drummers and percussionists playing simultaneously in Brazil. He said it was transcendent and overwhelming. A spiritual experience to say the least. He said the people in South America are so passionate with their emotions on their sleeves. He said it is so different down there than it is here in the US. I had never met a person that had so much experience going out and seeing the world. It was refreshing to meet someone like that.

With everyone on the same page as far as work ethic and vision, the band picked up on the songs and started to gel. Gary had a 24-track digital recorder we used for practice. We decided to use this recorder to seriously record our record. One of the songs we played was called "Ambulance" about a cynical ambulance driver having a spiritual awakening when he sees a child die in front of him. And how he discovers the value of life. The driver had become hard, seeing so much hardship. In the song, there is this clean ascending break where Nick would normally play this drum part in practice. When we recorded it, I wasn't prepared for his record level performance and didn't expect what he did at the time.

This is what it felt like... I was down on Santa Teresa Road in San Jose with my old green Pontiac Firebird with the two-barrel carb and I saw a new Corvette next to me. When the light turned green, I punched it and got ahead of him by about four car lengths. When suddenly, I heard a hellish rev from the Corvette, then a sound like the cross between a locomotive passing by and the growl of a male lion combined. It almost scared me. My stomach dropped in my abdomen like I was descending from a roller coaster.

That is how I felt when Nick unleashed his record-level performance. I felt so honored to be standing in the same room with him. And Gary is such a tactful and creative songwriter and bass player. He is consistent, with a solid handle on groove and heavy riff playing. Gary thinks in the pocket. He is truly a musician that never leaves the pocket. Totally immersed. When I think of our original drummer Phil, he can't be compared to any other drummer. Like most inspirational players., Phil has a solid metery progressive sound with a deep sense of groove. When I think of playing music, it's almost impossible to think of looking to my left or right side and not seeing Phil behind the kit. He is like a metronome when it comes to keeping meter, rarely if ever missing a beat. In fact, the only reason we sought other drummers was Phil was unavailable. He was the first person we called.

Around the same time, we got a show at Eli's in Oakland, a beloved historic venue. We were the opening act because I remember them giving us a sound check. Usually only the headliner gets a sound check. I was running my 100-watt fender combo amp into the 4 x 12-inch speaker cabinet Tom had sold to me years prior and a Roland JC combo amp with 2 x 12-inch speakers. It looked like a full stack. I rarely used this much gear in the '90s.

This guy named Greg was doing the sound. The clean sounded awesome. And when I clicked over to dirty, it was so punchy, solid and loud. It sounded perfect. That honestly was the best live sound ever for me. Nick's girlfriend at the time Annie was there taking pictures at the show. Turns out there was this giant crimson half circle above the stage that looked like one of those Asian fans open. It was about 5 feet above our heads I didn't even notice it when we came in, but I am sure it looked really cool to the crowd. I saw it in her pics later.

The show went awesome. Everyone played so well. The only problem was Hanks Rhodes piano didn't get mic'd, so the crowd had trouble hearing him until after the first song when it was corrected. I remember Nick really digging in live.

Shows are honestly the best part about being a musician. Although I get the introverted allure of production and sitting home writing songs. But it's just like with Greece. It is best to step out of your comfort zone. You can miss out on the fun parts of the experience or the experience altogether. I hate to reiterate but that has been such an important lesson I really want to drive that home to any of my fellow introverts out there.

Shortly after the show, Nick broke the news – Annie was pregnant, and he was going to have to take on more hours at work to help with the extra expenses of fatherhood. We were happy for him but also disappointed to lose such a valuable musician to the project and a friend. And realistically, we knew you often lose track of people once you stop working with them.

Hank, Gary and I continued. The song "Anomaly" took up an enormous amount of our time. It had so many difficult parts. We rehearsed that song for months and months. For me, it was getting to the point of frustration with that song and its energy. I was starting to get concerned with the music being too dark and not wanting to fixate on those emotions.

After talking to my mom and sister, I decided to quit the band for the time being until I could figure out my next move. That was right around the time I'd just released my first full-length solo record *Art of Solitude*. I was starting to see I may also be able to pursue a music career in that direction with an alternative to heavy music. I'm a gentle person. By that time, I was listening to Tom Petty more that I was Black Sabbath. In fact, I hadn't listened to heavy bands in years. My worst musical vice had become sad music. I'd gotten beyond the angry music only to discover songs with layers of sadness.

The guys understood and just wanted me to do what was best for me. Gary had known me forever and knew my whole story. He wanted the band but wanted me to find balance and happiness even more. I think he knew once things settled down with me and I felt better, we might work on more music in the future with different energy I felt more comfortable with.

I was also spending time with Nichole again. She would stop by on Fridays and we'd bake a rack of pork back ribs. I would buy potato salad or even cook my own little menu ideas that she always loved.

But I was really drinking a lot at the time. Kessler Whiskey was my poison. And as I discovered, it truly is as smooth as silk. Just like it says on the bottle.

We'd usually watch a movie together. It was so nice having her there. It gave me something to look forward to. The funny thing about depression – you go from being down in the dumps when you are alone and wishing you could just die, to wanting to live forever so you can enjoy your newfound companionship. I guess that's why they call it bipolar, right?

I'm learning to find peace of mind despite circumstances. If you let circumstances dictate how you feel, you are always going to be on an emotional roller coaster. So, the question is how do you do that? For me, I decided to establish a loving relationship with God. I know people who do not want to go to church because they feel they aren't living clean enough. God loves you. He knows you will make mistakes. He just wants you to be humble and try your best. He is also everywhere, including in your heart. If you don't feel he is there, ask him to abide in your heart and take residence. Once your faith gets stronger, you start to trust in God's plan and don't question every step. Then you can enter in his rest and peace. A peace that can't be taken away and doesn't change with the circumstances.

After a few years of working with Annie, the woman who trained me at Sutter Gould, she informed us she was moving back to Arkansas to spend time with her family. It was always her dream to have her own little house to call her own. Her sister had a good job, so she was able to buy one for her as an investment property. Annie and I had been on one date while we worked together. Although she was considerably older than me, we really liked each other but nothing came of it then.

Annie gave me a whole cabinet of liquor that day. Annie drank beer instead and she hardly ate at work. She was thin from that. That week was very festive to say the least. I drank a LOT of liquor. To the point I almost couldn't function normally. That was the problem with me and hard liquor. I couldn't keep it around because I would drink it too much. Every day until it was gone. So usually I would buy a half pint at a time and just drink one session at a time, usually on Friday night and sometimes on the weekend. If I was being bad I might do it a couple times during the week too. Due to stress at the job.

The Saturday before Annie left, her family threw her a party. Nicole and I were tore up from the Friday night before. I remember Nicole wearing her shades to avoid sunlight in her eyes which intensified her headache.

When we got there, I was nervous as always when I go into a social situation. I knew Annie had been raised in Arkansas and didn't want me to feel awkward being the only Black guy there. And it turned out, I was the only Black guy there. I remember Annie told me her ex was prejudiced and tried to instill that into her kids. I had a lot of respect for Annie because she told her kids he was wrong and not to think like him. She told them that it was a great big world out there and some day they were going to be around a lot of other cultures and they needed to be open minded.

When we walked out into the backyard, we were greeted by Annie who made a comment to Nichole about not wanting to steal her boyfriend. Which was ironic because that is exactly what she wanted to do. Annie offered us drinks. Nicole had a vodka and cranberry juice and I had a beer.

They had a nice set up out there. To the left was a makeshift little stage area for a cover band her family was friends with. Within a few minutes of us sitting down, Annie's sister came and whisked me away to dance with Annie. I really didn't realize Annie wanted to dance with me at that point. I was aware that there were feelings there, but it just surprised me. I knew Nicole wasn't the jealous type, so Annie and I danced for a full song. Left and right, as the music played like a backdrop to a developing story. She looked cute in a knit sweater, just off her shoulders and capri pants. I usually saw her in scrubs.

After the dance, before I sat down, I decided to sing a song with the band. I know Annie knew I was a recording artist. She and I had collaborated on a song on *Art of Solitude* called "Just Like This" from lyrics she had written and I reworked.

The crowd was kind of a country and rock crowd. So, I figured a good song to break the ice with would be "Folsom Prison Blues" by Johnny Cash. I had always admired Johnny. He had a great voice and was a downright bad ass rock star with a country twang. The band there had a female singer, a bassist, guitarist and drummer. I wasn't totally familiar with the vocal melody of the song. So, I asked the singer to sing it to me. Once she did, it sounded familiar and I knew what to do. She also had the lyric sheet. What a coincidence the band knew how to play it, given all the songs out here.

Suddenly, I heard the shuffling two-step beat start and the guitarist say, "I'll even give you the intro." And he picked it out on the guitar. Then I just heard the bass going, back and forth between the two notes for about two bars as the crowd anticipated what my voice was going to sound like.

I'm pretty good at impersonating voice, so I rifled right in:

> "Well I hear a train a comin'
> rollin' round the bend,
> I ain't seen the sunshine,
> since I don't know when."

The crowd roared in response – loud for such a small group. For an instant, it was 1957 and June Carter was standing up there, boppin' left and right beside me. It felt so good, like I'd stepped into Johnny Cash's shoes for a moment. And I felt what it was like to have the genuine adulation of the crowd. It was different than experiences I'd had on stages before. Because I was always trying to prove myself to crowds. But this was immediate acceptance. Something special since I felt so out of place when I walked in. It just showed me you can always find something in common with people.

After that, I felt like I knew everybody. I had broken the ice. A couple people even came up and struck up a conversation at my table when I sat down. The rest of the afternoon went great. Great food, drinks and conversation. I was just sad that when all the festivities died down Annie was going to be heading to the other side of the country. I knew that I may never see her again. I learned to appreciate people. You never know where life will take us and how long we have in each scene with each set of characters.

About a year later, Annie came back to visit from Arkansas. I didn't get to see her outside of her visit to the office because she was there with her daughter and relatives. But this time she made it very clear to me that she liked me. She said, "You better be careful because I might just flirt with you."

I don't think most of the people in the office thought I would date her. I was liking several unattainable women in the office. A total waste of time but all I had to make me carry on. I was going on very few dates and relations were few and far between. Nicole was my only reality and an unsteady one at that. She also had feelings for Donald.

I regretted not seeing Annie in private on that trip. Not just for intimate connection. Just to spend time with a woman I loved and respected. Soon after, I received word Annie was ill and wasn't doing well. A few days later I received a postcard she sent. Telling me she'd ridden a carriage at the Biltmore Estates, a grand almost castle-like place she loved in North Carolina. And a famous country musician had called her to wish her well – something her sister had arranged. She also mentioned I should call her.

I'd been putting off calling her. I thought she was going to be fine. I thought she was going to have more time. But one day I found out she was on her death bed and couldn't speak. My friend Susan, who also knew Annie, said I should call her and have her sister put the phone to her ear.

I decided to sing to Annie. She had been so supportive of my music when so many were so cynical and could care less. There was one woman in the office who had told me I should just quit. Annie never had and never would have told me that. She loved me too much. Maybe this is the type of woman I'm waiting for now. One to be by my side until the end.

When I called, her sister answered and put the phone to Annie's ear. I honestly didn't feel I had ever written a song that was worthy of being the last song someone ever heard. But one song came to mind. It is an old '70s classic from Jethro Tull. They had some of the most beautiful ballads I've heard. I chose "Wond'ring Aloud."

I couldn't imagine Annie there in bed, so I just focused on singing as close as I could from the core of my being. I had not visited. I had not called until then. And I was going to give her spirit something to dance to in the last minutes and hours. I softly and steadily started:

'Wondering aloud.
how we feel. today.
last night sipped the sunset,
my hand in her hair ... "

Before I could get to the next verse, her sister came on the phone in tears, "She's not responding."

I said, "I loved Annie."

Never take the ones you love or your own life for granted. We never know when things are going to change. And change is the only guarantee we have.

Annie believed in me. I promised myself if I ever won an award, I was going to mention her name.

When I first met Annie, she pushed me to go to the local *Modesto Bee* newspaper to do an interview. The reporter took a picture of me and wrote a full-page article about my journey as a songwriter and musician in 2007. I still have that article in a frame upstairs. God only knows where I would be if I had a woman like that in my corner to motivate and inspire me every step of the way. I still have that old postcard too. I know a spirit dwelled within Annie and she carried on beyond death. As with others who've passed to the other side, I hope to see her again someday. Around the time Annie passed, I met a special coworker. She was hired to replace Annie when she moved away. It was her responsibility to look up the patients MRN number which is an identification number and distribute the referrals to the appropriate nurse. The first thing I noticed is she had a combination of everything a man could want in a woman.

She was attractive, young, sharp, intelligent, perceptive with an enthusiastic sense of humor. She loved to laugh. When we were in that office together, that is in fact all we did. A lot of laughing and a little work. At least that was our goal. We did have to get things done. Her and I became good friends and were inseparable. I was like her older brother.

9

New Momentum – Leaving Dark Music and Alcohol Abuse Behind

In late 2009, I was listening to depressing music nonstop. Music that kept me down in the dumps. I related to those feelings. Being paralyzed by the fear of being alone forever and never being able to see the fruits of my efforts. I had feelings for women I liked that I couldn't express. It was all so frustrating, to say the least.

I remember being so depressed to the point of lethargy. I had so little energy it was hard to keep my head in an upright position. My head actually hung forward. I have bad posture until this day, in part because of years of depression. The medicine I took balanced me chemically for the most part. But unhealthy habits were sucking me under like a strong ocean undertow. I was drowning. Like in real life, I felt like I couldn't swim. Overwhelmed by the waves. I was afraid I was just going to go under and sink to the bottom of the murky depths of the unknown.

Sometimes I dreamt I was stuck on my back, a position that gives me nightmares. It makes me feel vulnerable. Pulled into the darkness. Terrifying. I'd kick my legs to wake up and jar myself from sleep. I would wake with a feeling of relief, realizing it was just a dream.

Three of my favorite artists at the time were Beck, David Gray and Pink Floyd. Their dark, dismal songs allowed me to connect with the deep sadness.

Beck had this record called *Sea Change* which was beautifully melancholy. Although it allowed me to find the beauty in my sadness, it was really perpetuating it. And David Gray had a song called, "Nightblindness" that could make the hairs on the back of my neck stand up and give me chills. Especially the live version. His album *White Ladder* had a profound impact on me as he too struggled with loneliness and alcohol abuse.

Pink Floyd has a few songs that immediately take me to the place of helplessness, insecurity and crippling sadness. I don't know why I was doing that to myself. But I guess it was something I had to go through.

Once, in winter of 2009, I was laying on my back in the bed. Staring at the ceiling. Mind wandering. The buzz of the alcohol and the chill of night on my face. Which was the only thing uncovered on my body. I had never felt so cold and alone in all my life. I felt like I was in a vacuum of doubt and insecurity, anxiety.

I thought to myself, "I am not alone right now. God is with me and he loves me." It was the first hint of compassion I had for myself in months. And I am sure God put it in my heart. The lyrics for "I'm Not Alone" off *Feel Something* started to form:

"I'm not alone,
but it's cold in this room,
and I choose to believe in you."

That was the beginning of a spiritual bond I never felt before. I had experiences at the Pentecostal church in '97, but I never thought too deeply about God's omnipresence and how I am never alone. When I look back on my life and all the close calls and bouts with the unknown, I know God was with me through it all.

In late 2010, my faith in the Lord's protection was put to the test. It was first thing in the morning and I got to work a few minutes early. So, I sat in my car a few minutes. This time I noticed, across the parking lot by the road, a white SUV with a man sitting in the back seat. Door ajar, as if he was going to jump out and confront me. Glaring at me as if he wanted to attack me. I thought is he going to shoot at me when I get out of the car? No one could convince me this was my imagination.

I got out of my car and rushed in, heart racing at the idea I may be having a beef with someone. I went out into the lobby of the doctor's office where I could see him, but he couldn't see me. He got out of the passenger rear door, went around to the drivers' side, jumped in and drove off.

The rest of the day I was on edge. At lunch, I decided to look out the front door to see if anyone was in the parking lot. To my dismay, I could see the same SUV parked across the street. By then, I was really starting to freak out. At that point, I decided to go home early. I went for a long, out-of-the-way drive up Highway 99, out to 120 over to 205 in Tracy. I eventually ended up home. I shared my story with my mom and dad. My parents told me I was just making assumptions and there are a lot of white SUVs. I was probably just overreacting. So, I decided to go to work the next day.

I didn't see any sign of an SUV that morning. I went on with my day hoping for the best. At the end of the day when I went out to my car, I saw the SUV drive up right as I was leaving. I jumped into overdrive with my paranoia. Assuming the absolute worst. Not knowing what was going on. I was afraid I may be under judgement for some of the sinning and bad decisions I was making.

I headed off for home and called my family on the way. They thought I was either in danger or having a mental breakdown. I was having such anxiety I could hardly breathe. My family suggested I make an emergency visit to my psychiatrist.

When I arrived, the doctor treated my situation as a psychiatric condition of extreme paranoia. He thought I was losing touch with reality. This was all in my mind.

I was convinced it wasn't just in my mind and hell bent on the idea I was in danger. My doctor decided to take me off work for a month. This was the first time I had that type of leave due to mental illness. I felt like Kevin McCarthy from the 50's *Invasion of the Body Snatchers* who was convinced aliens were taking over the bodies of his friends, family and fellow citizens. It was not a delusion to him. It was a reality he had to cope with.

This is the biggest problem with mental illness. Too many people are coping with anxiety, depression and bipolar without coming forward because of the stigma of mental illness. That's one of the reasons I'm sharing such personal things from my journey. To show people you are not alone and give you courage to seek the help you need or help someone you love get help.

When I went to stay with my parents, the change helped relieve my symptoms. Surrounded by people who truly loved and supported me. I remember this popping in my head while lying in bed, "This is the safest place you can be."

One of the most healing musical discoveries during this time was recording artist Mat Kearney. One day I was driving around, anxious and on edge, when Kearney popped into my mind. I remembered him from Pandora. So, I drove straight to Tower Records and bought his LP *Nothing Left to Lose*. I listened to the whole record, over and over in my car, as I drove for hours.

One song that stood out was "In the Middle." Like the song was made to get me through my feelings at the time. It was all in the chorus:

> "No parachutes no safety nets here,
> One foot on the water to face these fears,
> I'm coming out strong like I can't be wrong,
> I said, 'hey, I won't fall in the middle."

Since then, I've become a huge fan of Kearney, buying four of his records and seeing him live twice. I don't think some artists are fully aware of the impact their songs can have on people. Being an artist myself, I humbly wonder if my music has ever done that for anyone.

After a couple weeks, I went back to my apartment and things had settled down in my psyche. I no longer noticed that white SUV again. And it was nice having a couple extra weeks to recover. It is awesome to have a health care system that has taken such good care of my mental health. I have good insurance because I work in the medical field. Now we just need to get single payer, so everyone can have health coverage like most of the other developed countries.

Years ago, my mom had bought me a Jimi Hendrix guitar frame, that had a miniature fender Stratocaster glued to it about 6 inches long. I mean it was an exact replica of a Strat. It had a white body and pick guard, and a rosewood neck. Which was a little different than the Strat that I had been playing for years. Mine has a vanilla colored body with a white pick guard and a maple neck which is a light wood that looks kind of tan. The rosewood is a dark wood. One day my mom and I met Anne at Applebee's for lunch. Anne told me that she had a surprise for me. I had absolutely no idea what it was. It was not my birthday or a special occasion, which Anne is known for celebrating religiously. After we ate and went out to the car, Anne said, "Look at what I have … "

A guitar that looked a lot like my Strat. It was discovered in a shed, so I knew the neck would be warped and it would most likely be a show piece. So, I put it in the trunk of my car and didn't think much of it. When I got it home, I looked more closely at it. What occurred to me is it looked a lot like that guitar from the frame that my mom had given me many years before. In fact, when I took the frame out it was painted white, with a white pick guard and a rosewood neck. It was the same exact guitar. Which is also a little unusual because this isn't the guitar Jimi was most known for playing. The one I had was so similar to the one he used in Woodstock, one of the most iconic guitars he used. Jimi Hendrix and my family have a special connection. Both me and my cousin were born the day he died. The whole thing kind of blew me away. What a trip.

For my 40th birthday, Anne told me she was taking me somewhere but would not give me a hint as to where. Even once we pulled up, I still didn't know where we were. Until I got to the sign that said Safari West. I was in Marin County at one of those safari adventures where you ride through the wilderness and watch the animals in their natural habitat. The safari truck had two levels. The lower level where my mom, sister and her friend Carla sat. And the upper part above the driver that was about 9 to 10 feet off the ground. I rode up there along with Carla's husband and their two kids. Which were the perfect age for a trip like this. About 7 and 10. We had to be strapped down into the seat as it was going to be a bumpy ride. We observed a wide range of animals. From long horn steers, to zebras. The fact the Lord made such a variety of wildlife is beyond amazing. And we get to share the planet with them.

My favorite animals were the rhinos and the giraffes. The rhinos looked like giant dogs. The way they laid on their sides, exhaling and causing a plume of dust to kick up. Sounding kind of like the shutter of a horse's nostrils.

The guide mentioned zebras are impossible to break. Aggressive and hostile. I was thinking they were right – I'd never seen anyone riding a zebra!

And one of the biggest highlights of the excursion was the giraffes. As we rounded the corner, the giraffe's started to appear taller and taller, larger and larger. They told us whatever we do, don't touch them. A request Anne found difficult to obey. Even with us up as high as we were, the giraffes were still about 6 feet taller than the vehicle. The guide told us the males fight by hitting their necks together. I've since seen video of that and it's hilarious.

Unintentionally, I made eye contact with the tallest male giraffe. It looked like he was sizing me up, to see if I would be a threat or a good opponent as he leaned into the truck with the lower part of his neck, right at the level of my head. My sister got a great picture of me with a look of absolute anxiety and panic that simply looks like awe in the photo.

After we finished the tour, my sister had a final surprise for me. As if the safari hadn't been enough, she presented me with a voucher for a flight to Hawaii valid for a year. I was so shocked I couldn't speak. And she said she and Mom could go with me. Which made me feel relieved because I'm not one to travel alone. I like to have someone I can trust at my side.

Fast forward to a year later, August 2011. All the plans had been made for a five-day Hawaiian trip. I couldn't help but think about the *Brady Bunch*, *Charlie's Angels* and *Sanford and Son* Hawaiian specials I'd watched on TV growing up and all the clichés surrounding them. I loved those campy shows and wondered what Hawaii would be like. I was soon going to find out for myself.

When the cab driver picked us up at the airport, he let us know a firework display happens every Friday night at the hotel where we were staying and it could be heard from across the island. That night we found out firsthand what he meant. The sheer volume and concussions from the blasts of the fireworks shook the building we were in, as bursts of color lit the night sky. As Anne and I went out on the balcony to fully experience the bombardment, Mom exclaimed, "Get back in here! You could get hurt!"

The next day Anne had a special excursion planned – a submarine ride. She knew submarines were my favorite apparatus in the world. I used to design and draw them. Even with my limited knowledge of science, I sketched a half-fact, half-fiction sub. Zebra striped for the zebra twins, Gary's and my nickname for each other. The irony? I was afraid to swim but loved the idea of diving down in a submarine.

We took a boat out about a half mile where the sub was waiting for us, cigar shaped and able to hold about 30 people. We climbed down through a narrow portal into the sub which had a long bench down the center, to sit back-to-back and look out under water on both sides. The ocean floor was like the bottom of a pool. We watched florescent yellow fish drift by, about the size of the palm of my hand. Even a small shark, hovering at the bottom. Mesmerizing.

During our visit, we found a ukulele shop. I was familiar with ukuleles but never really played one. Like a mini nylon-string acoustic guitar. But only four strings. The woman at the store showed me a couple chords and in no time, I was strumming along. Anne offered to buy me one. I decided on one with a quarter-inch plug, so I can play it through an amp or sound board. I had my eye on a black one. Lined around the edges with a pearl like inlay. When we got back to the hotel, I got out the little book and started learning more chords. A minor, B diminished , C major, D minor, E minor, F major, G major all the chords for the key of A minor. I pieced together a simple song I later recorded in 2013 on *Proof* called "Little Song" with alternate picking rather than strumming, for a new sound.

The weekend after we got back from our travels, the band had a show at a little warehouse in Oakland called the Buzzard. A venue loved by local heavy bands as well as those from out of town. An awesome friend of mine Dominique from back in the days band was on the bill too. They were called 'Lady of the lake' from the old Camelot lore with King Arthur and Guinevere. She was the one that gave him a new sword after he had broken it to defeat Lancelot. They had a projector in the venue that was used for visuals during the performances. Lady of the Lake used dry ice so the whole room filled with what looked like smoke. But it didn't have the effect of making you cough or anything. Their music was rad. And as usual Dominique's vocals were great. It felt like old times playing on a bill with a band from the old San Jose scene. We had a rehearsal hall across from her old band Mother Earth in the mid 90s.

When it came time for us to play, I was nervous as always. This was my first real show with a band in a couple years. Gary dropped into a bluesy bass improv line. Inviting me to unload the energy I'd built up over the course of the night. I burst into warm bluesy runs that were so comfortable it was like having a conversation with a good friend over coffee.

Music between the guys and I was just like a conversation. Phil created a time frame and a meter within which we could speak. Gary and I established our own key and cadence in the conversation. And all of us had he freedom to just express ourselves uninhibited. I remember pouring sweat as I unleashed everything my body and soul had to offer to the group of people who so graciously chose to spend their time with us that night.

A few months later, we'd arranged another show. This one was at Gilman Street in Berkeley. Where we'd played our very first real show, almost two decades prior.

My biggest revelation that night? So many of the people at the show looked like zombies. It's funny how crazy people look when you're somber and they're high.

I asked one of my friends, "Were we like that back in the day?" I'm sure we were on some level.

After, I asked Joe over donuts, "I wonder how many more of these we are going to have to play to get where we're trying to go?" I wondered if grassroots performing was the way to Shoreline or if times had changed so much, it was a thing of the past. I realized with online marketing many musicians have taken total control of their careers. Cutting out middlemen like labels. On the other hand, you have artists like Owl City who write such good songs they get picked up by a label just from music videos on YouTube.

Some fans of my music say I should go on *X Factor* or some show like that. I should try to win my way to the top, like hitting the lotto. One thing most people don't realize is you don't have to have a stellar voice for a career in music. I know many artists who make a living at music that don't sound like Kelly Clarkson or Ruben Studdard. The bands I know have infectious music that resonates consistently with a certain crowd. If they write music in that genre, the fans follow. I think the internet can be used to artist's advantage to grow a fan base faster, without playing so many shows.

After those shows, the band refrained from playing shows for some time. I think in part, we knew there had to be a better way. Plus, the heavy crowd just wasn't our crowd anymore. We had too many clean parts. We had to find our crowd again.

Around May of 2012, I was sitting at my computer desk in the living room of my apartment. I heard the same steady quiet voice I knew was God say, "You are a prisoner here!" I sat there for a few minutes with my hands pushed beneath my knees stretching below the seat of the chair, head down in disillusionment and said to myself, "I'm out of here. I refuse to be a prisoner another moment"

Obviously, I wasn't in a literal prison. I had my freedom to come and go. But escaping using my coping mechanisms as bad habits had gone on for way to long. All the vices I've mentioned. A prisoner to the routine. Medicating instead of finding the source of the problem and resolving the core issue. I realized I'd been suffering for years. Suffering became so normal to me. It was my life. Everything. I needed to change the scenery and break the cycle. I remembered how much better I felt when I stayed with Mom and Dad. How supported, safe and loved I felt. And how much healing I did in just that 2-week period in 2010. How much more healing could I do with more quality time around my parents?

I was going to find out. I called my landlord and asked if I was in a lease or a month to month contract. She said month to month. So, I put in my notice for the end of that month.

Over the next week I made many trips to the storage with boxes. One time on the way to Storage, I was driving down Sylvan road and heard the most all-inclusive message I had ever heard from God. He said, 'I am going to make it clear to you who she is, what to do with your music and will be with you until the day you die.' I felt so re-assured and comforted by these statements. But that is God's nature. He is a comforter. He would much rather love us than discipline us. Many believe the other way around. They are anticipating discipline and judgement instead of love and acceptance. As Christians, we must lead with love.

Once I could get everything into storage, I settled in with my parents. Never did I think I would choose to move out of my apartment to live with my parents after having that sense of freedom. But there was another reason to move – I was thinking of buying my first house. I'd gotten a pre-approval before, but I wasn't ready financially for the payments and expenses. At the apartment, all my money was just going to a landlord. At my parents, I could save money and build up my credit. I decided to start making big payments to both of my cards bi-weekly for several months to improve my credit. Then I checked my credit score – raised from 620 to 720 into the good range. I then took out a $5k loan from my retirement account that I could pay myself back over time. At that point, I was ready to go forward, or so I thought. After further analysis, I realized $5k wasn't going to be enough to get in and pay for expenses. It just wasn't the right time.

So, I decided to produce my next record *Proof* in 2013. At the time, I had a crush on a woman I was working with. I think she may have had feelings for me too, but as usual, she wasn't available. There were so many mixed emotions surrounding this record. I wondered how she was going to respond to it when she realized it was for her.

In the studio, I was being attacked by demons, either literal or figurative. I don't know. The voice was telling me, "This record is going to fall on deaf ears." Looking back, there was some truth to that. But I don't know if it was a self-fulfilling prophecy. Or the power of suggestion placed by an enemy in my psyche or demon. Later in the session, I heard another voice that sounded more like God, was reassuring and comforting. It said, "I wrote these songs. You must record them." I may have just been struggling with good old-fashioned insecurity.

I told the violinist Benito about the situation at work. And he said it wasn't a good choice for me and I should move on. Phil and Gary played on the record too. Much of the music was recorded to a metronome, so the songs sounded very solid and tight. Our favorite song to record was "Reflection." We played it over and over because it was live with no metronome click track and so many parts. After we finished the project, I was stoked. Cicily, Nicholes' amateur photographer daughter with a good eye, got some great shots over by Lake Chabot in Castro Valley. Even a short video performance. Afterward Nichole, Cicily and I went to my favorite BBQ place and took the food over to Alameda Beach to eat in the car. One of my favorite things to do. It was nice spending the afternoon with my ex and her daughter.

Around that time, we played a couple West Coast Songwriter's Competitions at Freight and Salvage in Berkeley. We decided to perform "Little Song" that featured that ukulele from my Hawaii trip. I felt it was the most assessable and heartfelt track on the record, an expression of love I'd felt. Not just writing a ballad for the sake of writing one. The song starts with the phrase "I love you" spoken three times in a row. That is exactly what I wanted to say to the woman I cared so much about but couldn't say. It was like I was a prisoner to my own emotions. Trapped in a stoic state, unable to truly and freely express myself. Which is especially difficult for an artist, I can be so passionate. To have to bottle that up can be almost unbearable at times.

We got a roaring response from the crowd following our performance. I am not sure what the judges said, but we didn't make the cut that night.

I performed a second time by myself to support the record. I didn't make the cut that night either. I was competitive with sports when I was young, but I'm not big on competition when it comes to artistic things like music. Art is expression and it is subjective. A hundred people can listen and have a hundred different responses to the same song. A person may not even like the genre you are singing in. I think the point is, anyone can express themselves. And it helps if the music is infectious.

Unfortunately, after those two performances, I felt as if the record was a failure. I was being so cruel and unsupportive of myself. Sad looking back on how devastated I was. What I should have asked myself is what would a friend say to me if my record missed the mark? Or what did my friends say about the record? The musicians and close friends I worked with thought it came together well. Failing to accept my friend's critiques, I chose to fixate on the negative, or what I perceived as negative. I missed the opportunity to be kind, loving, empathetic and supportive of myself. I should have been celebrating the accomplishment of producing my first solo record with a full production and live drums.

Looking back the record was not a failure. I chose to not have faith in the record and follow through with the necessary marketing to make a splash. What I didn't understand is no one knew who I was. I had to go out and sell myself and my music to the people. I simply needed to find my fans. The people that loved the kind of music I was creating.

One day I called in sick of work. Some days it was unbearable going there and dealing with my depression and insecurity. I decided to head out to the Bay Area first thing that morning. Which is something I would normally never be able to do during the week. I headed out to Carl's Junior near Highway 12 for breakfast. I ordered a sausage biscuit meal with orange juice and a cup of ice. I love my orange juice ice cold. It felt so nice sitting there in my car. I could just exhale, knowing I could do whatever I wanted with my day. I felt like Ferris Bueller minus the cute girlfriend and my version of Cameron for company. Maybe I'd wind up singing in a parade down Pacific Avenue in Stockton, narrowly missing being seen by my parents who thought I was at work.

I just needed a break from everything, including being home with family.

After breakfast, I headed out west on Highway 12 toward the Bay Area. About 25 miles out I ran into the little city of Rio Vista. Just big enough to have a diner and a mom-and-pop gas station. I headed down the two-lane road divided with yellow bumps and 3-foot-high yellow cones to hinder head on collisions. Although I tried to stay on the right side of the lines I occasionally would be somewhat startled by a loud zipping sound accompanied by a rattle of the steering wheel.

As I headed around the bend, I began to see tall white three-prong windmills growing from the ground. As I got closer, I could see them towering over the rolling lush green hilly landscape. Some of them revolving around like out-of-synch clocks. The black and white cows peacefully grazing below. That was all they had to do. They didn't have to buy or sell something. All they had to do is exist. Just graze and sleep.

As I zipped through the landscape up and down over the winding hills, I wondered, "Why do I have to go somewhere all day and do something I have no interest in for eight hours a day to just have enough money to barely survive?" I didn't have an answer to that question but drew inspiration from Bruce Hornsby:

> "That's just the way it is,
> some things will never change,
> that's just the way it is,
> ah, but don't you believe them."

Once I got on I-80 West, I finally found myself at the Jack London Square exit in Oakland and took it. Just up the road toward the water was one of my favorite places in the world to eat – Everett and Jones BBQ. A Black-owned BBQ spot complete with a wood-burning brick fireplace to smoke the meats. This place reminded me of Flint's BBQ off East 14th in Oakland, where we used to go when I was a child. A real part of my African-American heritage. I ordered brisket with potato salad and chili beans and headed back to my favorite spot at Alameda Beach. There's a road that runs parallel to the beach about 20 yards from the shore where I liked to park. So, I sat there in the car enjoying my meal. The taste of the molasses. The salty, tender, juicy meat. Home-made potato salad. All washed down with a tart and sweet grape soda.

After, I headed out to the shore, shoes still on and walked the length of the beach. As my shoes sank down in the sand, I watched the seabirds plunging their beaks down into the moist sand, fishing for baby crabs and some people out in the water on surfboards propelled by a kite-looking apparatus hovering above them 15 feet in the air. They weren't behind a desk pretending to work or pretending they liked to work. What I was realizing is there were people living their lives instead of just enduring them. Tired from trudging through the sand, I sat on an old dried out sea log and thought about the record and the woman that inspired it. And how she had told me she wanted to marry another guy. I was amid my feelings. I couldn't see past my flailing emotions. Reaching up out of the water. Hoping for someone to grab my hand and pull me onboard.

I got back on I-80 and headed back toward the Valley. During the week, you have to leave by 2 p.m. or you hit terrible traffic. When I got over by Albany, where

I'd worked back in 2003, I heard the distinct, calm voice of the Lord. I was so wound up with tumultuous feelings, it was like an abrupt release of tension. Like the hammer on a gun discharging a bullet. "You are suffering because you don't have faith." The message could not have been more concise or clear. I was choosing to wallow in and be distracted by my fears, rather than having faith. I know now it's impossible to fixate on your fears and have peace of mind at the same time. It is a choice that must be made every day. Am I going to be fearful or am I going to have faith?

The truth is self-doubt had become a crippling hindrance to any progress I could hope to make. My fear was chronic and deep seated. One part is staying balanced on medication and the other is being positive and supportive to oneself. What the Lord said was empowering, to say the least. The idea that faith could be a liberating force in one's life. And it is tried and true. Many people in the Bible and many people since the Bible was written have had their lives transformed by the basic principle of faith and trusting in God to provide them with the good things he's planned for them from day one.

Much like the Israelites, I was promised things by the Lord and for two decades I doubted what he had promised me. I worried, fretted and worried some more. I had no experiences to confirm these things were his will. So, I leaned on past failures and imprisoned myself in those doubts. God pointed me toward a spiritual change. I was beginning to realize spiritual freedom was partially a choice and partly God's grace. Most of the progress I had made was done through prayer and God putting his seal of approval on it.

I wondered what would happen in my life if I let go of all fear and just trusted in God's vision? I think at this point, it was still more conceptual in my mind. Not something that was going to affect my actions and the choices I was making. Looking back, I don't know how I couldn't have been on fire with faith after I heard that. I was just so accustomed to going back to my cage that I did just that.

The next day, I had the reality of going back to work and grinding out which was a total waste of my time. Something that didn't use my talents, gifts or skills. I couldn't see how faith was going to get me out of the situation I was in or improve my daily life. It was an unproven concept from my perspective. Something that I would have to experiment with more and test out. I was taught to question everything and this turned out to be a huge hindrance to achieving my goals.

One day I had a notably strange dream. Which for me is a big deal, because most of my dreams are strange and creative. Sometimes I see worlds I've never seen. Like in a movie. In this dream, I was wearing baggy orange prisoner pants and a light grey sweatshirt with the neck cut out like bodybuilders in the '80s and orange flip-flops with no socks. It reminded me of when I was in jail in Merced. My head was hanging down. I was pouring sweat, nauseous and bleeding down onto my shirt. Guided down an aisle way with cubicles on each side in an office building.

The people on either side of me were holding me up at my armpits as I slumped all my weight down, creating the maximum burden for them. Giving them no assistance in my transport. I needed to be carried. Before we got to the little room on the left at the end of the hall I said aloud, "I've grieved the Holy Spirit!" They sat me up on the floor against the wall. My head was slumped down, my chin was touching my chest. There was what appeared to be a nurse in the room to my right, sitting in one of those swiveling doctor's stools. She let one of the other people know she didn't want to be left alone with me. She feared for her safety. That's where the dream ended.

The next day at work I decided to look up "grieving the Holy Spirit" online. I'd never heard that term before. When I researched it, I found this basic definition … you are basically insulting God. So, the question became, how did I grieve the Holy Spirit? It wasn't something I was familiar with. Maybe some of the things I was doing were upsetting God and I didn't know it?

It turns out our own moral compass is a good guide. If something makes you feel guilty or bad, there is a good chance it would be upsetting to God too. The dilemma is some sin is habitual. It is not sin to the person. It is their lifestyle. I believe the Lord just wanted to make me aware that some of the things I was saying and doing were insulting to him. It made me aware of God's feelings. It is kind of like an earth father. You want him to love, accept you and be a blessing to you. But you must have a good relationship with him to receive his blessings. God knows the work he is doing in you will take years to come to light.

Sometimes a person doesn't know what God's purpose is for their life, so they just do whatever they want until they are guided in a different way. Then they must have the strength, discipline and courage to be obedient to God. This makes me think of my Mother Mable. She was such a good girl and young lady coming up. She always helped with the chores in her family of ten children and 2 adults. She loved school, she had no interest in drinking and smoking etc. She was a young lady that her Earth Father and Mother could be proud of. She was one of the apples of their eyes. She loved and respected her Mother and Father. So, she was obedient, kind, loving and supportive of her parents. I know not everyone has that experience with their parents. But this is what the Lord wants. We show God we love him by being respectful and obedient. Much like my mother I have always done my best to be respectful to my parents. I believe that is all God wants. Us to love, respect him and appreciate the incredible gift that he has given us. Not because we earned it. But by his grace. He knows that we will make mistakes along the way. He just wants us to maintain that sense of awe and respect as much as we can. What I have learned is that change is a process and it is a journey more than a destination.

There is so much to learn in such a short time. But some of the simplest lessons can take us a lot further that we ever imagined. There is power in simplicity. Anything complex is a series of simple things put together. There are some experiences that are beyond words. Imagine if we had to live by things being described to us and never got to experience them. Our vocabulary would get bigger, but we still wouldn't get to feel the dew on our arms on the beach at sunset. Or watch as the sky transforms before our eyes. This is just another way he shows us that he loves us. He gives us access to the whole human experience. For the longest I felt that if God loved me, he would bless me. Like God had something to prove to me. I was withholding my love from God and being bitter because I felt like he wasn't giving me what I wanted.

The truth is God has nothing to prove. He is the author of everything. The things we understand and the things we don't understand. I had a role in this story as Lance before I was born on this planet. A specific purpose to serve. That only I could serve. A certain skill, a certain temperament, a certain undying vision for what I am supposed to be. Revealed to me as I go through each day and turn the page. I didn't know it was going to take me more than two decades to really start taking solid steps toward the spiritual change. But the master craftsman did. My path. I am exactly where I am supposed to be. Doing exactly what I am supposed to do. This is not a mistake, stutter step or stumble. This is my destiny. The path to the life I have always wanted and beyond.

Hope is a seed that takes careful nurturing and consistency to grow. It reminds me of when I've tried to grow houseplants. They always died. Because I didn't water them enough or watered them too much. One of them was a cactus. Yeah, you read that right I killed a cactus. I watered it too much. It requires knowledge and love to make a seed grow into a plant.

Hope resides in our hearts. However deep or close to the surface. Plant it in fertile soil. Whenever my mom gets a plant, she takes it out of the store-bought plastic pot and puts it in a larger ceramic pot with lush soil from the hardware store. Hope cannot grow in negative soil. It needs constant nurturing with positive reinforcement. Being around positive and supportive people is imperative.

In early 2014, I decided to take another Ferris Bueller day off from work. I was so wound up, I decided to call the Behavioral Health number on the back of my medical card to see what therapist I could see in my area. They listed several names, but one stood out to me Briar. I was a caregiver to my cancer patient when he lived on Glenbriar and I lived in Greenbriar apartments. So, Briar was a reoccurring theme in my life. (At the time, I wasn't making a correlation between the troubling things that happened with my client's death and me having such a lonely and painful time living in my apartment.) After speaking to her briefly, I arranged to see her later that week.

The next day when I got to work, I was pulled aside by the manager Mary and several other coworkers. They told me to sit down. The news was shocking. They informed me Janice had died and several coworkers had found her body the day before at her apartment. What struck me immediately was the timing. Had I come in the day before, I probably would have been with them when they discovered the body.

Janice was a good, dear friend of mine. When I had that bout with paranoia in 2010, she was there for me – asking me if I was ok when I had to tell everyone I was taking a month leave. She'd always stand beside me at the time machine before we clocked in. We both liked clocking in exactly at 8:00 a.m. I had shared so many of my ups and downs with her and her roommate in the office Susan. Janice was one of the only people in the office I could borrow $5 or $10 from if it was Wednesday and I'd run out of money. We had a line of credit with each other.

One time I went to her house to buy a computer she had for sale. She had this little Chihuahua mix that was a bit bigger than the average Chihuahua. She was so feisty and angry with me when Janice had brought her to the office before. She would growl and snap at me if I tried to pet her. When I got to Janice's house, she was a little angel. She ran right up to me and reached her cute little snout up closer for me to reach her. She suddenly loved me. I was her favorite uncle.

The loss of Janice was so sudden. No time to feel anything but numbness. The next thing I knew, we were at the funeral. Oddly like a reunion, many of the people that had left the office in 2010, four years earlier, attended. Janice's son came in from somewhere in the South. A nice guy.

"Simple Man" by Lynyrd Skynyrd played as the montage of memories played in pictures behind the little podium where an urn of her ashes were perched:

> "And be a simple kind of man,
> oh, be something you love and understand,
> Baby, be a simple kind of man,
> oh, won't you do this for me, son, if you can,
> oh yes I will."

A previous coworker Anita sung a tribute with beauty and soul. Mesmerizing, touching and selfless. She wasn't nervous at all. It was all about Janice.

The whole funeral setting just put me in this place where I wondered about death and who would be there when I died. What would they say about me and the legacy I had left? It touched on the sensitive area of how finite life is in the physical world. How urgent and pressing living appreciating and enjoying life is. The end of life can happen to anyone at any time, but I think that is predetermined too and not something to worry about too much. I think we all have a purpose to serve in this life. And we can't leave here until our purpose has been served. It makes me think of those stories where a married couple of 50+ years dies hours apart, holding each other's hand. Their purpose has been served. They loved and supported one another until the end. The idea of being apart was so unbearable there is no way they could have carried on, like the bond between Carrie Fisher and Debbie Reynolds.

I had a friend named Michelle when I worked for Nelson's Cleaners. She told me she was there when her father passed over to the other side. And she could feel his spirit rise and leave his body. This is another thing I contemplate when I think of death. Christianity teaches us we go to heaven. And some say we just leave our body and meet up with loved ones. But what do you do once you are out of your body? What do you do in heaven? Do you have a job or purpose just like here on earth? These are some of the questions we will all eventually get an answer to. That's what is awesome. Someday all the things in darkness will be brought to light.

I wondered where Janice was. Was she at the funeral hearing how everyone felt about her? Feeling the love and the loss we felt? My ex Nicole told me some interesting things regarding her take on heaven. She said she remembered being in heaven. It was her job to put fresh fruit on an altar. She had to pick the ripest shiniest fruit suitable for a king. She said she knew where God was, but she couldn't go there. There were places where normal spirits couldn't go. She said there were beings made entirely of light. They were so pure you couldn't go near them. They were in a special chamber in the building. Looking back, I don't know if she just had an active imagination or if she really had those experiences.

I know some people have even reported déjà vu or remember things from a past life. These experiences are incredibly interesting to me. In my family, there are many cases where supernatural things have been occurred. One of my aunts sees spirits in the form of their human selves when they were alive. When my grandmother on my mom's side died, grandma's spirit came to the head of the couch my mom was sleeping on in a black shadowlike form. She couldn't see through it. It was a standing shadow. Her heart was jumping out of her chest. She closed her eyes and opened them again several times, and the form did not go away. After about a minute or two, one of her sisters in the other room up the hall said, "Momma's here in the hallway. You can hug her!" Still terrified, my mom didn't want to go into the hallway. She was afraid her Mom had come to take her, and she said she was ready to go because she missed her mom. Later the hospital called and said Grandma had passed in the night.

When my Aunt Dorothy's husband Uncle Nevil died, he came into my dream. My favorite thing about my uncle was he reminded me of Rodney Dangerfield, my favorite comedian in the world. Except he had a heavy Jamaican accent. He loved to tell stories and it kept you on the edge of your seat. In the dream, he was standing on the water like Jesus, out in an aqueduct. I was sitting on the side. He came to the edge and told me I was going to see what it was like to have a son. He started to head back out into the aqueduct, hovering on top of the water. I asked him to stay longer. He said he had to go. That saddened me. The interesting thing, I hardly spoke to him over the years. He came to visit with my aunt once years ago and I believe I saw him once in New York.

In late 2014, I decided to produce the record Gratitude. I intended to bring honor and glory to the Lord. To thank him and show him respect for all he had done for me. I really wanted to use my gift of creativity he had given me to praise him. One of the things I decided from day one is there would be no songs about human relationships on this record. It was totally going to be spiritual.

First thing, I headed over to Bear Creek Church to get prayed over and receive divine inspiration. I wanted the record to be pleasing to the Lord. I didn't want to have the negative mixed emotions I had with Proof.

The prayer session was powerful. It was like I was on an eighth of a tank and filled the rest of the way with the Holy Spirit. I didn't drink for the full seven months it took me to write the record. And I worked with discipline after work, four to five days a week in 2 to 2.5-hour sessions. My goal was to do a song a month. From the first note, to a fully produced song on my Tascam Neo 24-Track in my personal studio. These served as reference tracks, so I knew exactly how to produce the songs in the studio.

Then I kept a continuous metronome on five of the tracks to keep meter easily. I really loved playing my new Fender Jaguar Bass, so I played that on five tracks of the seven-song record. I specifically chose seven tracks because seven is a perfect number. Six tracks like on Feel Something felt like an incomplete number. This record had the potential to have a positive impact on the listener, turning them on to Christian philosophy if they weren't aware of it already.

One of the songs "Your Way" had a very profound message that took me years to grasp. I'd tried to do things my way my whole life and I could never get anything off the ground. I realized it was time to do things God's way. All I'd done over the years was perpetuate my problems by medicating with unhealthy habits to cope with my depression. I had never tried not sinning and being consistently righteous over an extended period. (I would not drink but still struggle with lust, porn, unhealthy food and not exercising.) I made a promise in this song:

> 'I surrender all to you,
> and forever promise too,
> I'll do it your way …
> from now on I'll do it your way."

However, after the production was done, a friend told me I needed to go back to the drawing board. A keyboard vocal melody line that I was using as a reference was supposed to be mixed out in the final production. I didn't catch it, and no one made that suggestion to me before I got it up online and digitally distributed. Plus, I was planning to share this record with Pastor Jebby, the music coordinator at Bear Creek Church. I was inspired to do the record in part because of a sermon the Pastor Bill had done. It was my vision the music could possibly be used by them in their Sunday production. I really had my heart set on that.

I am shy so, I sent Pastor Jebby an email instead of just approaching him after service. Looking back, that was a huge mistake. He never responded, and I took it like my music was unacceptable to the church. As if it wasn't pleasing to the Lord. Which meant I had failed in my mission to be pleasing to the Lord. What I realize now is the Lord put it on my heart to do the record. And he would never reject me. He loved me and knew I had the best intentions in the world.

Unfortunately, I slipped back into my old self-destructive habits of drinking and eating a lot of fatty food to cope with the perceived rejection of my work. I didn't realize God is love and wants to share his love and appreciation toward me. I felt guilty going back to bad habits because of the promises I'd made to the Lord. I felt deeply discouraged and disappointed in myself, and I felt I needed to medicate to survive what I was going through.

At some point, I went back to private prayer night, which was much like therapy and told them how I was feeling. I needed the strength to go back to living a righteous life. They were excited to hear I'd written a record with the intension of sharing it with the congregation. They were honored they had inspired me to action with the project. They reminded me that when it comes to sin, you can't give up the fight. Be patient and kind with yourself and keep trying to do better.

I've found prayer is an immense help as far as motivation and inspiration to do better. Prayer reminds you of the promises you have made and holds you accountable for your actions in front of a group of peers. The first thing I'd do when I fell back into sin was isolate myself and stop going to church. I didn't want to be held accountable. I wanted to take the easy way and escape the feelings I was having.

Another song on the record was called "Dormant" about receiving the Holy Spirit and renewing the Spirit. A pivotal lyric:

> "Finally ignite, the dormant flame
> lost in my heart, awaken me …
> awaken."

Even though I'd received the gift of the Holy Spirit in '97, I was actually talking about where I was at in 2015. The dormant flame was lost in my heart. Waiting to be rekindled. I couldn't feel the love in my heart anymore. A love that physically abided in my heart. Like I felt in '97. I desperately missed that feeling.

After that private prayer night at the church, I realized I'd missed the whole point of my own record. How could I be so cruel and unkind to myself again? No remorse or sympathy for myself. The Holy Spirit is like a pilot light on a water heater. Sometimes the wind blows through and puts it out. No more warm water. Or like the pilot light in those old wall heaters like the one I had in my apartment on Coffee Road. If the pilot went out, no heat. Then you begin to get cold inside.

I had to go back to church, fall to one knee and turn the pilot light in my heart back on. Sometimes a person can get used to that winter chill. Then when they finally turn that pilot on they wonder how they ever went without heat. Sometimes we have a space heater but it's not strong enough.

For emotional and spiritual survival, stick to the essentials. Keep love and hope alive in your heart and maintain a healthy mindset in which a spirit can grow and flourish. My introversion often keeps me from getting more involved in church groups. I think about all the interaction I'd have to be part of and it scares me off. Strangely, I have no trouble talking to someone once the conversation starts. I'm just not good at starting a conversation. But humans have a lot of common ground to talk about. Sometimes I've felt like I have so much to share but not a situation where I feel comfortable sharing. I think that's why I love being in a band. You make close friendships with a small circle of people with similar interests.

The band's music comes up in conversation at the sessions at church. I was concerned the band's music was too dark. One day I realized that dark music came from inside me. And I had a lot of the same bad habits as my friends. And God never condemned me. He loved me. He worked with me. He never gave up on me.

I realized I loved my friends and I was going to love them all the way down the line, like God has done with me. That gave me even more inspiration to break free from my own cage. So, I can help my friends with things they may be going through and give them some emotional shelter from the storms of life. I believe seeing beyond my own struggle is imperative. One of my friends Hayes at Kinko's used to say, "Come out of yourself. You're only thinking about yourself. There's so much you could do in this world if you would just look beyond yourself." That was some of the greatest advice.

In 2016, I learned there was a possibility of my department at Sutter Gould moving to Sacramento. It wasn't etched in stone, but I heard rumblings from management. I really didn't think too much of it. I was planning on hanging in there until the very end if it came to that. In late 2016, it became a reality.

The management from Sacramento and the Human Resources representative called a meeting with the whole staff and informed us the department would be moving and our entire staff was going to be laid off on February 3, 2017. They also informed us we'd get a severance based on how many years of service we put in and we would be eligible for unemployment from the layoff. Even though it was somewhat troubling news since I'd become so comfortable with the routine, I was relieved there was light at the end of the tunnel. I had wanted to leave the job for so long. And it was happening exactly the way I wanted it to. I desperately needed a long break from the doldrum and oppressive environment of the job.

It was hard seeing people go as the time went by, down to the final days. I decided to just wait until the end and collect the severance. My awesome best friend stayed until the end too. In fact, we were the last ones to leave the office on the last day.

It felt so liberating when I was driving down the freeway back home to Mom and Dad's on that last day. When I was about a mile from the Eight Mile Road exit, I heard, "This is meant to be." Leaving Gould. I knew it in the core of who I was.

I remember when my dad retired from United Defense in the mid-2000s asking him how it felt to drive down that freeway for the last time. He commuted for more than 25 years from Stockton to San Jose, five days a week, and he never missed a day of work. He said it felt surreal. As if it hadn't really sunk in that he never had to go back there. He said the first few weeks he couldn't believe he could get up whenever he felt like it and do whatever he wanted to do and still get paid. (God bless the person that came up with Social Security and those that made it happen.) He said someday I would feel that way.

That drive for me was like a mini retirement. I didn't know how long I was going to be without a job, but I had 11 weeks of severance to find out.

The Monday after the layoff, I started writing more for this project. In the month of February, I was only doing a couple pages per session three times a week. In March, I decided to do four-page sessions four days a week. That month I wrote 58 pages. In my sessions, I noticed I could sometimes even do seven-page sessions.

Most of the time, I was going for drives during the week, often on days when I did my writing sessions. In that time, I would hone my vision and revise it each day. I was starting to see I could write a book. And it wasn't some lofty goal on a mountain top. I could have a career as an author.

Plus, I could still perform as Lance West and with the band Human Anomaly to generate income, also selling products and downloads on my websites with almost no overhead costs. Humanomaly's music feels loaded with more potential to draw people in than it did before … the sound is more assessable, uplifting with a strong sense of groove. More people will relate because they can move to it. More parts in standard 4/4 timing but still switching it up sometimes with our favorite 7/8 signatures and others.

I realized it's possible to have a life where I make a living doing things I'm passionate about. Things I have control over. Aspirations where I can set short- and long-term goals and have the discipline to stay on track, like with this book.

When I left my job I also had some money saved. For once, I was able to buy the things I really wanted and needed for my craft. The next generation of gear. I could get my dream guitar – a Mystic Green Fender Jazz Master with the new Roland GR-55. Honestly, the best feeling in the world. Getting good gear to last me another 20 years. Passion manifested.

One night about a month ago, I was lying in my bed and heard the Lord say clearly, "Focus on your vision and I will bless you." That made me feel so reassured and confident. The idea that God would endorse my vision. I had always felt like my prayers were going unanswered, but I was just on a negative wavelength that God was not on. You gotta be on the right frequency. For once in my life, God was assuring me I was on the right frequency.

One time I drove to the Shell gas station on highway 12 to get a half pint of whisky and God said, "Don't do this. It means a lot to me." I got back in my car and drove off. It's hard having a habit you're leaning on for an escape and feeling guilty because you're hurting God by doing it. But I've felt so liberated since I made the commitment to writing this book and being sober. Soon the months will add up to years.

Now when I go to band practice, my friends know I don't drink and don't even offer. They understand and make me feel comfortable. One thing about the Lord – if you're trying to do something positive, he will give you all the help you need. Even surround you with people who respect the positive changes in your life. He will give you the strength to push through the uncertainty – be it mental illness, life challenges, bad habits, wrong relationships – and so on.

Be the momentum that doesn't stop.

10 Steps to Generating and Maintaining Momentum in Your Life

I believe we can all benefit from having the vision to consistently pursue the goals that move our lives forward. Here's some of my ideas to motivate and inspire …

1. Determine what it is that you are trying to accomplish.
This can be anything from being a race car driver or an astronaut (why not!) to just feeling peace of mind and balance in your life.

2. Find and replace any unhealthy habits you have.
In your thoughts, your speech, the way you treat yourself and others. This step is huge and often an ongoing process. Sometimes we need something to inspire and motivate us to make better choices – like the birth of a baby, wanting to live to see your grandkids. Prayer can be a huge help. Avoid negative self-chatter. Words can heal or wound.

3. Be patient and kind to yourself as you are attempting to change.
You are never going to have peace if you let circumstances determine how you feel. Faith allows us to enter a state of rest and peace of mind. We are no longer chasing our tails, trying to figure out something we have no control over. Love and trust God to provide. Many people think being obedient to God is putting them in bondage. They can no longer do what they want to do. But faith gives you freedom. And a healthy love for the Lord can satisfy the soul.

4. Commit to the process and follow through.
Committing to the process means it is a continuum. You are on a trajectory. Even when it seems like you are off the track in the wilderness, God is with you. He knew you were going to struggle with this. Despite ups and downs, I've produced 5 records and written this book in the last 10 years. I committed to the process and pressed through.

5. Hold yourself accountable.
Find someone you can confide in, who you can check in with periodically, maybe once a week or every month, to see how much progress has been made. Be honest with yourself and the person you confide in. You don't have to share things that make you feel uncomfortable. Just things you feel are pertinent to your growth on your journey.

6. Go to church or have a friend pray with you.
Start to engage with God and build a close, honorable and respectful relationship with him. One where you trust him to be supportive and loving toward you through thick and thin. A relationship in which you can admit your mistakes and faults but know the Lord still loves you and would never condemn someone trying their best.

7. Set long-term goals.
Break your long-term goals into short term, attainable goals you can be proud of as you achieve them. Momentum is putting one foot in front of the other. We do it every day. Add in something productive, that you love to your schedule each day in pursuit of those long-term goals.

8. Momentum requires consistency.
Anything that helps you be disciplined and consistent is going to get you to the ultimate goal. Many people use a system of rewarding themselves. I suggest you make it something healthy. Like buying yourself a book, eating a healthy snack, going to dinner with friends. Positive reinforcement can be great to help you along.

9. Believe in lifetime goals.
This is also where destiny comes in. If you were meant to climb all the way to the peak of that mountain in the distance, you will. Forge on and keep making attempts. Feel a sense of pride in simply trying.

10. Life is a journey of momentum, not a destination.
We are always growing, learning and sharing with others. Let the possibilities fill you with joy and bless your journey.

Lastly, if you or a loved one needs mental health help in the U.S., please call the SAMHSA treatment referral helpline: 877-SAMHSA7 (726-4727). Don't take this journey alone.

Join me at lancewestmusic.com to continue this journey with a free song download from the momentum companion album.

Editor's Note – Serendipities

I'm normally the behind-the-scenes person who silently wrangles words without anyone the wiser. But this project carries an extra bit of serendipity to cause me to step forward for just a moment.

First, I met Lance on a connecting flight from Chicago to Sacramento, coming back from time home with friends and family. As an introvert myself, the first thing I thought when I saw Lance in my seating row, "Oh crap, how much talking is enough without being rude?" But Lance was more than gregarious and fun to talk to with about music and creative pursuits. He even spoke about wanting to write a book and I gave him my business card. I had no clues of the bipolar diagnosis he was dealing with under the surface.

Fast forward a few years later and an email from Lance asking if I would edit his story. I was swamped with copywriting and screenwriting projects, but I soon realized that raw everyday accounts of life dealing with bipolar deserve a bigger place at the reading table. People coping with mental challenges or those with friends and families suffering from the disorder need more insights on the inner workings of what it means to be bipolar. We can all miss the signs to help, and we often have no reference point to begin to understand the mental illness.

I lived with a roommate in college who I was none the wiser about her mental struggles. All the time my other roommate and I marveled at the seemingly strange impulses that would keep her up all night, doing God knows what in her bedroom. I would only discover my old housemate's inner compulsions years later when I heard about her bipolar diagnosis. Editing this book has become a mea culpa of sorts for my youthful ignorance.

Finally, as a fellow creative, I understand the tiniest of tickles the brain can toss at you. I've only had to deal with the most miniscule organizational OCD that was far worse when I was younger. At 12 years old, I would be just shy of tears as I wrote, erased and rewrote my name countless times at the top of my homework, aiming for a perfection that my brain only allowed out of sheer exhaustion. I've always thought to myself, "But for the hand of God, I might have slid further down the OCD rabbit hole."

I hope Lance's words resonate and uplift while pulling back the curtain on mental illness. We can all benefit from more glimpses of our shared humanity.

ACKNOWLEDGMENTS

I would like to take the time to thank as many people that have shared this journey with me as possible. If I do not mention you here, it is not because our connection wasn't meaningful. It is almost impossible to really share how I have felt about everyone, but I will try. Special thanks to the following people:

Cheryl Laughlin, my editor, for countless hours of reading and helping make this content as concise as possible. I know we met on that plane for a reason. I hope to use your services again in the future; you did such a great job.

Annie Daiva Kelly, my photographer. You have a great eye and are one compassionate, lovely person. It has been such a pleasure working with you. Your strength and tenacity are beyond inspiring.

Curtis Hudson Jr., my father, for inspiring me to take writing seriously. You taught me to work hard and never give up. You showed how a man is supposed to be. I am so grateful having you in my life. Many young men have had to find their way alone, and are often misled. But I had your wisdom and knowledge on my side. Thank you.

Mable Hudson, my mother, for your generosity, warmth, kindness, and unconditional motherly love. You showed me the power of love and faith in the Lord. You have supported me through everything, never once questioning if I would succeed. Having you, a teacher, as my mother was such a gift. Much of my diction was learned by making mistakes and being corrected by you in real time. I am so thankful for that. I couldn't have even considered writing a book without that type of background.

Anne Hudson, my sister, for being motivated, positive, and focused no matter what adversities you faced. Your life is proof of the power of having a positive attitude and walking in it. You have achieved so many of the things you have dreamed of, and I am so proud of you. Your belief in the idea of putting positive energy out there has taken you to places most people fantasize about and has added such a glow to the world. Your constant, unwavering support of me has been beyond a blessing. It has been a lifeline at times. I can never thank you enough, but allow me to express my deepest gratitude: thank you, thank you, thank you!

Nicole Quismondo, my muse for many years. Thank you for being there for me through those years when I was struggling and floundering. You always believed in me, no matter what endeavor I took on. I will never forget the times we shared. I truly believe we crossed paths for a reason and the Lord's will has prevailed in our lives.

Robinmarie Rowen, my long-time friend and inspiration. I will never forget the day you walked into Kinko's in Mountain View with that beret on. We have been through so much together, and we never gave up hope on one another. We served as beacons of light in each other's lives. I don't regret how our relationship has evolved. Thanks for being patient with me in my introversion.

Annie "Weegie" Heffley, my late friend, whom I met in the Utilization Management Department at Sutter Gould in Ceres. You were so welcoming and accommodating from the moment I met you. When you started training me on that first day, you said, "No question is stupid. I don't care how many times you ask me; at some point you will know it, and you will never ask me again." I will forever treasure that slow dance we stole while singing Johnny Cash's "Folsom Prison Blues" for your friends at the going-away party. I really regretted not pursuing a more intimate relationship with you. I know you heard those last heartfelt words I sung to you from "Wondr'ing Aloud" by Jethro Tull. I will see you again someday, I am certain.

Gary Niederhoff, my longtime friend from high school and bassist for the band Humanomaly. You have been like a brother to me. When I had no food, you fed me. When I had nowhere to live, you shared your spaces with me. We have shared the same visions, dreams, and goals for many years. I am sure we will see the fruits of our efforts. We just have to keep focusing on the work and everything will fall into place. I think God puts certain people in our lives that are like companions and guardians through the entire journey of life; you and Phil have been that to me.

Phil Romero Jr., my longtime friend from high school and drummer for the band Humanomaly. I was blown away by your drumming ability from the first time I heard you play. Your friendship has been just as consistent as the steady beats you provide us with. I consider you a brother. I have grown so much over the years, having a friend like you to talk to and share ideas with. As I said with Gary, we will see the fruits of our efforts soon. You too have fed me and shared your awesome tequilas and whiskies with me. I am forever grateful for yours and Gary's friendship.

Lisa Ballard, You rock, Lisa! You remind me of my sister in many ways. You are so positive. You don't put up barriers, which allows ascent into the stratosphere.

David Galbreath, you took me in when I needed our friendship most. I was actually living with you when I had my first full mental breakdown. You are so laid back, and it is refreshing to be around you. You have also been there through this entire musical and writing journey with us. You produced our videos at the Mountain View public access and some of our shows over the years. I also really enjoyed adapting that horror story I wrote in college, "The Trunk," into a screenplay. I still believe that you could see your name scroll by in the credits at the end of a film. This book, Momentum, is all about motivation, putting one foot in front of the other, and most importantly believing in the possibilities. Just take it one step at a time. I am willing to help you with that endeavor too. You have helped me so much over the years. I would love to reciprocate.

Nicholas So, whom I met in Berkeley, working for Sutter. You and David Galbreath share a similar vision, wanting to be directors and producers of movies. I know that seems like a huge, daunting task. But it can be broken down into individual steps that can be tackled one by one. A vision starts with belief and faith. As you begin to take the steps, you start to get more and more excited as you see progress. That is the essence of Momentum. People like you and Dave inspire me. I want to see your dreams become a reality, because I like to see people live their passions and not watch life pass them by. I hope and pray both of you pursue your dreams and goals. I believe sometimes something is put on our hearts to do. It is our destiny. That is why we can't let it go. Before I could write this book, I had to take the dream out of the stratosphere and bring it down to earth. It turns out that the seemingly insurmountable and almost impossible goal, from my perspective of writing a book, became a reality. My reality included about thirty, two-hour writing sessions, rereading and rewriting, hiring an editor, finding a publisher, and completing the whole process with the publisher. This book exists because I made it a goal, not a dream.

Benito Cortez, violinist on my records and live music. You bring such a warm sound to our recordings and a thoughtful kind voice to our conversations. We've talked for hours about our spiritual philosophies. I definitely have you to thank, because our conversations actually led up to this book. Many of the principles we talked about are included. Thank you for giving me your perspectives. It is so important to be open to the thoughts and ideas of others. We have so much to learn that we can't afford to miss out on the nectar of knowledge others have to share. Religion can be used to divide us, or it can be used to bring us together. In our case, it brought us together and that is so inspiring. *That is what the world needs right now, a universal voice of love and truth that resonates with humans in general, not just one group.*

Nicholas J. Pack Jr., you are all-pro, man. It was so refreshing to meet such a stand-up musician and man like you. Working with you came so naturally. Everything was smooth, and you always kept us reaching for the highest standards in our productions. Gary and I are still in awe of your performance on that recording we did. It truly should have been released, but circumstances claimed another project. I look forward to hopefully working with you at some point in the future.

Hank Chang, I swear you are one of the fastest learners I have ever met. You are consistent as the sun. We must have practiced for a year and a half, and you never missed a practice. We really could count on you. I'll never forget when we finally got the ending of that one song down. It was such a feeling of accomplishment! Projects like that make life worth living. I'm glad to see you are traveling with music; that looks like fun. You are another pro musician that I wouldn't hesitate to contact in the future.

Bil Bowman, it is not often that I meet a character like you. You are basically the "Ferris Bueller" of drummers. It was really fun working with you. I'll never forget that hush puppy character you would do.

Tom Choi, you inspired me from the first time I heard you play guitar, back when you were living behind Target on Capital Expressway in San Jose. For me, Asbestos Deaths' music was a turning point in how I thought about music. It was true art. I will never forget the clean tone you got out of that Crate half stack with the chorus effect. You always had such great tone and your own style of playing that could not be emulated. I absolutely loved your work with "ItisI"; it was truly transcendent at times. In the early 90s, when I moved to the South Bay, we were inseparable. I really enjoyed those times so much. Like when we wrote that country song, which was a genre I had no idea you liked being in such heavy bands. I can still remember some of the lyrics: "Don't need a job or money to feel free, got a quart of wine to keep us company." We haven't been around each other in many years, but you will always hold a special place in my heart and this story of life. You are great! I still want to hear the music you are working on. I am so curious about that.

Joey and Bobby Coelho, *Joey*, your bass work with "ItisI" was impeccable. I could tell it was Bootsy inspired, even though it was in a heavy context. The sliding with the two top strings together gave the band that incredible low-end sonic boom. You are also really fun to talk to. You add so much to the conversation with your knowledge of so many different things. *Bobby*, you remind me so much of the really awesome old blues players on guitar. I loved your playing with "Dragonfly" so much. The tone and the clean licks were so refreshing to hear live. You are also a really stand-up guy. Real. I really respect that.

Roy Page, you have always been there for Tom Choi like a brother, and I think that is awesome. You and Tom remind me of me and Gary—a friend that is just there through everything. It is awesome to see you are living your passions, working with amps/guitars, playing in bands. It was so fun going over to your house back in the day and hanging out. You added your own special touch to quite a few bands over the years. I hope to see you guys some time soon. Also, it was an honor being on the *Lova Appamatics* (I hope I spelled that right) cover.

Brian 'Terrorizer' Rubio and Ozwaldo Aguilar, you guys really brought it in "ItisI" too. *Brian*, I have never seen a person with as much pent up energy as you. You were relentless, and that added something special to the band. *Ozwaldo*, you tied things together for this relatively controlled chaotic band. I remember camping and that brisk run at the winery. Fun times.

Angie Thurman, we haven't spoken in many years, but you have always been a magical person to me. I am happy to see how you and your family have grown. God bless you guys.

Al Cisneros, it is awesome to see how you have grown so much over the years. I am so proud of you! I have really cherished those conversations we have had over the years about the pocket: the note on "Machine Gun" Jimi Hendrix Band of Gypsies at the Filmore, Black Sabbath, Maha Vishnu Orchestra, etc. You have such a good heart and such wisdom beyond your years. I wish I could see you more often, but with traveling and living out of area it is hard. Everything you have done from *Ear Wax, Asbestos Death, Sleep, OM* has inspired me on a deep profound level. I wrote my first song in high school, "Societies Humanoid," based on *Ear Wax* song structure. I am glad to see you are living the life you want. So many of us compromise and lose a little bit of ourselves every day doing things we don't want to do but have to. You have shown me that it is possible to do what you are passionate about for a living. I appreciate that, brother. I will always be here for you.

Matt Pike, you were a rock star from the moment you picked up a guitar. It is so awesome to see you playing with the musicians who inspired you when you were young. It is like things coming full circle. You have become exactly who you aspired to be. I have so much respect for you, for not compromising and just being you. You inspire me on so many levels. You have the courage to believe in yourself and follow through. I plan to follow your lead. The band is almost to the point where we are ready to really shine. I hope to see you soon.

Chris "Goat" Hakius, you are an incredible drummer who has influenced me in so many ways. You are solid and consistent. You are the kind of person one can depend on. It was so much fun going to all those Sleep shows in the early 90s and seeing you guys grow over those years. Your passionate, thundering drum sound really gave a solid foundation to those songs. I hope to hear you behind the kit again someday, my friend..

Chiyo Nukaga-Jacobus, I have known you since the "Wood" days. I remember when "Noothgrush" was playing shows back in the day, you guys were super heavy. It was cool with you pounding away on the drums. Thanks for encouraging me and the band over the years and attending our shows. You have always been so supportive of us.

Kelley Donahue, you are one kick-ass woman! I remember the Campbell days like it was yesterday. We had such a special time at that house. Like you said, a lot of Kessler and Weinerschnitzel were being consumed. You are one of the coolest, down-to-earth people I have ever met. Maybe we should have a Campbell house reunion party sometime.

Jeff Gilleland, you were like the dad of our crazy, dysfunctional house. I always looked up to you as a responsible guy. You were like a role model to me in a lot of ways in my early 20s. Thanks, man.

Josh Reineke, you were one of my favorite people in the old scene. You had an infectious laugh, and we shared the same sense of humor and musical taste. I remember the tower books days with Al Cisneros too. It was fun just being around you. If you are ever down in the Bay, let's get burritos.

Jason Albertini, you are one of the best and most dedicated bass players I have ever met. I remember leaving for work in the morning with you playing bass and coming back hours later, and you were still playing bass. It is so awesome to see that you are making a living as an artist. That is what I am planning on doing. You are a really mellow, cool dude. It would be rad to hang out with you again someday and catch up.

Ari Rosenschein, it was awesome to see that you pursed a higher education in creative writing and have a book coming out right around the same time as mine. That is really inspiring, man. You are doing a great job at marketing your book. I am taking notes. I wish you the best with your creative pursuits.

Dominique Bauelos-Matz, you are a rad, powerful singer. I remember when "Mother Earth" rehearsed right across the hall from us. I have always looked at you as the person that holds the scene together. You know all the contacts. Thank you for introducing me to Rabiah and Liana.

Joseph Vastano, that little bit of time we spent together in the early 90s really made a big impression on me. You are such a wise soul. You have taken the time to ponder the most meaningful things in life and grown accordingly. Thanks for your writing and sketches, which are equally incredible. You inspired me to write, man. The way you brilliantly describe things down to the tiniest detail resonates with the reader. You are a really visual writer. I still have some of your writings and a few of your drawings. I have a really awesome one of Jim Morrison. You were a role model to me when I met you. You showed me how to be a stand-up guy. That trip with my mom to Petaluma and the ensuing adventure was rad, which included sleeping in a 1985 Buick balled up in the fetal position, you in the front and me in the back. I also enjoyed playing for the senior citizens in the old age home. That was something that I always wanted to do but didn't have the courage. I remember just strumming my guitar and not even saying a word, I was so shy. You were confident and did all the speaking. When I come to Austin to play "Austin City Limits" (which my mom always tells me is going to happen), I am going to take you up on that place to stay, man.

Rabiah Harrison, you are one of my favorite people. I will always hold a special place for you in my heart. You are such an intelligent, compassionate, strong, independent woman. I really admire and respect that. You will always be a reference point for me as to what to look for in a woman.

Liana, you always have a smile on your face; I love that about you. And you have a little edge, too, that adds another dimension to you. I miss seeing your smiling face. Look forward to the day when I can see you again.

James Toledo, you were like my little brother growing up. We had so many adventures on our bikes, in the trees of the field and the creek. It is awesome to see how you have grown and become a business owner. I am proud of you, man. I am planning on following your lead and pursing life on my own terms as an author and recording artist. I look forward to seeing you, as it has been many years. I am sure we will pick up right where we left off. I will never forget those summers and all the cool things we did. Those memories will always be a part of me and alive in my heart.

Dani Gasperson, you will always be special to me, like my little sister. I remember all the animals you had. Zeus, the Great Dane, who could stand up on his hind legs and peer over the fence, the rabbit cages on the side of the house and the cats. It is like those memories will always tie us to that time and place. I wouldn't have it any other way.

John Rogers and Phil Day, the funka-groove-adelic drummer and riffy guitarist. It was those first experiences with you guys that put me on a life trajectory toward music. Thank you so much for that. It was so fun visiting you guys up in Arcata, so many cool memories.

Dave Rogers, Bob and Dina Petit, those cool summer nights sitting out on the porch are etched in my psyche forever. I have never felt so relaxed and at peace before. Dave, remember us pretending we were the cops on Sanford and Son: "Hey Smitty it looks like we have a situation out here." And then killing all the flies that had congregated in the kitchen. Thanks for sharing those times with me.

Ray Cunningham Jr., thank you for sharing your experiences of loss, pain, joy, and hope. I realize how sheltered I was from the experiences most black males were having in the early 90s, and how lucky I was not to have experienced those things firsthand. I really hope that us black males will learn to have compassion for one another and we can someday see peace on the streets instead of gang violence. Here we are twenty-five years later and the murder rate is still staggeringly high. The only way all that loss will ever be vindicated is through peace. I hope for that, man. And I hope your son has grown to know peace.

David Edwards, you were like a father figure to me, man. Your wisdom was leaps and bounds beyond your years. You learned from your experiences and didn't allow them to be a constant source of strife. I started doing desktop publishing following your lead. I really regret that we lost touch and hope the best for you and your family. Contact me through my website, if you see this.

Special thanks to the educators over the years that encouraged me to pursue creative writing. I have finally followed through!

Also, in the last twenty years I have spent my time with a very small handful of friends. I am an introverted person by nature and like to be one on one rather than in groups too much; it just stresses me out. I have had very little contact with and lost touch with many people that I care about dearly and sincerely hope that I didn't hurt any of you in the process. I didn't realize that isolating oneself too much could also alienate the people one cares about most. I am truly sorry for that and any hurt I may have caused.

And finally, and most importantly, I want to thank the very Creator of creativity, God. He created us and the entire context in which we exist. There are three qualities that God has that I would like to share. Understanding these concepts has really helped me change my perspective on life.

God is Omnipotent: He has unlimited power and is able to do anything.

When we feel powerless, we must remember God is all powerful and capable of doing all the things that make us insecure. Trust in Him will give us the strength to do the things we don't think we are capable of through Him.

God is Omnipresent: present everywhere at the same time.

There is no hiding from God. We cannot close the door and assume He doesn't see what we are doing. Eventually all things that are done in darkness will be brought to light. This serves as a reminder to us that God is with us at all times and we need to remember to be respectful. God doesn't expect perfection; He expects us to make an effort and be cognizant of the effect our actions have on the world around us.

God is Omniscient: knows everything.

We have to remember to seek knowledge at its source. And seek truth, not to distort the facts for selfish purposes. Reach out to God in prayer if you want an answer to something not written in doctrines that is specific to your situation. As they say, knowledge is power. And power can corrupt man. It is intended for God because He has the knowledge to take all the variables into account when making a decision on how to use His power. Humans don't have access to all the variables. Humans can't control all the circumstances that affect them. Circumstance is God's territory.

About the Author

Lance West is a singer, songwriter, musician and medical biller who hopes to assist in liberating as many people as possible from the perpetual cycles of doubt with his faith filled music and literature. He lives with his family in Stockton, California.

You can check in on Lance's journey at **lancewestmusic.com**.

www.ingramcontent.com/pod-product-compliance
Lightning Source LLC
Chambersburg PA
CBHW052031070526
44584CB00016B/1989